Journeys

JOURNEYS
How travelling fruit, ideas and buildings rearrange our environment

Edited by
Giovanna Borasi
/
Stories by
Kozy Amemiya
Anders Bell
Giovanna Borasi
Ilaria Brancoli Busdraghi
Lev Bratishenko
Ian Chodikoff
Curtis C. Ebbesmeyer
Bernard L. Herman
David Howes
Serge Michel
Riitta Oittinen
Wouter Oostendorp
Maureen Power
Peter Sealy
Jouke Sieswerda
Jean Teillet
David Theodore
/
With illustrations by
Erika Beyer

/
Canadian Centre for Architecture
ACTAR

TABLE OF CONTENTS

FOREWORD
MIRKO ZARDINI — 7

SCENES — 10

STORIES

WHEN A CUCUMBER IS NOT A CUCUMBER: AN E.U. TALE OF CUSTOMS AND CLASSIFICATION
LEV BRATISHENKO — 89

RE-CONFIGURATIONS: A TOWN IN NEWFOUNDLAND GROWS WHEN HOUSES ARE FLOATED IN FROM FAR-FLUNG OUTPORTS
MAUREEN POWER — 101

RETURNING TO A NEW LAND: HOW THE ARCHITECTURE OF THE OLD SOUTH MADE ITS WAY TO ARTHINGTON, LIBERIA
BERNARD L. HERMAN — 117

OH BUNGALOW, BORN BY THE BAY OF BENGAL, YOU CONQUERED AN EMPIRE—AND THEN THE WORLD—REDEFINING SUCCESS EVERY STEP OF THE WAY!
DAVID HOWES — 129

ON THE MOVE OF IROQUOIS, ONTARIO: HOW CHOOSING A SITE TO THE EAST OFFERS AN OPPORTUNITY FOR FUTURISTIC LIVING
PETER SEALY — 137

DEADLY RE-EVALUATION: WHEN THE IBIS, ONCE SACRED IN EGYPT, BECAME AN ALIEN MENACE IN FRANCE
ANDERS BELL — 151

EXPATRIATE EXPERTISE: WHEN THE ARRIVAL OF SKILLED ITALIAN WORKERS TRANSFORMED THE VERMONT GRANITE INDUSTRY
ILARIA BRANCOLI BUSDRAGHI — 165

THE BACK-AND-FORTH CYCLE: HOW TEMPORARY SENEGALESE WORKERS LIVE ON THE EDGES OF ITALIAN SOCIETY AND RAPIDLY TRANSFORM THE BUILT ENVIRONMENT BACK HOME
IAN CHODIKOFF — 179

CALL SHOPS: A NEW ARCHITECTURAL TYPOLOGY FOR CALLING HOME
RIITTA OITTINEN — 191

LEARNING IDEOGRAMS: A STORY OF HOW CONGO'S
BRAZZAVILLE IS BEING BUILT ANEW BY CHINESE
COMPANIES
SERGE MICHEL — 203

FEELING FOREIGN: WHAT HAPPENS WHEN A HOSPITAL
LOOKS JUST LIKE A SHOPPING MALL
DAVID THEODORE — 215

INTERPRETING MODERNISM: HOW AN AMSTERDAM
HOUSING DEVELOPMENT CHANGES WHEN SURINAM
GAINS INDEPENDENCE
WOUTER OOSTENDORP AND JOUKE SIESWERDA — 223

COMPROMISE IN THE CASBAH: HOW THE RESIDENTS OF
A SICILIAN TOWN NAVIGATE SEVERAL LANGUAGES AND
MANY DIFFERENT IDEAS ABOUT HOW TO USE SPACE
GIOVANNA BORASI — 237

THE PRAIRIE IS VAST AND ENDLESS, UNTIL IT ISN'T:
A MICHIF STORY
JEAN TEILLET — 249

HOW RICE, PERSIMMONS, SOY AND A WHOLE HOST OF
OTHER CROPS FROM JAPAN RESHAPED THE BOLIVIAN
COUNTRYSIDE
KOZY AMEMIYA — 261

PERPLEXING PEREGRINATIONS: ON THE TRAIL
OF DRIFTING COCONUTS
CURTIS C. EBBESMEYER — 277

BIOGRAPHIES — 292

REFERENCES — 294

LENDERS AND COPYRIGHTS — 299

NOTE FROM THE EDITOR — 300

ACKNOWLEDGMENTS — 301

FOREWORD

In recent years, the Canadian Centre for Architecture has undertaken a number of projects addressing themes that lie at the heart of contemporary life: the perception and use of urban space in *Sense of the City* (2005-06); the exploitation of environmental resources in *1973: Sorry, Out of Gas* (2007-08); the processes of urban transformation in *Actions: What You Can Do With the City* (2008-09); and speed in *Speed Limits* (2009). In a period that is witnessing ever-increasing movement of people and things, it was inevitable that we should turn our attention to the theme of migrations and examine their transformative impact on the areas they affect.

One of the first expressions of this research project is the exhibition *Journeys: How travelling fruit, ideas, and buildings rearrange our environment* and this companion volume. It does not focus on the phenomenon of migration itself or the contemporary conflicts and disputes it engenders, nor does it focus on modern-day barriers and interdiction schemes, those problematic and likely vain attempts to control or regulate this flow. Rather, it examines the consequences and results of these displacements.

What is happening today to the historical courtyards in the centre of Mazara del Vallo, Italy? How has a grand housing development in Amsterdam managed to accommodate an unexpected surge in newcomers from another continent? What generates the continual flow of people and goods between Senegal and Italy? How did the arrival of different cultures and crops alter the landscape of Bolivia? How is the urban landscape changing with the advent of call shops—the physical expression of a new dimension in global communications? What can we learn from events in the recent or distant past, for example the appearance of bungalows in California, or the shifting location of housing in Newfoundland? These are only some of the questions considered in this book and exhibition. Though based on actual facts and documents, they are presented here in the form of fictional stories. By a variety of authors, these narrative-based essays explore migrational factors behind real transformations of place, providing an initial contribution to any potential history of these phenomena's effect on cities and regions.

Migrations, both within national borders and internationally, are constantly on the increase, and forecasts for the coming decades indicate they may eventually involve as many as a billion people. For the foreseeable future, wars, poverty, conflicts, natural disasters and the simple desire for better—or different—working and living conditions will continue to fuel new streams of people, things and animals. Considering the growing ease of transportation and the gradual reduction in the limits of time and geography, this type of movement seems set to become a permanent part of life for a larger and larger proportion of the world's population.

FOREWORD

Journeys: How travelling fruit, ideas, and buildings rearrange our environment presents new avenues for reflecting on the complexities of this theme. The exhibition and book are the result of the diligence of many people, some at the CCA, others part of a broader network of collaborators and researchers. This project was brilliantly conceived and enthusiastically guided by Giovanna Borasi, Curator of Contemporary Architecture at the CCA. To her, my special thanks for having given us the opportunity, through these narratives, to observe the hybrid territories of the contemporary world with new eyes.

MIRKO ZARDINI
Director and Chief Curator
Canadian Centre for Architecture

CLASSIFICATION:

Cucumbers grown organically can develop with a wide range of forms and gradients of curvature. In 1988 the European Economic Community (EEC) adopted a law that included new regulations for fruit and vegetables sold directly to consumers. The law included a mathematical definition for the acceptable curvature in the highest class of cucumber. This was intended as a way of standardizing the contents of shipping crates, but an unintended consequence of the law was that, for the purposes of retail, some cucumbers ceased to be cucumbers.

Organic cucumbers,
Montreal organic food growers co-op, 2009

CLASSIFICATION:

The 1988 EEC law was superseded in 2009, and the new
legislation allows for many nonstandard fruits and
vegetables to be sold directly to consumers as long
as they are labelled "intended for processing."
The variety of what we grow and eat is shaped by the
power of abstract classification, ultimately affecting
the landscape and its biodiversity.

Commission Regulation (EEC) No 1677/88, laying
down quality standards for cucumbers, June 15,
1988, from the *Official Journal of the European
Communities* No. L 150/21
Courtesy of the Publications Office of the
European Union

COMMISSION REGULATION (EEC) No 1677/88
of 15 June 1988
laying down quality standards for cucumbers

THE COMMISSION OF THE EUROPEAN COMMUNITIES,

Having regard to the Treaty establishing the European Economic Community,

Having regard to Council Regulation (EEC) No 1035/72 of 18 May 1972 on the common organization of the market in fruit and vegetables (¹), as last amended by Regulation (EEC) No 1117/88 (²), and in particular Article 2 (3) thereof,

Whereas Council Regulation No 183/64/EEC (³) lays down quality standards for cucumbers;

Whereas a change has occurred in the production and marketing of those products, particularly as regards the requirements of consumer and wholesale markets; whereas the common quality standards for cucumbers should therefore be changed to take those new requirements into account;

Whereas such changes entail alteration of the definition of the supplementary quality class as laid down by Council Regulation (EEC) No 1194/69 (⁴) as last amended by Regulation (EEC) No 79/88 (⁵); whereas account should be taken, in defining that class, of the economic importance to producers of the products concerned and of the need to meet consumer requirements;

Whereas the standards are applicable at all stages of marketing; whereas transportation over a long distance, storage for a certain length of time or the various handling operations may bring about deterioration due to the biological development of the products or their tendency to perish; whereas, therefore, account should be taken of such deterioration when applying the standards of marketing stages following dispatch;

Whereas in the interests of clarity and certainty as to legal requirements and for ease of use the standards thus changed should be consolidated in a single text;

(¹) OJ No L 118, 20. 5. 1972, p. 1.
(²) OJ No L 107, 28. 4. 1988, p. 1.
(³) OJ No 192, 25. 11. 1964, p. 3217/64.
(⁴) OJ No L 157, 28. 6. 1969, p. 1.
(⁵) OJ No L 10, 14. 1. 1988, p. 8.

Whereas the measures provided for in this Regulation are in accordance with the opinion of the Management Committee for Fruit and Vegetables,

HAS ADOPTED THIS REGULATION:

Article 1

The quality standards for cucumbers, falling within subheading 0707 00 11 and 0707 00 19 of the combined nomenclature shall be as set out in the Annex hereto.

Those standards shall apply at all marketing stages, under the conditions laid down in Regulation (EEC) No 1035/72.

However, at stages following dispatch the products may show, in relation to the standards prescribed a slight lack of freshness and turgescence and slight alteration due to their biological development and their tendency to perish.

Article 2

Regulation No 183/64/EEC is hereby amended as follows:

— the second indent of Article 1 (2) is deleted,
— Annex I/2 is deleted.

Article 3

Regulation (EEC) No 1194/69 is hereby amended as follows:

— in Article 1, the words 'and cucumbers' are deleted,
— Annex VII is deleted.

Article 4

This Regulation shall enter into force on 1 January 1989.

CONFIGURATION:

Between 1954 and 1975 the government of Newfoundland, Canada encouraged about 300 isolated communities to resettle in central areas in response to economic pressures caused by collapsing fish stocks and the difficulty of providing public services to remote communities. Assistance was made available only to communities where a majority signed documents promising to move.

Nomination form filled out by F.C. Paul Grubb, Moravian missionary, for Hebron, Newfoundland
ca. 1957
Courtesy of the A.G. Stacey Papers, Archives and Special Collections, Queen Elizabeth II Library, Memorial University of Newfoundland

Your Name F.C. Paul Grubb
Address Moravian Mission,
Nain,
Labrador,

Position or Minister of
Appointment Religion.

Name of Settlements you think should be vacated. (In order of priority)	No. of families involved. (approximate)	Note the reasons why you think the settlement should be vacated.
Hebron	Aproximately 50 ✓	This complicated matter. As general economy as good as any on Coast. But from health stand point and fuel is in very poor condition.
		But whole Northern Coast in very bad shape in regards to earning possibilities. These are reasons in very small nut shell.

CONFIGURATION:

About 30,000 people had to find new configurations for their existing social relationships and for their houses, enabled by a local history of flexible construction that allowed many homes to be moved whole. Moving one's house to follow fish populations to increasingly remote grounds was a long-established practice. Houses were often built with light foundations, perched on wooden structures on rocky outcroppings.

Pulling a structure across the ice Conche, Newfoundland, 1965
Courtesy of the Maritime History Archive, Resettlement Collection, Memorial University of Newfoundland

Pulling a house across the ice at Cook's Harbour Great Northern Peninsula, Newfoundland, 1953
Courtesy of the Maritime History Archive, Resettlement Collection, Memorial University of Newfoundland

CONFIGURATION:

Higher housing prices in centralization areas often made the purchase of new homes unrealistic and further encouraged transportation. Some destinations, like Arnold's Cove in Placentia Bay, became largely inhabited by resettled families whose homes lost their original references to topography, local agriculture and landscape, and traditional patterns of use.

Moving a house across the water
Trinity Bay, Newfoundland, ca. 1968
Courtesy of the Maritime History Archive,
Resettlement Collection, Memorial University
of Newfoundland

The Frank Drake house, constructed ca. 1880—1890,
moved November 1969 from Haystack
Arnold's Cove, Newfoundland, 2004
Courtesy of the Maritime History Archive,
Resettlement Collection, Memorial University
of Newfoundland

INHERITANCE:

Free American blacks and former slaves were encouraged to emigrate to Liberia, in Africa, by the American Colonization Society and other groups from 1816 until 1847. While some of the latter wanted to abolish slavery and spread evangelical Christianity, others supported emigration as a way to strengthen slavery by removing freed blacks from the United States.

Max Belcher, photographer
House built ca. 1880
Hertford, Perquimans County, North Carolina, 1986
CCA Collection

Max Belcher, photographer
The Simpson House, construction date unknown
Clay-Ashland, Liberia, 1978
CCA Collection

INHERITANCE:

Max Belcher, photographer
The J.J. Cheeseman House, built ca. 1885
Edina, Liberia, 1978
CCA Collection

Max Belcher, photographer
The Bricks, Bratton House, built ca. 1843-45
Historic Brattonsville, McConnells, York County,
South Carolina, 1987
CCA Collection

INHERITANCE:

Max Belcher, photographer
Interior, the George Stanley Padmore House,
built ca. 1880
Crozierville, Liberia, 1983
CCA Collection

Max Belcher, photographer
Interior, the Walker House,
built in the early 19th century
Bethel Vic, York County, South Carolina, 1987
CCA Collection

INHERITANCE:

About 17,000 settlers made the voyage, founded cities, built farms, and developed a culture whose buildings reflected their origins. The homes, churches, and other buildings they constructed, as well their organization of Liberian society, was part of their inheritance. Building in a style from the American South, with verandas and columned porches, the settlers transformed some of the hierarchies they had known in America and established themselves as local elite in Liberia, where they played a dominant role in society until the 1980s.

Max Belcher, photographer
Cove Grove, built ca. 1830
Perquimans County, North Carolina, 1986
CCA Collection

Max Belcher, photographer
The Rev. June Moore House, built ca. 1885
Arthington, Liberia, 1977
CCA Collection

DEFINITION:

"Dr. Brown's Bungalow," Plate VI
from the album *Views of the
Middle and Far East, and India.*
Sylhet, Bangladesh, ca. 1860s
CCA Collection

DEFINITION:

The definition and the form of the bungalow evolved in
parallel as they were adopted by different cultures.
In 17th century India the name was applied to Bengali
houses with a single story and porches all around, but
by the 20th century it also meant a house "suitable"
for Europeans in Africa and the Indian subcontinent,
a symbol of colonial power and occupation.

"A Cottager's Dwelling," Plate XIV from Joseph Gandy,
*Designs for Cottages, Cottage Farms, and Other Rural
Buildings Including Entrance Gates and Lodges.*
London: Printed for John Harding, 1805
CCA Collection

"Bungalow Design No. 2004" from Fred. T. Hodgson,
Practical Bungalows and Cottages for Town and Country.
Chicago: F.J. Drake & Co., 1906
CCA Collection

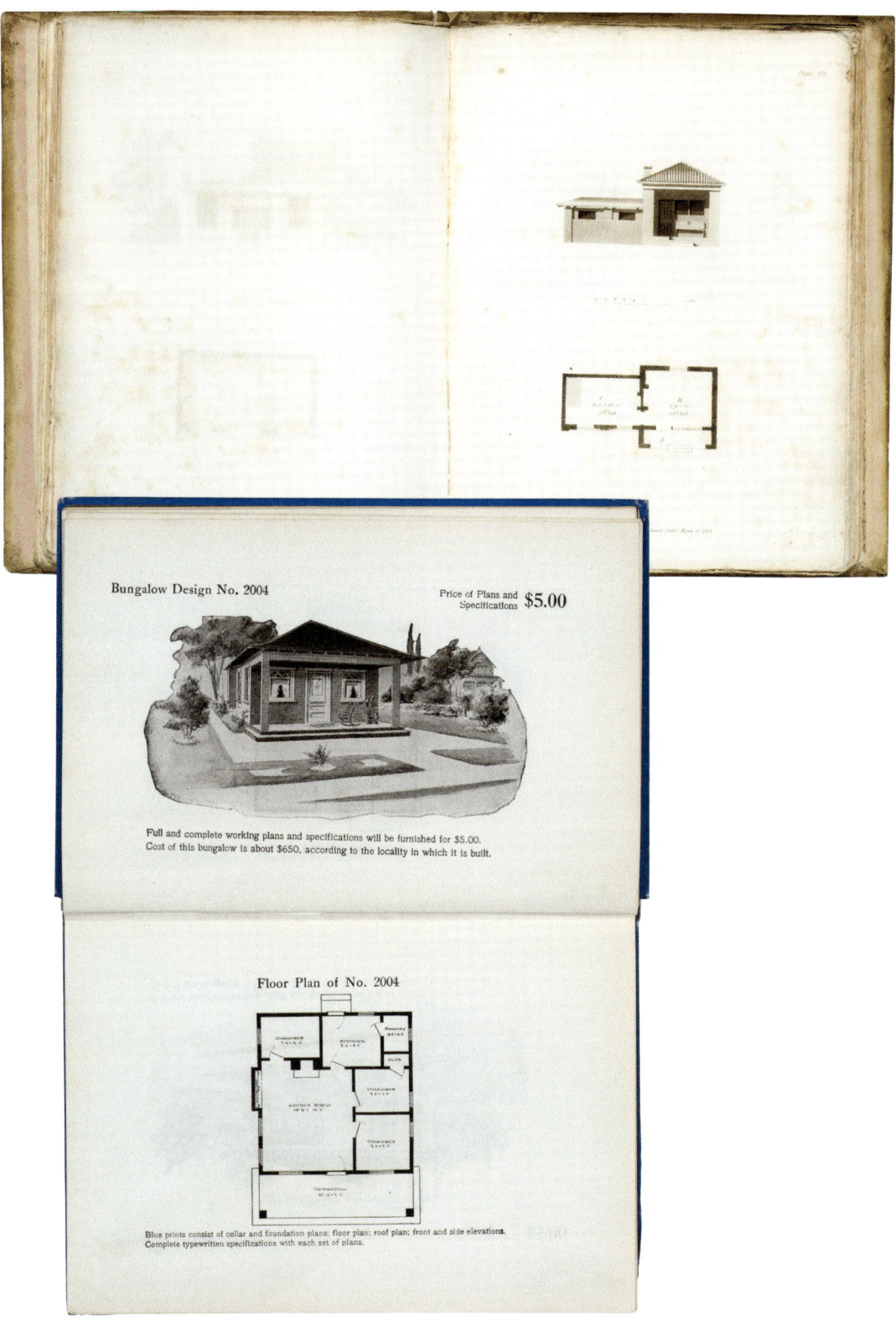

DEFINITION:

1   Radford's Artistic Bungalows: Unique Collection of 208 Designs; Best Modern Ideas in Bungalow Architecture.
Chicago: Radford Architectural Co., 1908
CCA Collection

2   Bungalowcraft: "Homes Not Houses"; Stucco, Colonial and Swiss Chalet Bungalows.
Los Angeles: Bungalow Craft Co., 1921
CCA Collection

3   The Homefinder Bungalow Plan Book.
London: Homefinders, 1957
CCA Collection

4   Castle Mountain Bungalow Camp, Banff Windermere Highway, Canadian Rockies.
Canada: Canadian Pacific Railway Company, 1930
CCA Collection

5   The Book of Bungalows: Designs and Floor Plans for 34 Attractive Practical Homes.
St. Paul: Home Plan Book Co., 1946
CCA Collection

6   Bungalows.
Minneapolis: J.W. Lindstrom, 1936
CCA Collection

7   Jack Fitzsimons, Bungalow Bliss, 2nd edition.
Kells, Ireland: Kells Art Studios, 1976
CCA Collection

4

5

6

7

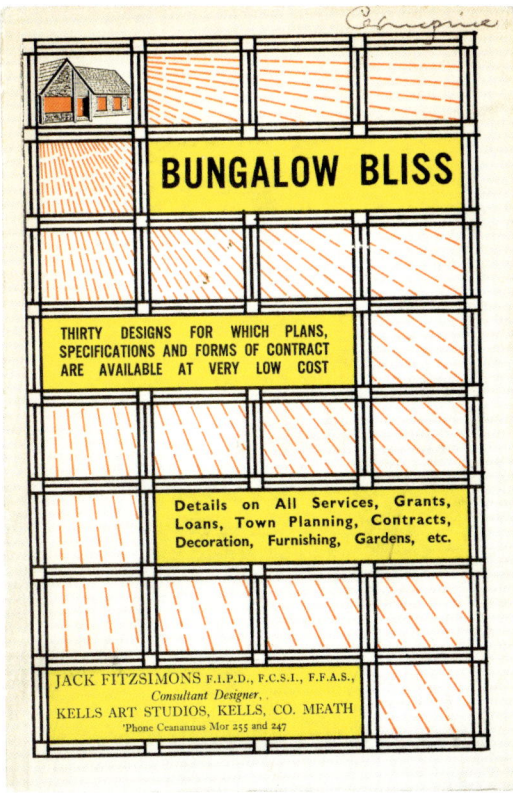

DEFINITION:

In 20th century Europe, especially in England, the bungalow was characterized as a second home and not limited to single storeys or simple designs. A flexibility of form, and associations with leisure, holidays, and good weather, may have played a role in the popularity of the type in North America, where it filled the endless suburbs built during the post-war economic boom of the late 1940s and 1950s. Bungalow plans were sold in catalogues, and prefabricated components could be delivered in short order.

Martin Parr, photographer
Bungalow
Keadue, County Roscommon, Ireland, 1981
CCA Collection

Martin Parr, photographer
Bungalow
Glencar, County Sligo, Ireland, 1980
CCA Collection

OPPORTUNITY:

Navigation improvements planned for the Saint Lawrence Seaway in the 1950s meant the flooding and relocation of several small communities in Ontario, Canada, particularly around the International Rapids section between Kingston and Cornwall. Forced to move one kilometre, the town of Iroquois sought an ambitious proposal for a New Town on the Saint Lawrence River.

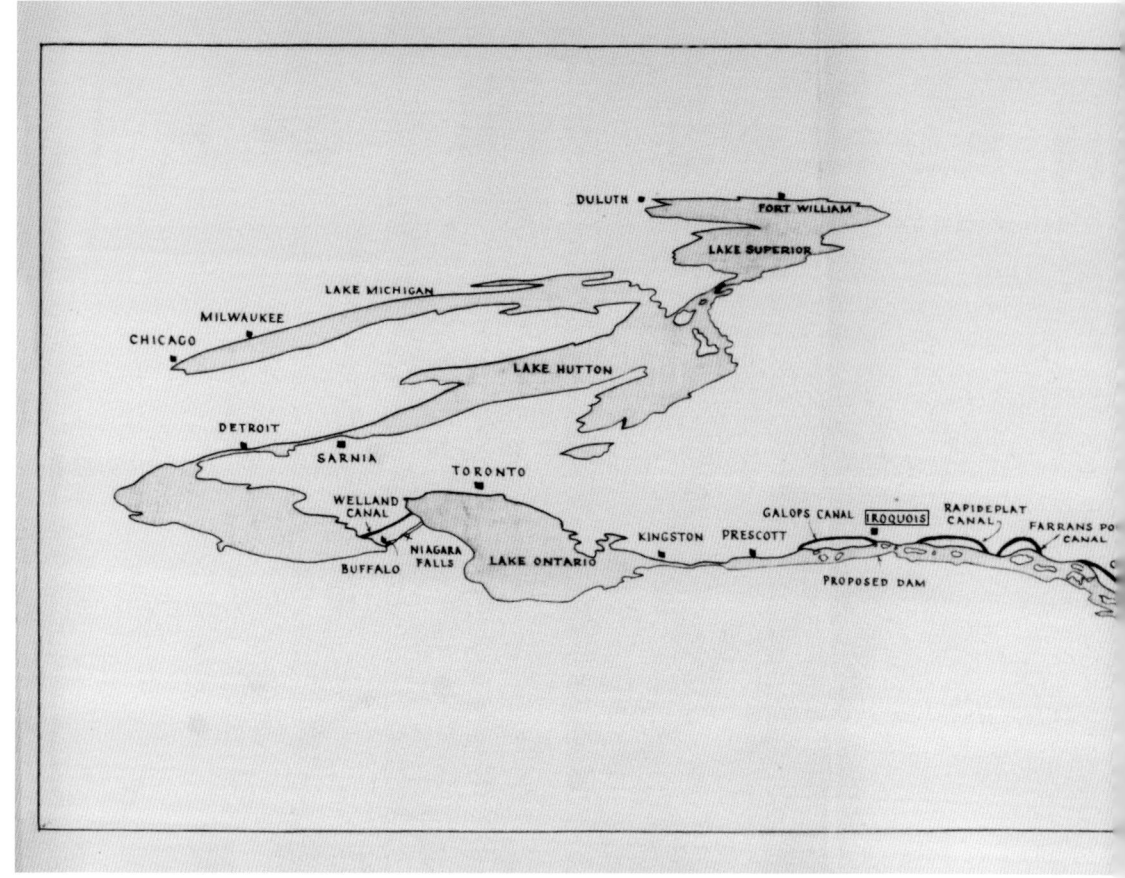

Map of the St. Lawrence Seaway from J.F.M. Wood,
The St. Lawrence Seaway: Iroquois Project.
London: The Imperial Life Assurance Co. of Canada,
ca. 1952—54
CCA Collection, Wells Coates fonds

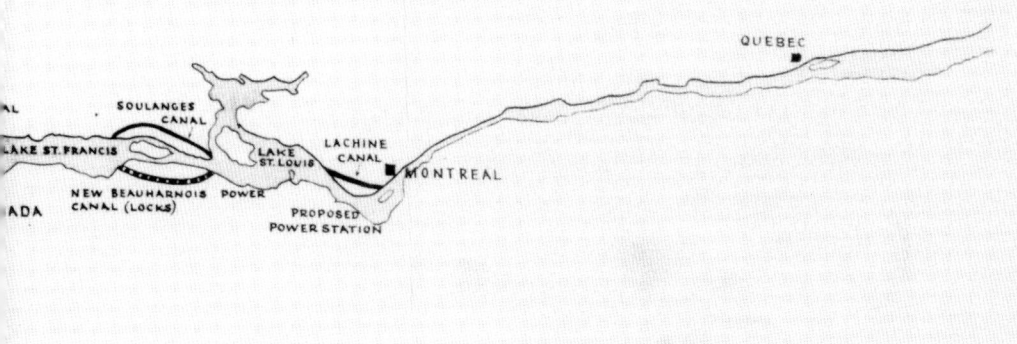

THE ST LAWRENCE SEAWAY

OPPORTUNITY:

In 1952, the town of Iroquois, with a population of about 1,100, hired the British architect Wells Coates as a planning consultant to prepare plans for the new town. Coates' proposal saw a move of only a few kilometres as an opportunity for an ambitious redevelopment that anticipated an eventual population of 40,000 and substantial British investment in this new town.

His Modernist design re-housed the original inhabitants in the centre of the new town near important public institutions. The new arrivals would occupy village-sized units he called "neighbourships." Following Modernist practice, Coates carefully planned not only zoning separation between industrial, residential and leisure spaces, but a hierarchy of transportation networks.

Coates' proposal combined his recognition of a strategic geographical location (in an age when access to transcontinental railways and shipping lanes was crucial) with detailed concern for transposing the original inhabitants of Iroquois to their new situation. While an Ontario Hydro plan was carried out instead, Coates' project remains important for its re-conception of urban design in Canada.

Wells Coates, architect
Sketch of neighbourships, Iroquois, ca. 1952-54
CCA Collection, Wells Coates fonds

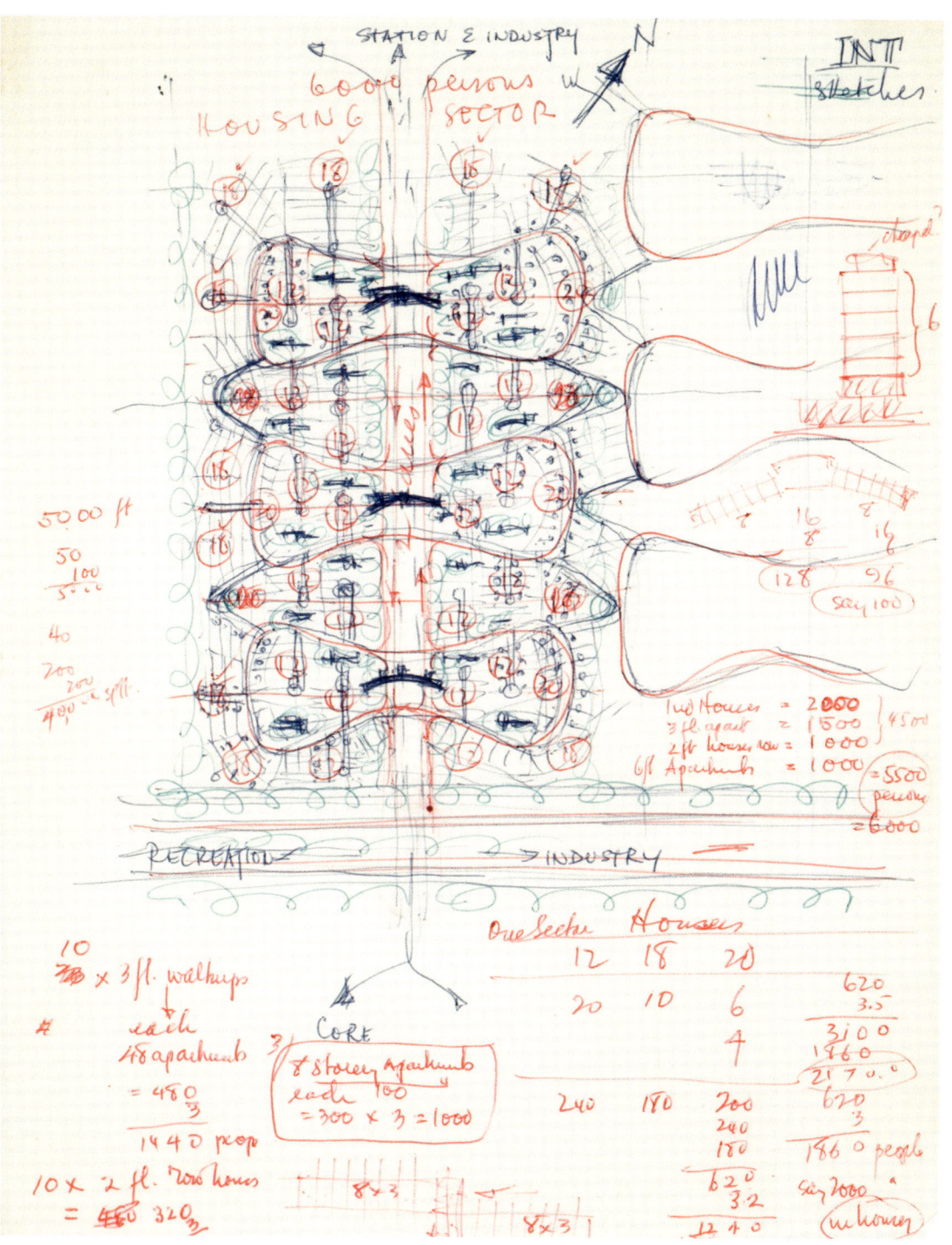

OPPORTUNITY:

Wells Coates, architect
Draft master plan for the New Town
of Iroquois, ca. 1952-54
CCA Collection, Wells Coates fonds

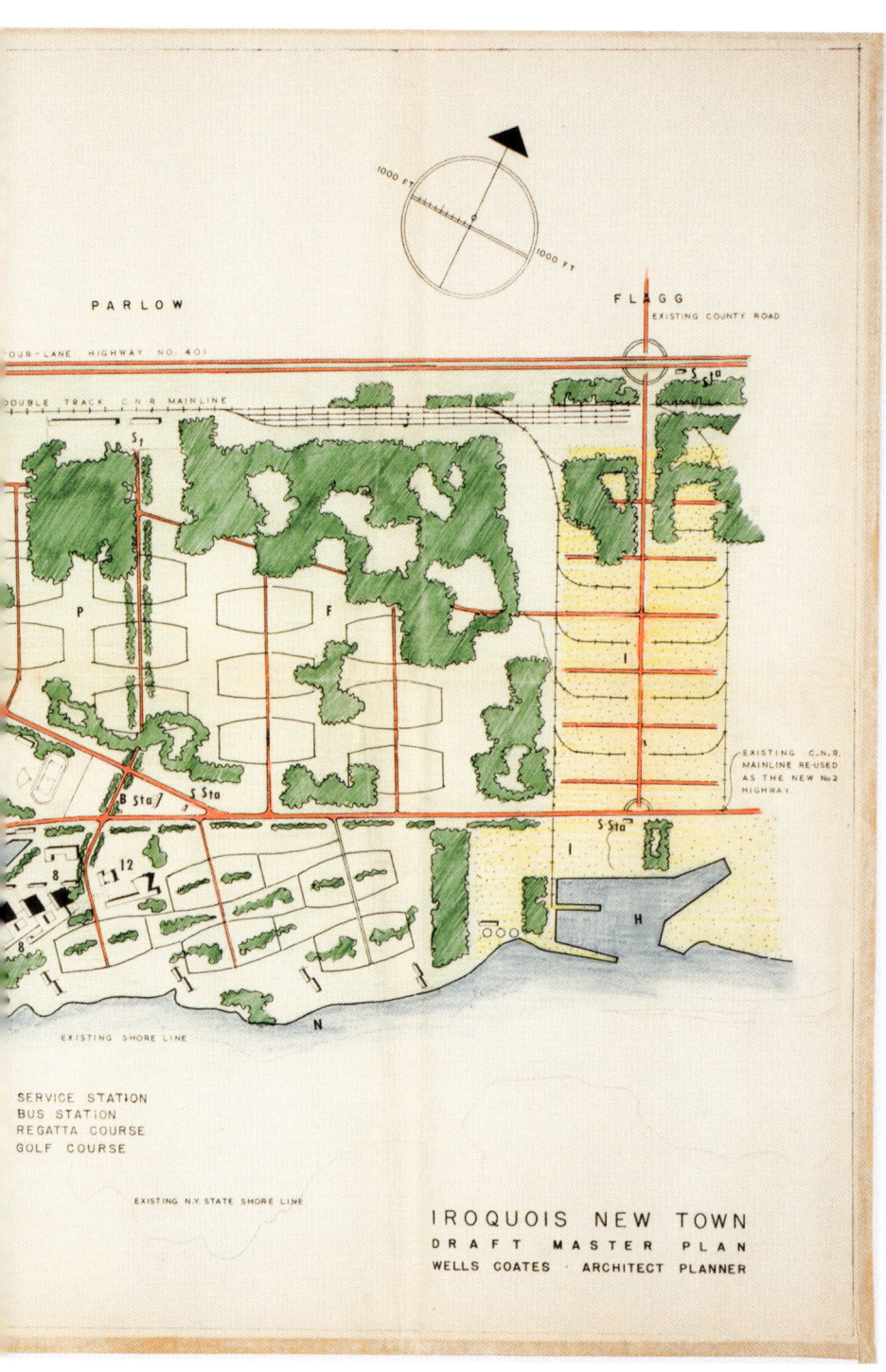

VALUE:

Associated with Thoth (the ancient Egyptian god of writing, science and magic) from as early as the 3rd millennium BC, the Sacred Ibis also became a popular sacrificial animal during the Ptolemaic period and was likely farmed for this purpose. In the late 1970s, a small number of Sacred Ibises were imported to a zoological park in the Loire estuary in northern France. These birds were allowed to fly freely and some nested outside the confines of the park.

However, in 2005, after claims that Sacred Ibises were feeding on the eggs of native birds, a detailed report on the Sacred Ibis and its effects was commissioned. The results, along with E.U. laws prohibiting the introduction of non-native species, allowed local officials to enact a total cull of Sacred Ibis colonies in the region. Movement over a long period of time resulted in a dramatic change in the value of the Sacred Ibis.

Colony of Sacred Ibises
Bilho Bank, Loire estuary, France, 2005
Photo by Pierre Yésou

EXPERTISE:

The population of Barre, Vermont almost quadrupled from 1880 to 1910 due to the availability of skilled labour, the proximity of a rail link, and the low iron content of the region's granite, which helps inhibit discolouration. The population's special skills and density of expertise determined the growth, form, and importance of this small town, which remains a national centre for the production of monumental granite, memorial sculpture and stone carving tools.

Edward Burtynsky, photographer
Rock of Ages No. 13
Active granite section, Adam-Pirie Quarry
Barre, Vermont, 1991
Courtesy of the Nicholas Metivier Gallery, Toronto

EXPERTISE:

Skilled stonemasons and cutters were recruited by American immigration companies in the 1880s and 1890s to work in the booming granite and marble quarries of New England. Many of these immigrants came from the Italian Alps and Prealps regions of Piedmont and Lombardy, as well as central towns like Carrara, a historical centre for marble work and political agitation. In Barre, Vermont, their expertise in fine work, monuments, and carving shaped the development of the industry, allowing for a complete range of production from architectural components to obelisks and decorative sculpture to funerary work.

Novelli and Calcagni granite cutting shed
Barre, Vermont, ca. 1900
Courtesy of the Aldrich Public Library, Barre, Vermont

O.J. Dodge, photographer
Novelli and Calcagni statuary used in the Burke Mausoleum, Lake View Cemetery, Cleveland, Ohio
Barre, Vermont, ca. 1960s
Courtesy of the Aldrich Public Library, Barre, Vermont

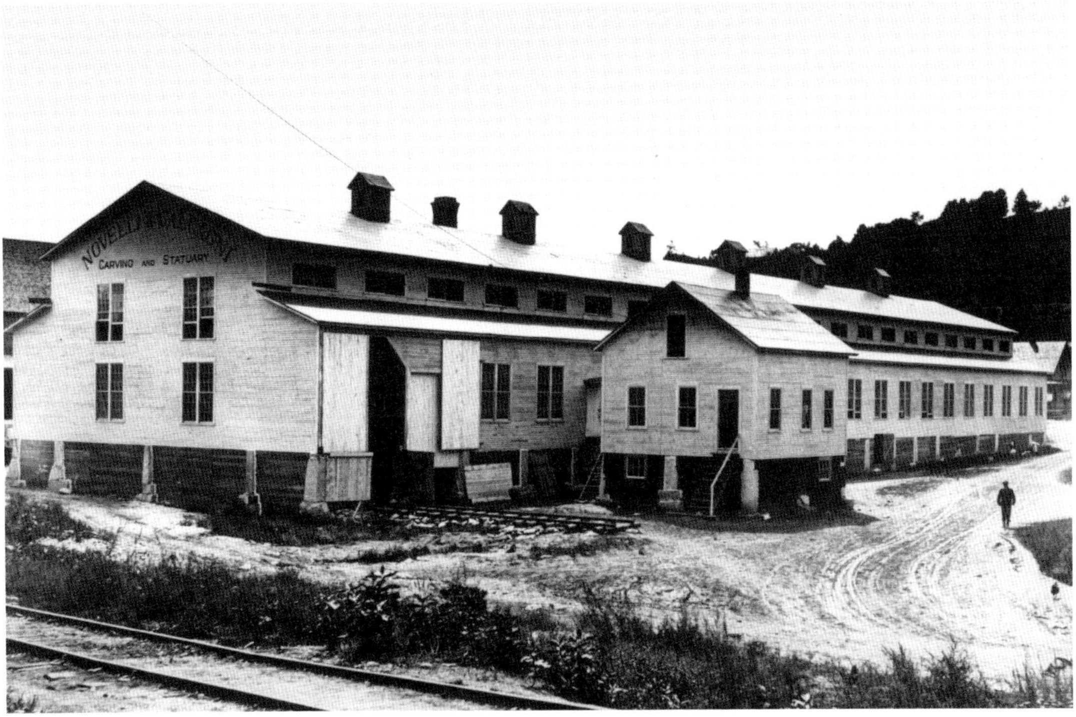
CARVING AND STATUARY

Cut by
Novelli & Calcagni
Barre, Vt.

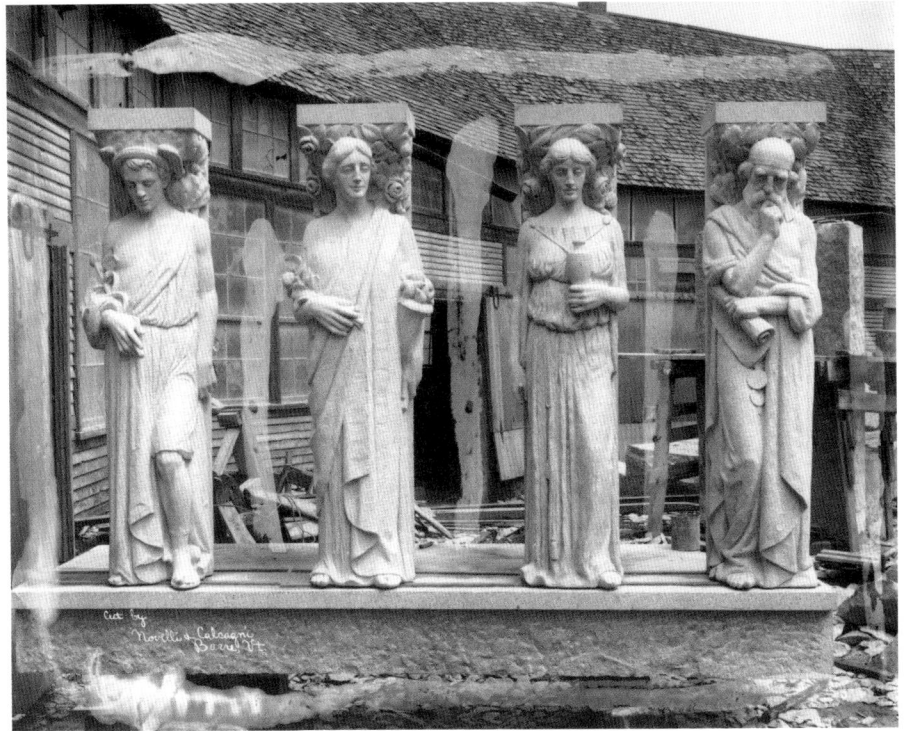

EXPERTISE:

F.W. Sherburne, photographer
Transporting a gable stone for the Leland Stanford Mausoleum, Stanford, California
Barre, Vermont, 1886
Courtesy of the Aldrich Public Library, Barre, Vermont

"The Mausoleum" from *Leland Stanford Junior University*.
Palo Alto, CA: H.W. Simkins, 1900
CCA Collection

In Barre. Part of Stanford Mausoleum. Wgt. of Stone 50 tons.

THE MAUSOLEUM.

CYCLE:

An established pattern of economic migration between Senegal and Italy typically begins like this: one member of a family is chosen to work in informal commerce, farming, or construction for three or five years in Italy. Their travel and employment are arranged through kinship networks, and they send money back. After their return another person is sent.

Senegalese economic migration to Italy occurs at a large scale and with a regular period of repetition and return, a cycle that provides capital for construction in Senegal and alters cities in both countries. This phenomenon provides about $400 million each year, much of which funds land speculation and rapid urbanization in several Senegalese regions.

Construction in Keur Massar
Dakar, Senegal, 2005
Photo by Ian Chodikoff

CYCLE:

The returning Senegalese workers also bring back products, materials, and habits they have learned while away. Used cars from Europe are regularly imported into Senegal. Some returning Senegalese workers construct houses for themselves and their families; others use their capital for speculative development. The sometimes strange and ostentatious buildings that result from this cycle have stylistic elements that do not seem local, and they appear faster than formal development projects.

Used cars
Rimini, Italy, 2005
Photo by Ian Chodikoff

Used cars
Dakar, Senegal, 2005
Photo by Ian Chodikoff

CYCLE:

Nearly complete private development facing
unfinished government-financed housing
Mbao, Senegal, 2007
Photo by Ian Chodikoff

TYPOLOGY:

Small "call shops" that provide telecommunications services are found in most urban centres around the world. These electronic service stations will appear anywhere there are travellers, tourists, immigrants, or temporary workers who want to contact somebody else. In countries with an underdeveloped telecommunications infrastructure, they fill this gap, and in developed countries they often serve groups with short-term or changing needs.

These specialized businesses have a limited range of functions and take their basic structure from a simple typology: they are almost always the same, often with standardized cubicle sizes, generic telephone booths, and taped-up advertising on the exterior that lists available services.

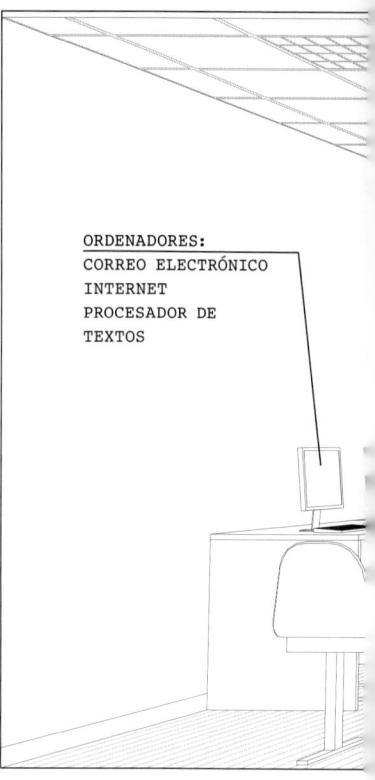

ORDENADORES:
CORREO ELECTRÓNICO
INTERNET
PROCESADOR DE
TEXTOS

The call shop "Jorge Locutorios: Real de envíos" also functions as a remittance exchange; a rival call shop is right next door.
Calle de Almansa 4, Madrid, 2010
Drawing by Matthew Fellows; documentation by Alexandra Atiya

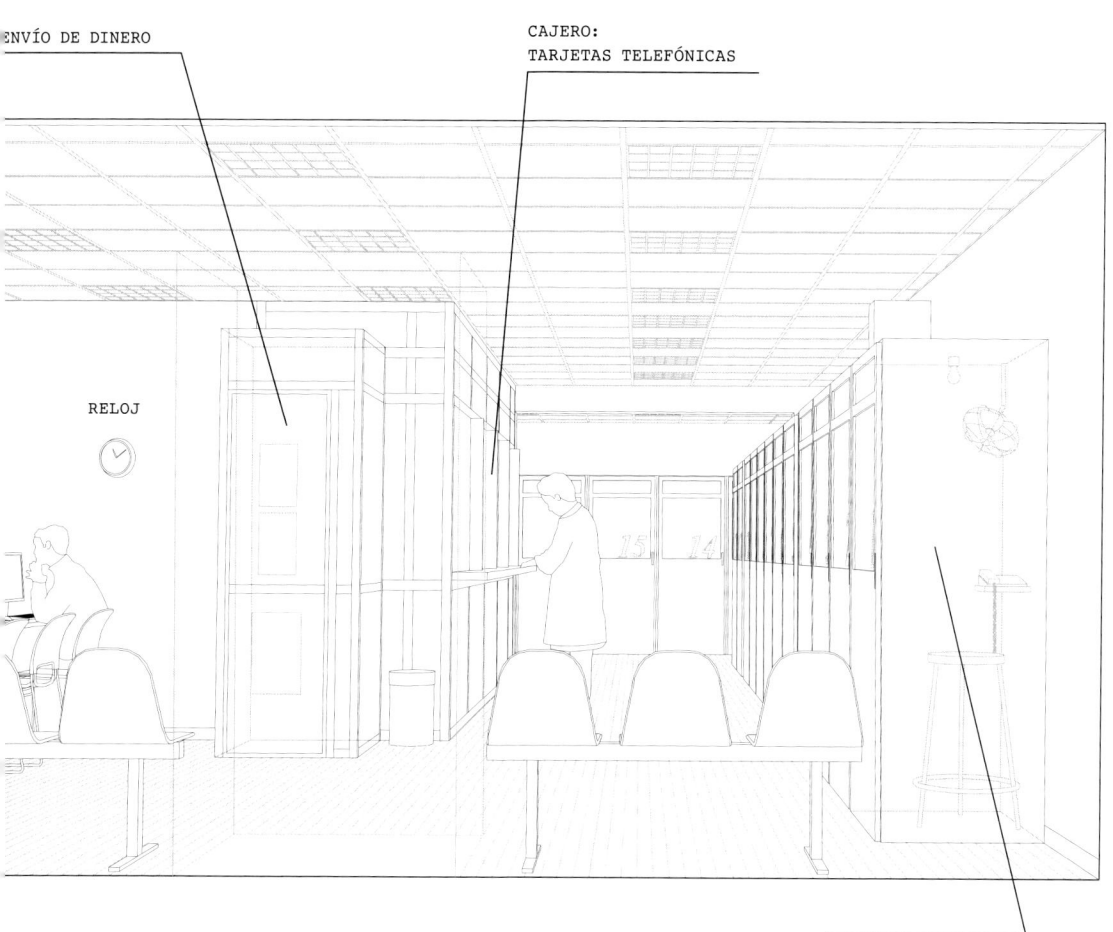

TYPOLOGY:

Because call shops primarily connect international customers, they must operate beyond normal business hours and frequently take on a variety of social functions, serving as community gathering places and developing sidelines as importers of foods and merchandise. Some even offer highly specialized services such as translation and assistance with filling out official forms, which can be difficult to obtain in some countries.

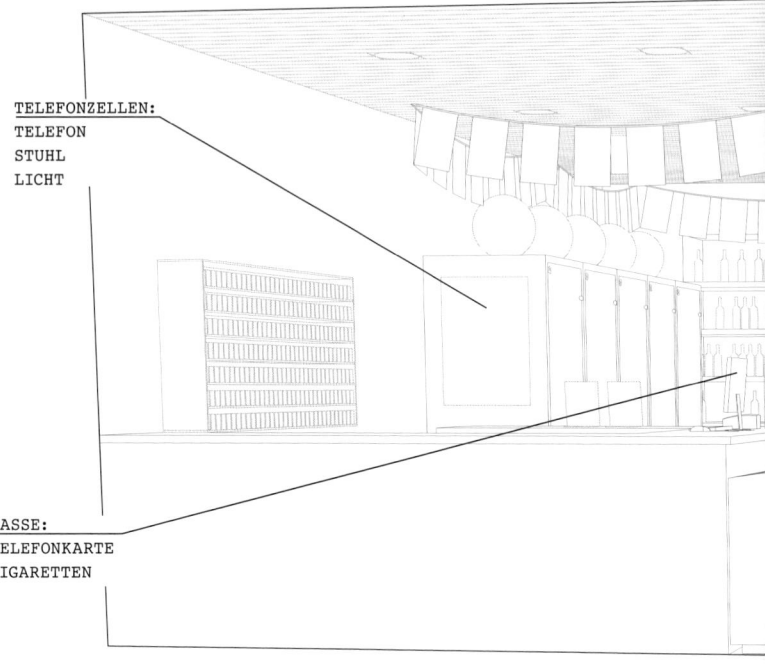

TELEFONZELLEN:
TELEFON
STUHL
LICHT

KASSE:
TELEFONKARTE
ZIGARETTEN

The call shop "Globus Surf & Call Point" has two levels: at the street level is a convenience/liquor store with phone stalls; the basement offers computer services only.
Claire Waldoff Strasse 2, Berlin, 2010
Drawing by Matthew Fellows; documentation by Trevor Larson

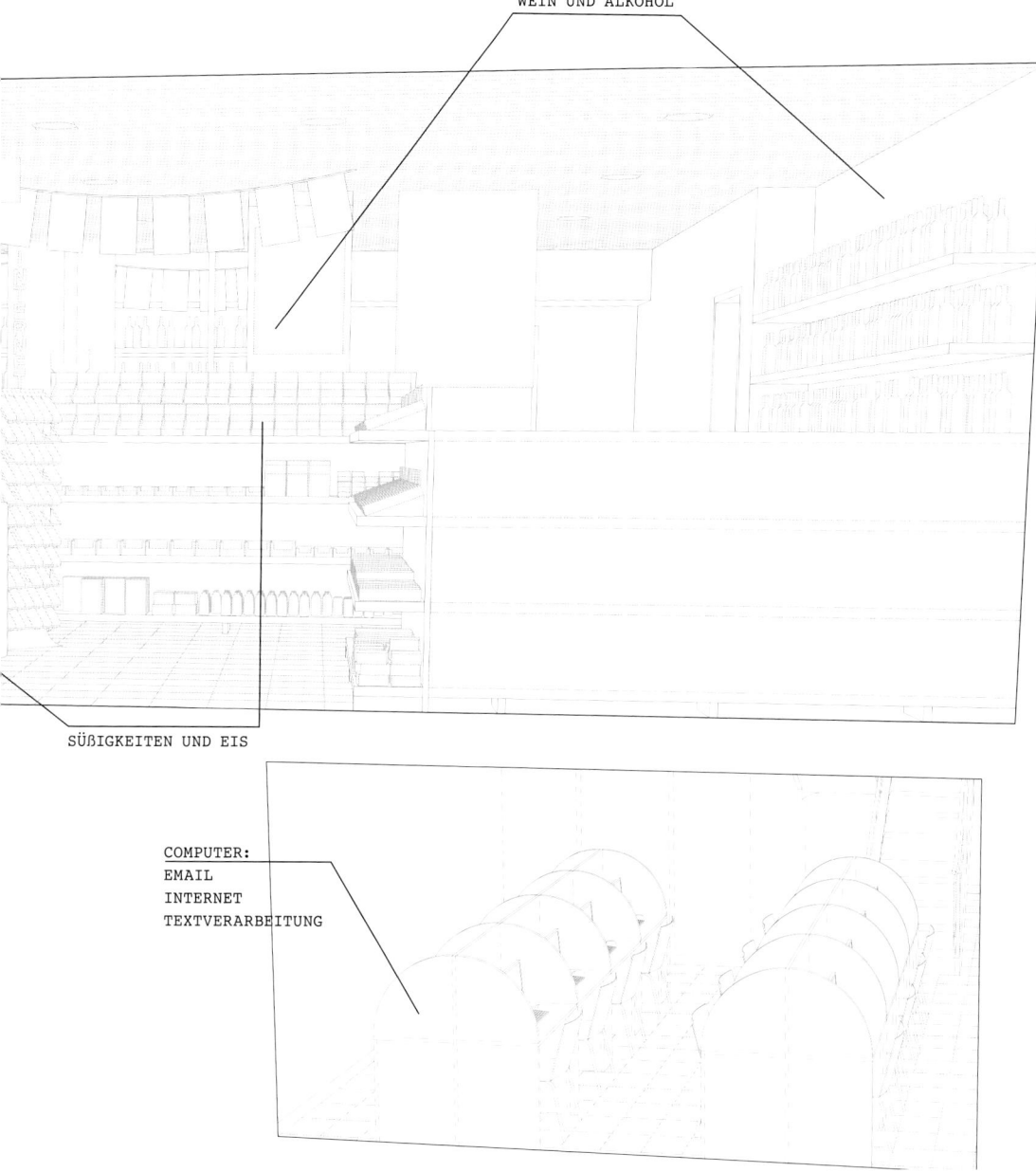

NEGOTIATION:

The capital of the Democratic Republic of the Congo is being rebuilt after sustaining heavy damage in the civil wars of the 1990s. The Chinese government and Chinese developers and investors have been instrumental in the emerging shape of the city, Brazzaville, which is taking form as a negotiation between local political forces and international economic interests.

In exchange for economic concessions in one of the world's richest wood, oil, and mineral zones, the Congolese receive a development package that provides complete building and construction projects, housing and infrastructure. Along with new attitudes towards leisure and expertise in business, labour, and political relations, the economic relationship is reshaping the built landscape of Brazzaville and the immense forests of the Congo.

Paolo Woods, Photographer
The Savorgnan de Brazza high school
Brazzaville, Republic of the Congo, 2007
Courtesy of the artist

Paolo Woods, Photographer
On the building site of the Imboulou dam
200 km north of the capital Brazzaville,
Republic of the Congo, 2007
Courtesy of the artist

INTERPRETATION:

The Bijlmermeer was a new addition to the city of Amsterdam planned by Siegfried Nassuth and the Department of City Development in the late 1960s. It was envisioned as an application of modernist principles of air, light, traffic separation and internal circulation, and its form as a guarantee of equal opportunities for its residents. However the Bijlmermeer was never fully inhabited from when the first tenants arrived in 1968: they were isolated from the rest of the city by the delay of a subway connection, subserviced, and faced increasing rents because of poor financial planning.

Postcards showing the Bijlmermeer, Amsterdam: the buildings, the public open spaces, and the elevated highway.
ca. 1970
Courtesy of the Office of Metropolitan Architecture (OMA)

Prettige Kerstdagen en Gelukkig Nieuwjaar

Groeten uit de Bijlmer

INTERPRETATION:

"De pioniers van de Bijlmermeer" [Pioneers of Bijlmermeer]
by Rene Zwaap from *Amsterdam Stadsblad*, Amsterdam,
4 February, 1987
Courtesy of the Netherlands Architecture Institute

le Bijlmermeer

INTERPRETATION:

Postcards showing the Bijlmermeer, Amsterdam:
the buildings, the public open spaces,
and the elevated highway.
ca. 1970
Courtesy of the Office of
Metropolitan Architecture (OMA)

Bijlmermeer, vissers bij Gerenstein

Bijlmermeer, gezicht op Kralenbeek

INTERPRETATION:

In 1975 the Dutch government offered newly-independent Surinamese a Dutch passport if they immigrated. The initial influx was dispersed in small groups across the country, but vacancies in the Bijlmermeer offered a longer-term solution to their housing needs. Other communities followed, each interpreting the modern buildings and collective spaces in a creative way. Though continued isolation, lack of facilities, and an increase in crime made Bijlmermeer the image of defeat of urban planning in the 1980s and 1990s, the self-organizing capacity of the inhabitants built much of what the neighbourhood lacked.

Since then, architects and experts have been repeatedly called to consider the Bijlmer: one of the first was Rem Koolhaas (OMA), whose 1986 plan was never carried out. The only solution implemented to date has been partial demolition.

"Allochtonen in cijfers" [Foreigners in Numbers], illustration with "Een blanke enclave in kleurrijk Zuidoost" [A White Enclave in the Colourful Southeast] by Frans Bosman, from *Het Parool*, Amsterdam, June 24, 1989
Courtesy of the Netherlands Architecture Institute

The text reads, "More than a quarter of the 150,000 inhabitants of Amsterdam is not of Dutch origin. In the area of Amsterdam Southeast this percentage is considerably higher, with 40% of inhabitants being of foreign origin. This number is even higher (51.4%) if we consider the Bijlmermeer alone."

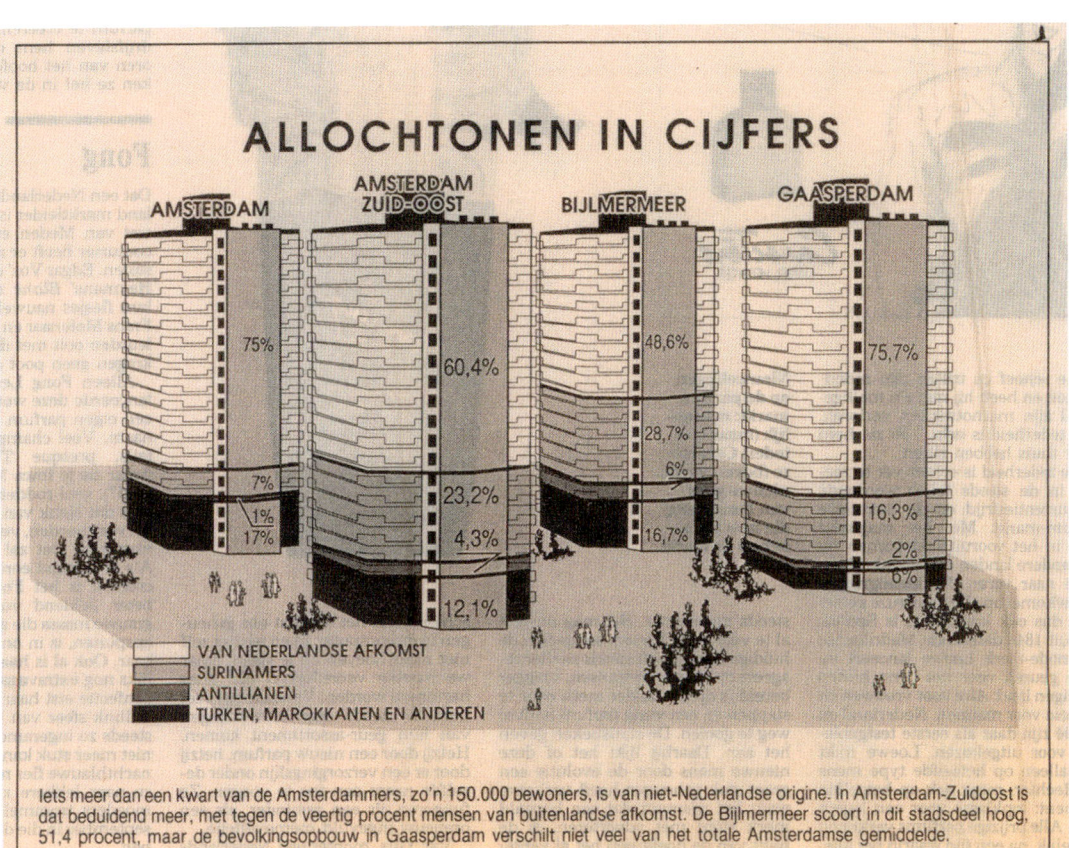

Iets meer dan een kwart van de Amsterdammers, zo'n 150.000 bewoners, is van niet-Nederlandse origine. In Amsterdam-Zuidoost is dat beduidend meer, met tegen de veertig procent mensen van buitenlandse afkomst. De Bijlmermeer scoort in dit stadsdeel hoog, 51,4 procent, maar de bevolkingsopbouw in Gaasperdam verschilt niet veel van het totale Amsterdamse gemiddelde.

INTERPRETATION:

A community church located in
a transformed parking garage
Bijlmermeer, Amsterdam, 2007
Photo by Jouke Sieswerda

A typical Bijlmermeer apartment
block Bijlmermeer, Amsterdam, 2006
Photo by Jouke Sieswerda

Shops and centres of informal
economy occupying the ground floor
Bijlmermeer, Amsterdam, 2007
Photo by Jouke Sieswerda

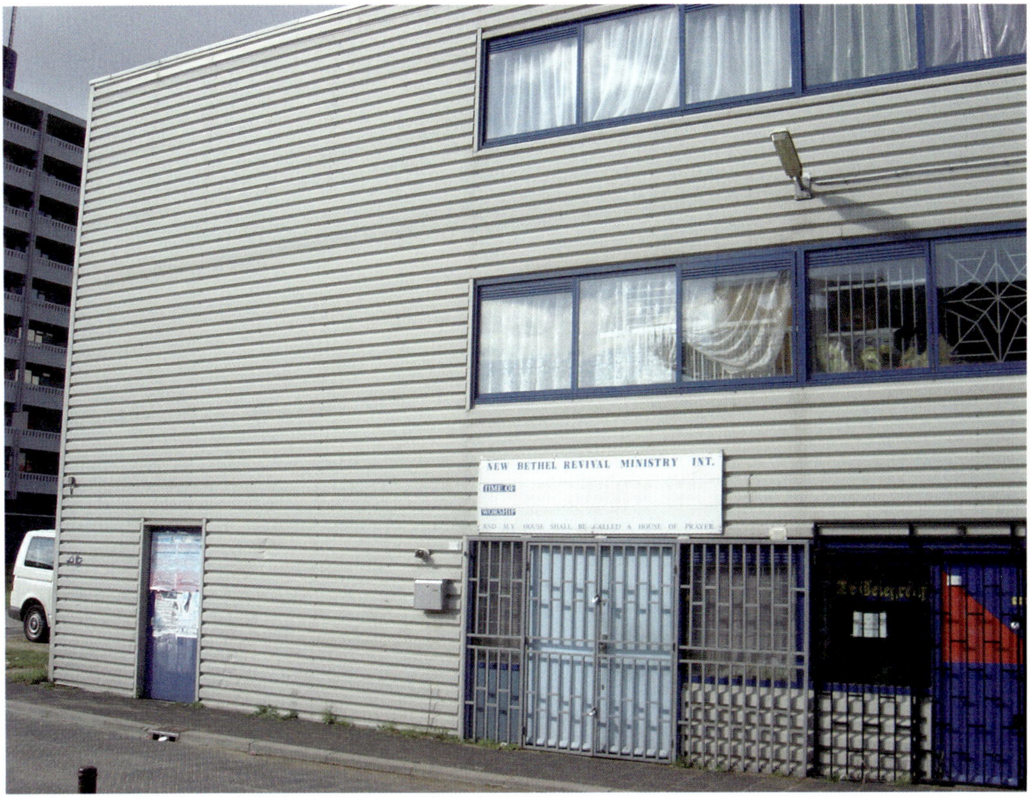
NEW BETHEL REVIVAL MINISTRY INT.
TIME OF
WORSHIP
AND MY HOUSE SHALL BE CALLED A HOUSE OF PRAYER

STICHTING
SIPALIWINI
TEL. 5992682

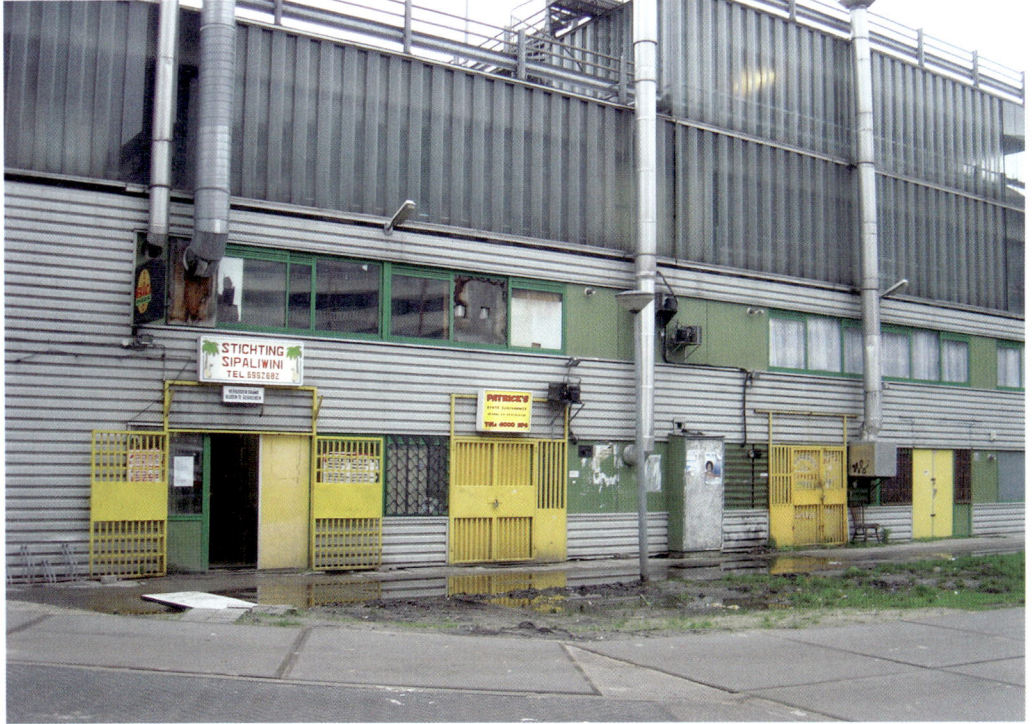

COMPROMISE:

A variety of nationalities inhabit the Casbah centre of Mazara del Vallo on the southwest coast of Sicily. Dating to the period following the Arab conquest of Italy in 827, the Casbah has become a complex space transformed in use and meaning—and rich in opportunities for architectural research and intervention.

The dense and complicated structure of the Casbah, built over many years, means that courtyards and rooftops are often shared by several families with different concepts of what normal use of those spaces means. Occupation includes friction and negotiation that requires compromise, while everyday activities like eating and playing are surprisingly good at creating new spatial situations.

A courtyard in the Casbah
Mazara del Vallo, Sicily, 2008
Photo by Fortunato Pappalardo

COMPROMISE:

Mazara is now one of the most important fishing harbours in Italy, with more than 400 ships and 4,000 fishermen. Most of the fishermen are immigrants, about half of them Tunisians who arrived after Tunisia's independence in 1956, but other groups are present as well. In 1981 an earthquake left the Casbah largely abandoned as Italians moved to housing projects on the outskirts and immigrants moved to the center, which remained affordable and near the harbour.

Plan of the Casbah, analyzing the courtyards system
Mazara del Vallo, Italy, 2010
Abitare Straniero research project,
by Marco Navarra (NOWA)
Courtesy of NOWA

Plan of a sector (the dark grey area in the larger plan) of the Casbah, showing the different nationalities of the inhabitants
Mazara del Vallo, Sicily, 2010
Abitare Straniero research project,
by Marco Navarra (NOWA)
Courtesy of NOWA

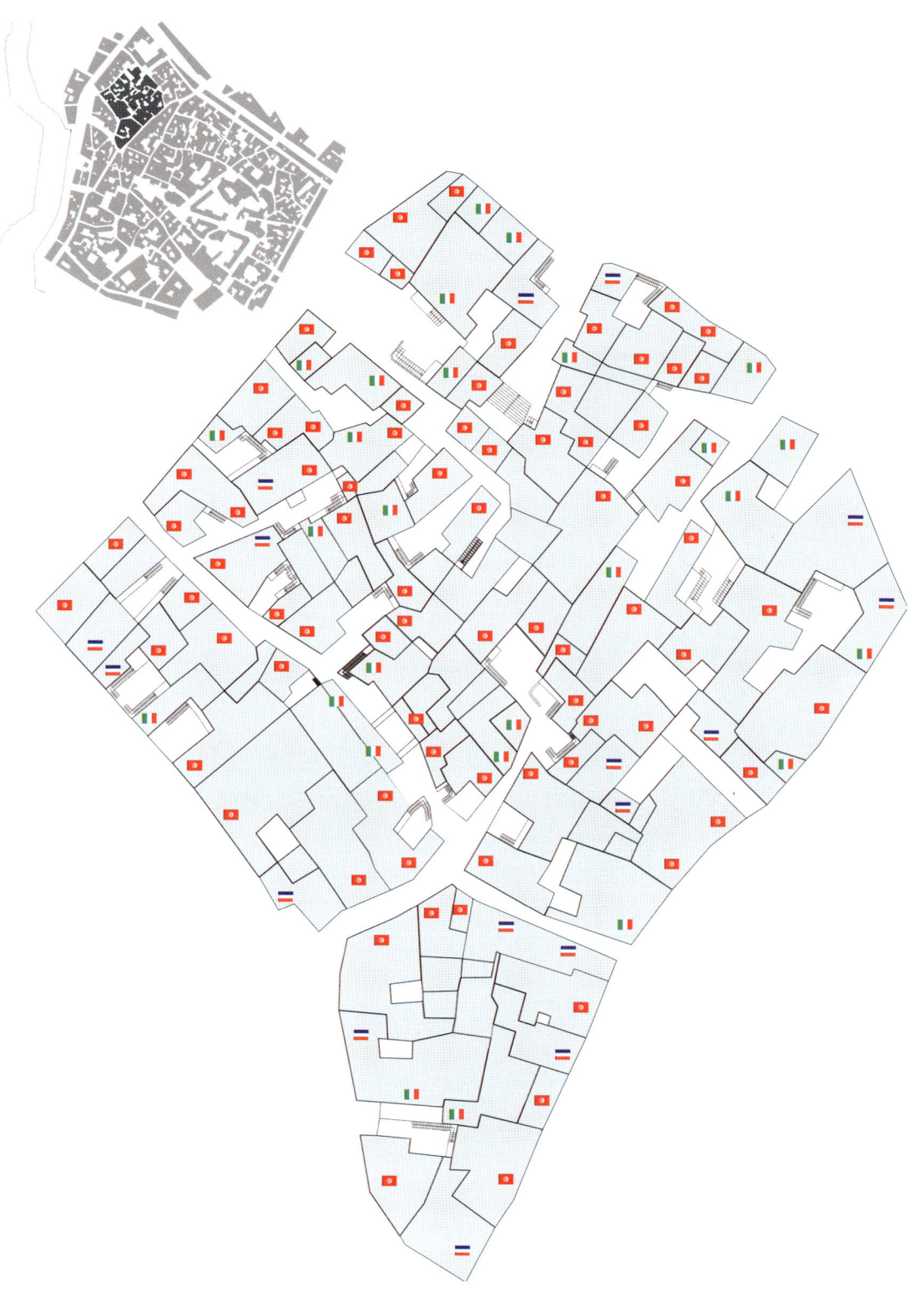

WAYFINDING:

For the Inuit, Arctic geography is rich with information: places are named in terms of how one gets to them, what the traveller will see on the horizon, in which direction the winds will blow and how they will shift, what shapes can be seen in snow drifts, and other useful information that can be observed without specialized tools or external referents.

Traditional methodology and sensitivity for movement in the arctic has passed down through generations of Inuit in oral histories and lifetimes of movement, as part of an experiential understanding of the Arctic. New tools like Global Positioning Systems are shaping the future of wayfinding—the orientation in and navigation of physical space—in the north, determining where people are present and which regions they avoid, and affecting settlement and use of the land.

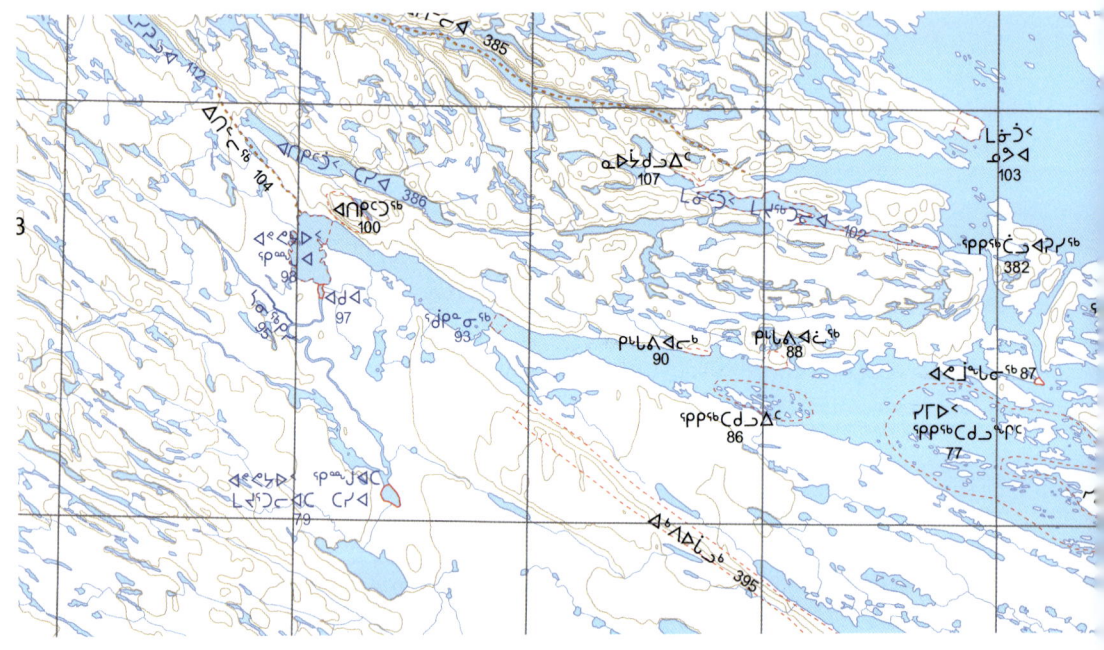

Detail of a map of the National Topographic System of Canada, showing Iglulik place names, 2008
Cartography and research by Claudio Aporta
Courtesy of Inuit Heritage Trust

No.	Syllabic	Roman	Feature	Meaning
43	ᐃᓗᐃᓕᖅ	Iluiliq	main land	"Main land". People used to refer to the land west of the island of Igloolik as "Iluiliq". In the old times, Baffin island was also known as Iluiliq.
44	ᐊᕐᓇᖅᑯᐊᒃᓵᑦ	Arnaqquaksaat	camp	Means "old ladies".
45	ᖃᓕᕈᓯᖅ	Qalirusiq	hill	There are two features of this name on Igloolik Island around the community. Qalirusiq means: "secondary, layered, one stacked on top of the other; the upper part [referring perhaps to the stratified limestone composing the hill]. The two hills are the highest features on Igloolik Island. Since the last Glaciation, about 4,000 years ago, the island has been continuously rising from the sea. The hills appear to have been occupied soon after they rose from the sea by predecessors of the Inuit. Radiocarbon dating has fixed the time of these first occupants at about 2,000 B.C. The community airport and water reservoir are situated on this Qalirusiq.
49	ᐅᔭᕋᓱᔾᔪᒃ	Ujarasukjuk	rock	Huge rock (under water). Dangerous for boat travel.
51	ᐅᒡᓕᐊᕐᔪᒃ	Ugliarjuk	island	Little place where walrus land or haul-out.
57	ᖃᓕᕈᓯᖅ	Qalirusiq	hill	Meaning: secondary, layered, one stacked on top of the other, the upper part [referring perhaps to the stratified limestone composing the hill]. The Igloolik cemetery is located on top of this hill, hence the name "Cemetery Hill" used by some of the community's English speakers.
69	ᐊᕝᕚᔪᑉ ᓱᓪᓗᐊ	Avajjaup Sullua	channel	A channel of Avvajja
70	ᐊᕝᕚᔾᔭ	Avvajja	former settlement and island	Meaning obscure, but may refer to the fragmented character of the area. Former settlement. Inuit used to spend their summers here and in the winter they would move to Iglulik. The Roman Catholic mission first established here in 1931. Its abandoned mission chapel still stands. The settlement of Avvajja was abandoned in 1950. The island is also referred as Avvajja.
73	ᓱᓗᕋᐅᒐᖅ	Suluraugaq	point	Long and thin [like the tip section of a dog whip].
74	ᕿᕐᖑᒻᒥᒐᕐᕕᔪᐊᖅ	Qirngummigarvijuaq	Island	Big place where one scans with binoculars or telescopes.
76	ᓯᒥᒃ	Simik	island	Plug.
77	ᓯᒥᐅᑉ ᕿᑭᖅᑕᑯᓗᖕᒋᑦ	Simiup Qikiqtakulungit	islands	The little islands of Simik. Simik means "plug".
79	ᐊᕝᕚᔪᑉ ᕿᙵᑕ ᒪᔪᖅᑐᓕᐊᑕ ᑕᓯᐊ	Avvajaup Qinnguata Majurtuliata Tasia	lake	The lake of Avvajja's bay. A good fishing lake.
80	ᓱᓪᓗᑯᑖᖅ	Sullukutaak	channel	
82	ᐅᖅᓱᕆᐊᑦᑎᐊᖑᔮᒃ	Uqsuriattiangujaak	three islands	Like Uqsuriattiak. Three islands with quartz outcrops.
86	ᕿᑭᖅᑕᑯᓗᐃᑦ	Qikiqtakuluit	islands	Little islands.
87	ᐊᕙᒨᖓᓂᖅ	Avamuunganiq	point	A place where one has the choice of going in a number of different directions.
88	ᑭᒡᒐᕕᐊᓛᖅ	Kiggavialaaq	cliff	Peregrine falcon chicks [nesting falcons]. Cliff. Peregrines nest in the cliffs.
89	ᐃᒥᓕᒃ	Imilik	island	Has drinking water.
90	ᑭᒡᒐᕕᐊᓕᒃ	Kiggavialik	cliff	Having nesting falcons.
93	ᖁᑭᓐᓂᖅ	Quukinniq	bay (part of)	The narrow part. Part of a bay.
94	ᕿᑭᖅᑖᓗᒃ	Qikiqtaaluk	island	Large island.
95	ᓴᓂᖅᑭᓯ	Saniqqisi	creek	Tributary. The current of this creek (before it enters the bay) is very strong.
97	ᐊᑯᐊ	Akua	river mouth	Refers to the front part of an amauti.
98	ᐊᕝᕚᔪᑉ ᕿᙵᐊ	Avvajaup Qinngua	part of bay	The end or head of Avvajja's bay or inlet
100	ᐊᑎᑭᑦᑐᖅ	Atikittuq	hill	Narrow beach between the sea and higher ground.
103	ᒪᓃᑦᑐᑉ ᓄᕗᐊ	Maniituup Nuvua	point	Point of Maniituq.
104	ᐃᑎᓪᓕᖅ	Itilliq	portage	Pleasant little land crossing between two bodies of water [usually by dog team or snowmobile].
105	ᒪᓃᑦᑐᖅ	Maniittuq	Area	Land with rough terrain. It is possible to see seals, narwhale and beluga whales here.
106	ᑲᙱᓕᕐᔪᐊᓕᒃ	Kangilirjualik	island	It has stones for sharpening knives.
108	ᓄᕗᒃᓯᖅᐹᖅ	Nuvuk&iqpaaq	island	The farthest point of land from the mainland.
109	ᐃᓄᒃᓱᒐᓕᒃ	Inuksugalik	island	Place where there is a stone cairn or inuksuk.
111	ᖃᐃᕋᑦᑐᔪᒃ	Qairattujuk	island	Large flat surface of bedrock.
112	ᐃᑎᓪᓕᐅᑉ ᑕᓯᕈᓗᐊ	Itilliup Tasirulua	lake	Lake of Itilliq
114	ᐅᓗᒃᓴᖕᓇᑦ ᓱᓪᓗᐊ	Uluksangnat Sullua	channel	Channel of Uluksangnat.
118	ᐅᖅᓱᕆᐊᑦᑎᐊᒃ	Uqsuriattiak	island	Quartz [of appearance similar to blubber]. This place has been used as a spring camp by the Inuit for many years.
119	ᒪᔪᖅᑐᓕᒃ	Majuqtulik	lake	A place for going up.
120	ᒥᑭᒃᓱᒍᑦ	Mikiksugut	island	Fish bait.
123	ᐆᒑᕐᔪᐊᓕᒃ	Uugarjualik	bay	Has big cod fish.
124	ᒪᓂᓕᒃ	Manilik	island	Has moss (of the kind used for wicks in soapstone oil lamps).
127	ᖃᒃᑭᐊᖅ	Qakkiaq	mouth of creek	Landing place.
129	ᐅᓗᙳᐊᖅ	Ulunnguaq	cape	It looks like an ulu.
130	ᐊᐅᒃᑲᕐᓂᕐᔪᐊᖅ	Aukkarnirjuaq	polynya	The big polynya. Polynya.
132	ᒥᑎᓕᒃ	Mitilik	island	Has eider ducks.
375	ᐃᖃᓗᓕᑯᓗᒃ	Iqalulikuluk	lake	A little lake with a little fish
376	ᑭᖑᓕᒃ	Kingulik	lake	Lake is not visible on this map
377	ᑲᓕᒑᖅ	Kaligaaq	Point	This point stops moving ice
378	ᕿᑭᖅᑖᓗᑉ ᓱᓪᓗᐊ	Qikiqtaaluup Sullua	channel	A good channel to boat when the sea is too rough
382	ᕿᑭᖅᑖᓗᐊᕈᓯᖅ	Qikiqtaaluarusiq	island	Smaller than the island Qikiqtaaluk (94)
385	ᒪᓃᑦᑐᑉ ᐃᑎᓪᓕᐊ	Maniittuup Itillia	Trail	Trail of Maniituq
386	ᐊᑎᑭᑦᑐᑉ ᑕᓯᐊ	Atikittuup Tasia	Lake	Lake of Atikittuk
387	ᖃᐃᕋᑦᑐᔪᑉ ᓱᓪᓗᐊ	Qairattujuup Sullua	Channel	A good channel for boat travel. It is connected with Uluksangnat Sullua (114)
388	ᒪᓃᑦᑐᑉ ᐃᑎᓪᓕᐊ	Maniituup Itillia	Portage	Part of a trail

EXPERIMENTATION:

Japanese colonies at San Juan and Okinawa in Bolivia were established after 1952 when revolution, agrarian reform, and Japan's domestic economic problems encouraged emigration. There was an opportunity to develop land in the sparsely populated eastern part of the country.

    The first Japanese arrivals, after clearing tracts of rainforest by hand, began to farm rice in the traditional Bolivian way, without flooding the fields; however they soon switched to the more efficient method of wet rice farming. With help from contacts in other Japanese colonies in South America, they also experimented with different crops, many of which had not previously been grown in Bolivia. The most successful were soybeans, cotton and macadamia nuts.

A pathway opened in the jungle by Japanese immigrants San Juan de Yapacaní, Bolivia, ca. 1957
Photographer unknown, Japan International Cooperation Agency
Courtesy of the Asociación Boliviana Japonesa de San Juan

EXPERIMENTATION:

The Bolivian government had hoped that the colonists would bring with them new farming techniques and provide a model for domestic farmers in the country to emulate. Today the eastern part of Bolivia is the centre of the country's growing agricultural industry, and the surplus of crops grown there are exported worldwide. The habits and knowledge of the Japanese settlers have changed the landscape of Bolivia.

Landscape of a virgin forest San Juan de Yapacaní, Bolivia, 1960
Photographer unknown
Courtesy of the Asociación Boliviana Japonesa de San Juan

Rice and soy seeds produced by Cooperativa Agropecuaria Integral San Juan de Yapacaní (CAISY), 2010
Courtesy of CAISY Ltda

CAISY LTDA.®
SEMILLA
DE
ARROZ
PESO NETO 50 Kg.
CALIDAD GARANTIZADA
COLONIA SAN JUAN DE YAPACANI
Telf. Central: 9347006 • Sucursal: SC. 3346557
SANTA CRUZ - BOLIVIA

CAISY LTDA.®
SEMILLA
DE
SOYA
PESO NETO 50 Kg.
CALIDAD GARANTIZADA
COLONIA SAN JUAN DE YAPACANI
Telf. Central: 9347006 • Sucursal: SC. 3346557
SANTA CRUZ - BOLIVIA
SOYA RESISTENTE A GLIFOSATC
SOYA RESISTENTE A GLIFOSATO

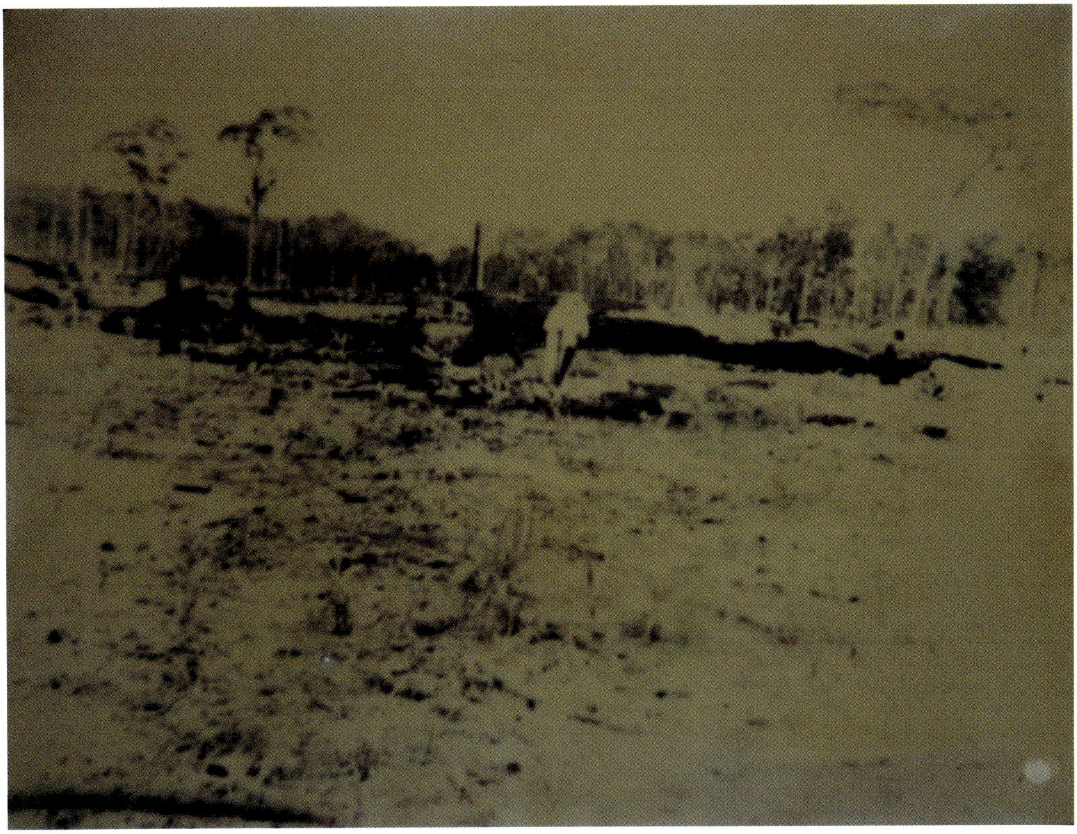

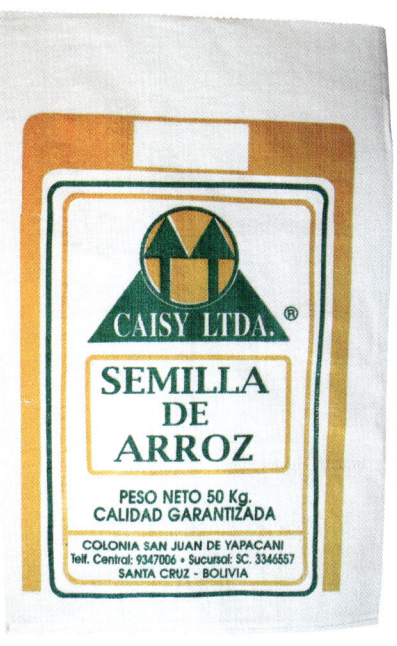

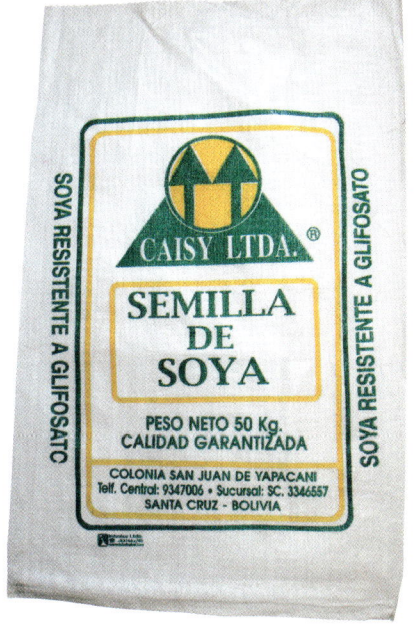

EXPERIMENTATION:

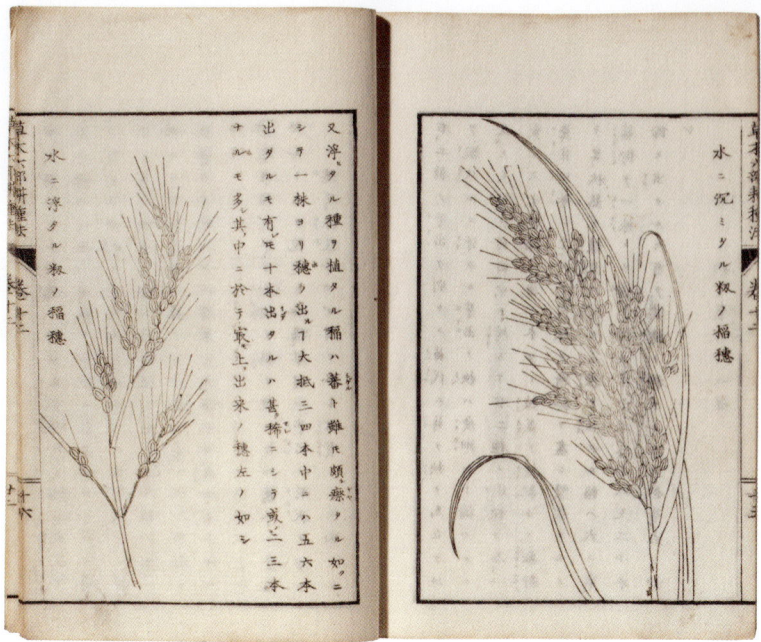

Illustrations of two rice varieties, from Sato Nobuhiro, *Somoku Rokubu Koshuho* [Cultivation Methods for the Six Parts of Plants], Vol. 11–12, 1876. CCA

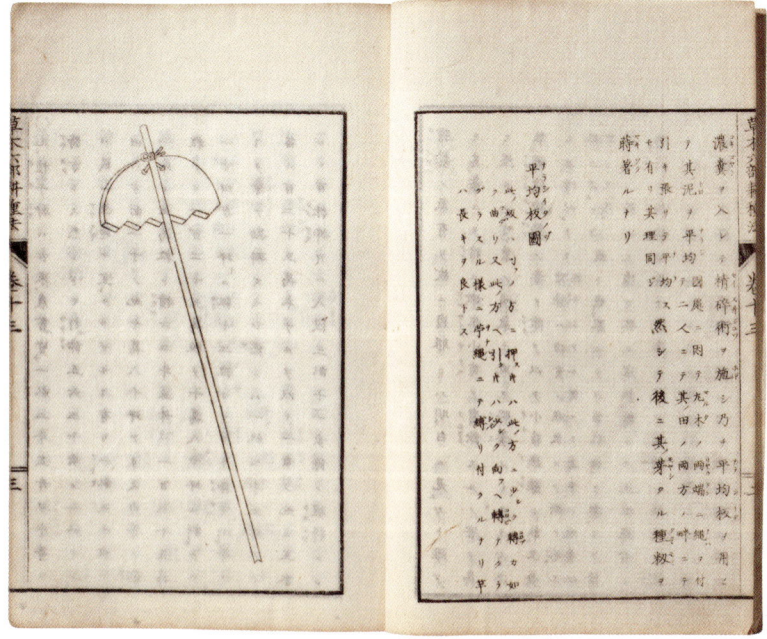

Illustration of a levelling rake, from Sato Nobuhiro, *Somoku Rokubu Koshuho* [Cultivation Methods for the Six Parts of Plants], Vol. 13, 1876. CCA

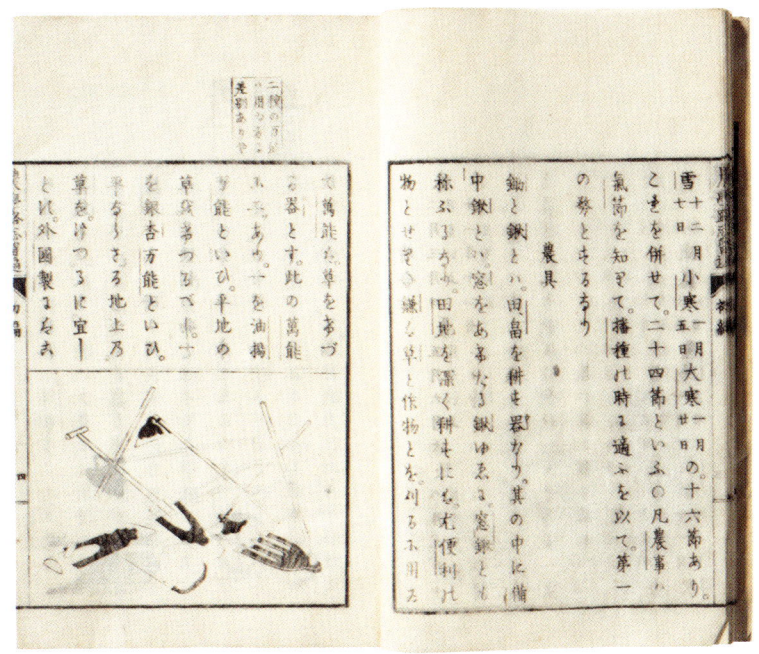

Illustration of various agricultural tools,
from *Nogaku Michi Shirube* [Guide to Agronomy], 1878.
CCA

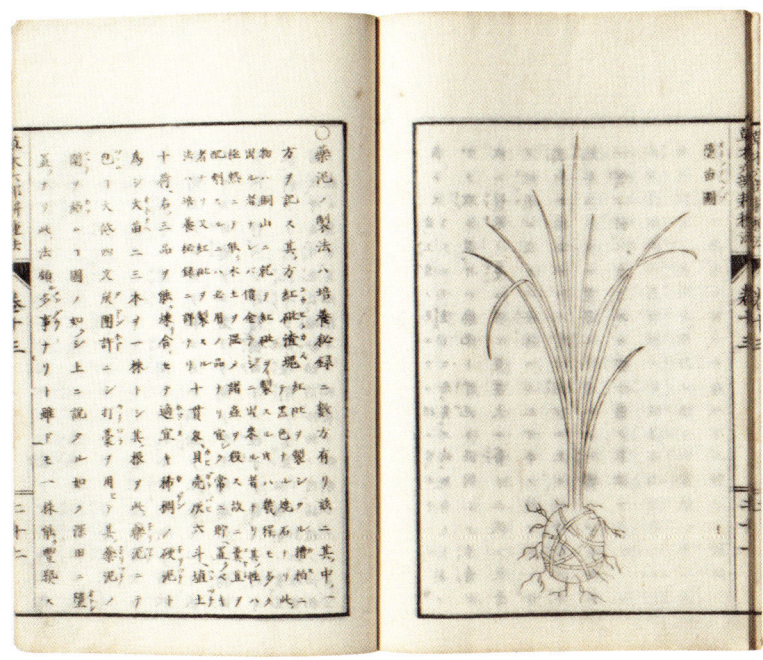

Illustration of a young rice plant, from Sato
Nobuhiro, *Somoku Rokubu Koshuho* [Cultivation
Methods for the Six Parts of Plants], Vol. 13, 1876.
CCA

DRIFT:

Wild coconuts are buoyant, and nobody can stop the ocean currents from moving them. The wild coconut evolved to be an efficient global traveller: its tough fibrous husk and air-filled seed allow it to float great distances and remain generally viable if it reaches suitable land within four months.

 The endosperm or coconut milk sustains growth until the roots are able to find fresh water and the first leaf fronds start converting the sun's rays to power further growth. Though the origins and first voyages of the coconut remain contested, its capacity for long-distance movement is certain. The coconut appears in a number of stories from India to the Pacific Islands and has had a long presence in human mythology.

Cross-section of a coconut
2010
Drawing by Matthew Fellows

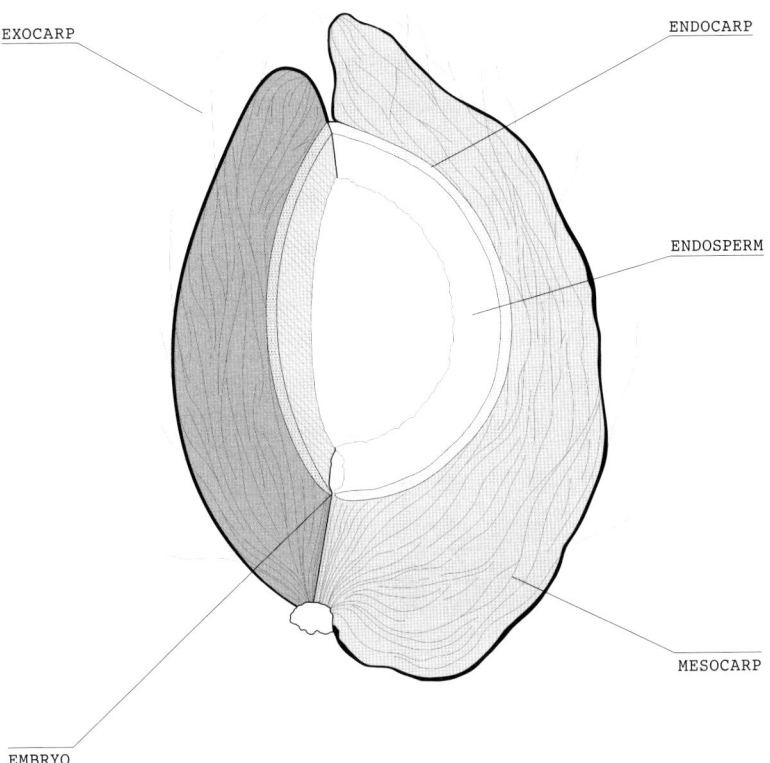

KISZOMBOR, HUNGARY, AUGUST 12TH-17TH, 2002

WHEN A CUCUMBER IS NOT A CUCUMBER: AN E.U. TALE OF CUSTOMS AND CLASSIFICATION

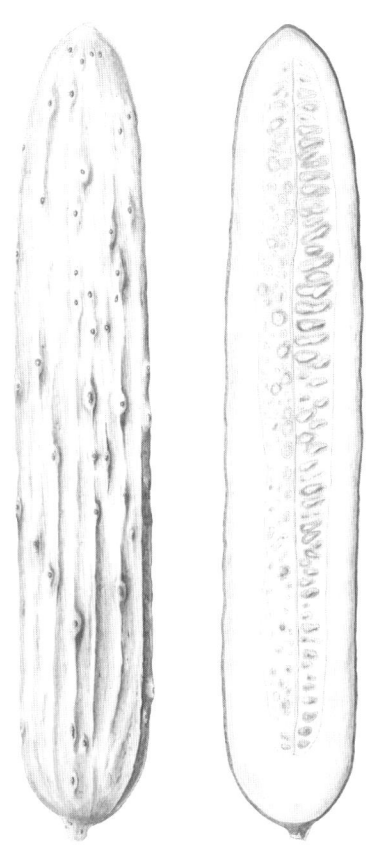

BY
LEV BRATISHENKO

Day One

At 19:32 on Monday August 12th, 2002, Darius Corneliu pulled into the truck lane at Kiszombor, a small border post between Romania and Hungary. Beside him a limp chain link fence ran behind a line of trucks and towards a concrete cube plastered with signs in Hungarian that he could not read. In the distance, fields weakly suggested cultivation. His Renault truck, a family investment, was carrying a blue 6 metre steel container holding approximately 26,000 kilograms of cucumbers, which came from his uncle's farm near Bistreţu about six hours away. No, he told the Hungarian customs officer, he did not know how his uncle grew them, whether it was in the field where he played as a kid, or in the rusting greenhouse next to the ditch. Did his uncle practice "Bulgarian gardening"? What was "Bulgarian gardening"? His uncle wasn't Bulgarian. Really, they were not his cucumbers. Darius was only doing a favour by taking his uncle's cucumbers to a wholesaler in Szeged. Normally he did not ship cucumbers. He preferred cargo with fewer border hassles, like televisions. He did not understand why the officer—a short man with dark circles under his eyes—was irritated with his paperwork. He only had what his uncle had given him, he explained in broken Hungarian. It should be in order. He was sorry. *Bocsánat*.

The weary Hungarian customs officer was disappointed with this amateur importer. Sanyi Szilágyi had been working his gate since early that morning and now he wanted to go home, but this guy's forms were a disaster and Sanyi could not just let him go. He would have to impound the truck. He lifted the gate and motioned Darius to park on the right of a small building about 400 metres up the road. This building served as the office of the Hungarian Customs and Finance Guard, where Sanyi had worked for twelve years, and where he would retire as long as he did not break too many tenets of Act C of the 1995 regulations governing customs law, customs procedures and customs administration, or Government Decree No. 45 on its implementation.

The office building that Darius approached was in rough shape, but Kiszombor was too small a border post to be a priority for the infrastructure upgrades that began when Hungary joined NATO three years earlier. Big crossings, some with up to twenty lanes, were getting automated disinfection stations, radiation detectors and x-ray machines. Most of them also got a phitosanitary officer or two, trained in handling suspicious produce. At small posts they could only cross their fingers. Kiszombor was 32nd on the list for upgrades.

As he closed his gate and walked after the truck, Sanyi tried to remember the last time he had been required to hold a produce shipment. He could not. Cigarettes topped the list of annual seizures, followed by alcohol, historical artefacts, animals, and finally drugs. Vegetables did not appear. Either they were not considered noteworthy, or they were confiscated in such enormous quantities that their inclusion in the statistics would have ruined the graph.

"Come back tomorrow," Sanyi said as he walked up to the truck. Darius did not seem to mind, he just shrugged and asked for a ride to Szeged.

Day Two

Darius never came back from Szeged to get his uncle's cucumbers, but Sanyi would not know this until later. He spent the morning of August 13th at his post stamping the passports of Romanians from Timisoara who were going shopping in Budapest. Sometimes he glanced over his shoulder at the truck, but he did not worry.

Over lunch in Szeged he watched Ferencváros defeat Békéscaba EFC on replay, ate a pork cutlet, and did not talk to anybody. The truck was gone when he got back to Kiszombor.

"Katy," he asked the receptionist, "who signed the Renault out?"

"Nobody. It's still there," she replied, twisting in her chair to look outside. "What truck?" she concluded. "I never saw one."

Nobody had seen the Renault leave or would even confirm that it had been there in the first place. Sanyi was glad the team was covering for him, but Darius had somehow ditched his cargo and an explanation would have to be made for the bright blue container on the parking lot.

Sanyi had held the truck because the amateur importer was missing a Certificate of Inspection. Since the passage of EU Regulation 1788 in 2001, vegetable shipments that originated outside the Common Market had to be certified by their national regulator, who issued a form that specified the variety, pesticides used, and the average length and weight of the vegetables in question. Sanyi would normally do a quick inspection based on this document, call in to the county office and reference the central database (he would not have his own computer until 2004), then estimate the cargo's market value. The EU certificate was not really required if the produce was only sold in Hungary, but the government thought early compliance would look good. Yet this amateur importer had not met even the lowest standard: he had not filled out the Romanian origin certificate beyond the word "cucumbers," misspelled.

Fortunately for Sanyi, the Customs and Finance Guard had prepared for such an eventuality: there was a flowchart in duplicate, with white and yellow copies, used for identifying the unknown. Selecting the right form required a level of judgement that the Customs and Finance Guard admitted even their junior officers probably possessed, and Sanyi proved them right. He found the one marked *növényi anyag*. Vegetable matter.

The form was organized according to questions about "qualitative," "quantitative," or "pseudo-qualitative" characteristics, the answers eliminating other questions, and so on, until all possibilities were narrowed down to one variety approved for Hungarian or pan-European sale. The benevolent authors of the form had included diagrams in case Sanyi had any difficulty identifying parts of plants; roots were drawn on the first page. The form also defined the four types of observation that he was approved to use: single measurement, group measurements, group visual assessment, and single visual assessment.

Sanyi took a ruler, left the container door open for some light, and began. It went well at first and in a few minutes he had narrowed the possibilities down to "gourds" before landing on a square with a recognizable silhouette. *Cucumis*. Good, everything past this point was a cucumber of some sort.

The tone of the document then became impenetrably scientific. The first question stumped him and he had to find a dictionary to look up "cotyledon," which turned out to be an embryonic leaf. The only leaf he could see in the darkness of 26,000 kilograms of cucumbers was brown and crumbled when he touched it, so he skipped the question. He hoped this would not screw up the worksheet. Next he had to count the length of the first 15 "internodes," which the dictionary told him were the spaces between leaf attachments on the stem. He could not see any stems so he skipped that question as well. Then there was a "pseudo-qualitative group measurement" question about the "leaf blade attitude." He thought this was unfair since he had already skipped the first leaf question, and he began to have doubts about the form. This continued for qualitative, quantitative, and other pseudo-qualitative questions about leaf "blade length," "terminal lobe," "intensity of green colour," "blistering," "undulation of margin" and "dentation of margin."

Sanyi turned the page over hopefully and found a "qualitative single visual assessment" question about "sex expression." Back to the dictionary, but he could not tell if the cucumbers had exclusively female or exclusively male reproductive organs, or some ratio of the two. Counting "female flowers" was impossible. Then he had to look up "parthenocarpy," which apparently meant that the cucumber plant produced fruit without fertilization. These cucumbers had seeds, so he filled in "no." This brought him a little satisfaction after having skipped so many questions.

Next was a section on fruit, though he was not sure cucumbers were fruit. He decided "fruit length" was "long." It seemed an appropriate category for the "quantitative measurement" approach, but there were only choices between descriptions. So, "diameter" was "small," making the "ratio length/diameter" in his estimation "very large." He was disappointed that he was not using the ruler. He groped at answers to qualitative assessment questions on "shape in transverse section," "length of neck," "shape of calyx end," "ribs," "sutures," "creasing," "degree of creasing," and "type of vestiture" (Were the cucumbers hairy? They were not.). Following that were questions about "warts," the "length of stripes," the "density and distribution of dots," the "ground colour of skin at physiological ripeness" and "length of peduncle." This finished Sanyi off. He could not bother to look any of it up.

The only question that had required a measurement was about "fruit curvature." Printed with a helpful chart, this question noted that Class 1 cucumbers could not bend more than 10 millimetres for 10 centimetres of length. Sanyi wondered what Class 2 cucumbers were used for, then realized that though all of this was interesting and maybe even educational it did not make the cucumber he held in his hand an official cucumber. And he had finished the worksheet. He had no way of measuring the curvature anyway.

Frustrated, Sanyi turned the page over, noticed a lengthy appendix of "Explanations and Methods," and upon closer inspection realized that many of the questions he had struggled with were not even applicable. He slammed the container shut and walked back to his office depressed.

Flipping through the sloppily filled out forms on his desk, Sanyi felt a growing anger towards the inventor of the worksheet. Some committee at the Community Plant Variety Office had written that thing, had deliberated on it, had considered the people who would use it, and had decided that those people would know what a "peduncle" was. He decided to call Szeged. It meant dealing with Ildi Mészáros, but he was getting nowhere alone. Maybe he could convince her to talk with her boss, the customs king Anatoli Király. Together they were responsible for the Szeged *megyei varos*, or urban county, and its handful of crossings.

He dialled.

"Post and identification number," Ildi barked.

"Kiszombor … 13975," he mumbled, twisting the badge on his shirt so he could read the number.

"Kiszombor is not a number. A number starts the file," was the reply. Sanyi swore under his breath and rifled through the papers on his desk for the post's identification code. There was a betting pool at work that Ildi was a computer. Nobody had ever seen her, so the idea seemed plausible.

"212," he said.

There was silence as Ildi accessed her databanks or filed a nail. "What do you want, 13975?"

"I have a problem. A vegetable shipment has been abandoned."

"Use a 6-Z form," she said with the warmth of a lawnmower.

"Doesn't apply. The shipment is unidentifiable."

"3-NA then," Ildi replied, even more coolly.

"Unidentifiable," he repeated. "Not unidentified. I tried the vegetable matter worksheet already."

"That is not possible, those sheets identify all vegetable matter."

"Have you ever tried filling one of these out? I never thought cucumbers could be so complicated."

"Did you say cucumbers?"

"Yeah, they're cucumbers alright."

"You just told me they are unidentifiable."

"The worksheet didn't work, but I can tell a cucumber when I see one, Ildi."

"Don't call me Ildi. Assuming that you are sober and correctly filling out the worksheet, these are not cucumbers." She paused to let the logic settle like concrete. "When was the shipment abandoned?"

"Yesterday. No contact information for the shipper. Are you being serious?"

"Dispose of it."

"Of the cucumbers. These are cucumbers."

"No they aren't." Ildi hung up.

But he knew they were. Sanyi took a cucumber out of his pocket and looked at it. It was bumpy and obscenely curved, twisting around itself with patches of pale yellow at the ends. It was an irregular cucumber. He cut it into chunks and offered it around the office. Everyone agreed it was definitely a cucumber, but there was no taste test on the flowchart.

He went to lunch with Tibor Komárosi, the ex-Olympic wrestler they employed as a security guard. When Tibor proposed they toast the cucumber, he agreed.

Day Three

The next day Sanyi started the paperwork to destroy the shipment. He had to call a trucking company and write a report, which seemed easy enough until he reached the environmental assessment.

When Sanyi had started at the Customs and Finance Guard in 1990, regulations were gently applied, pay was low and sporadic, and staff took home whatever was abandoned or confiscated. If it could be eaten, it was; if it could be sold, all the better; and if it had to be destroyed, there was an area about a kilometre from the post where the ground was black and cracked from fire. An orphanage nearby sometimes complained about respiratory problems, but otherwise you could say the system worked flawlessly.

Things became more complicated when Hungary entered negotiations with the European Union in 1998. Something called harmonization began and the paperwork changed, then increased, and gradually became something he had to take seriously. A year later this would culminate in the 14303/21 Customs and Finance Guard Deed of Foundation by Dr. László Csaba, Minister of Finance, which would state wryly that "The Hungarian Customs and Finance Guard does not pursue any enterprising activity," in case his employees had other ideas.

For now, the environmental assessment required Sanyi to attest that the destruction of the shipment would not pose a danger due to the release of chemicals or toxins during incineration. This required, among other things, a phitosanitary certificate and a classification code. There was none for 'unknown, obviously a cucumber,' so he called Ildi again.

"13975. Not cucumbers," she answered.

"The disposal papers need an identification code. What am I supposed to do?"

"Pass the telephone to a sober colleague."

Shortly afterwards, the staff at Kiszombor were ordered to take a sheaf of worksheets and a pencil, and form a line at the container. Sanyi fumed nearby and watched the vegetable matter worksheet defeat his colleagues one-by-one.

A cloud settled over the post and the container still sat on the lot. Kalman Kocsis, the paranoid elder of the customs guards who believed the Bolsheviks secretly remained in power, was convinced that the shipment was a test of their collective abilities. Failure meant "Siberia," he said, weeping, and spent the day packing a bag. Tibor could barely hold a pencil in his meaty hands but insisted on doing his part: he struggled manfully with the worksheet before pounding a dent into the side of the container. Then he went to the hospital. Traffic through the post slowed to an angry trickle as staff abandoned their gates to discuss the mysterious container; those who remained to check papers stopped Romanians, which meant everybody passing through a post between Hungary and Romania, and grilled them about agriculture. Your brother the botanist, where did you say he lives?

Later that day on the way to his car, Sanyi saw Attila Kepes bend over to pick up something on the lot. Sticking out of Attila's back pocket was a cucumber curled like a pig's tail. It was too much. Sanyi went back to the office and tried Ildi again.

"I can't destroy them. The 26,000 kilos of cucumbers I have on the lot don't exist because of a piece of paper."

"Then they never entered the country."

"But they are in the country! I can see the border from here and they are on our side of it. And they are definitely cucumbers. I tried one."

"There are many borders. The one you see is not the only one. The legal border puts the shipment in Romania."

"The border adjusts for cucumbers?" But Ildi had already hung up.

He slammed the phone on the desk. It rang.

"Fill out a P-7309 for the removal of the sample or you'll be fined."

Day Four

The next day he decided to try higher up the chain of command than Ildi because, he reasoned, the situation could not get any worse. He called the Customs and Finance Guard headquarters, a Beaux-Arts building on Mester Street in Budapest. After giving his personal identification and the number of the post, Sanyi was put on hold. He ate some cucumber while he waited. Then a friendly voice came on the line.

"Good morning valued colleague . . . Szilágyi!" the voice exclaimed.

"Thanks. My name is Sanyi."

"This call is being recorded!"

"Is that really necessary?"

"This is regarding an abandoned shipment, correct? Szeged office has made notes on your file."

"I wouldn't pay too much attention to those."

"Thank you for your concern, valued colleague . . . Szilágyi. Now, how can I assist you in raising the quality of service we provide?"

Sanyi explained the situation. He wanted to talk to somebody who could approve the destruction of unclassified cucumbers. He needed help.

"Thank you for your enquiry. You should submit a written request to the phitosanitary officer for your region." The voice continued, brightly. "There is no phitosanitary officer on record for your region. Please submit a written request after one has been hired."

"I can't, they'll rot."

"It is easier to maintain a high level of service if you take your time, valued colleague... Szilágyi. I can suggest that you fill out form CPVO-TQ/061/2 and submit it in writing to us. We will forward it to the European Union Community Plant Variety Office with a request for Community Plant Variety Rights. If your request is approved then the shipment would be identified as a new variety and it could enter the country. You could even name it... Szilágyi!"

"Do I need a phitosanitary officer to certify the form?"

"That is correct." The voice affirmed, effervescent. "There is no phitosanitary officer on record for your region."

Sanyi rubbed his head. "Why can't I just certify the shipment myself? I know they're cucumbers. Everybody does. It's obvious, want to come down and look at them?"

"Thank you for the invitation, valued colleague... Szilágyi, but I am not approved to make such a certification. Our protocols exist to ensure the safety and quality of goods entering Hungary and continuing into Europe. The rules as amended by Regulation 1117/88 exist to maintain common quality standards under new production and marketing conditions. The Management Committee for Fruit and Vegetables, the members of which are all approved to make phitosanitary certifications, submits an opinion that must be considered. You can obtain more details on the comitology procedure from Council Decision 87/373/EEC!"

Sanyi hung up, disgusted with everyone including himself. If he had not called Ildi in the first place then he could just dump the shipment. Instead he had followed protocol and now the cucumber situation appeared in his file. He was trapped. He had to destroy the cucumbers legally. Suddenly he felt nostalgic for the 1990s.

Did anybody at the office know a phitosanitary officer? No, they would already be working for the Customs and Finance Guard. But Katy had a botanist uncle, and that was better than nothing. Sanyi made her call because he could not bear to explain over the phone.

Day Five
A beige Lada in a state of mechanical distress pulled up to the customs office the next morning. The portly, bearded man inside was the retired Dean of Botany at Budapest University, originally from Szeged. The title gave Sanyi hope, and he took the professor inside the container. The professor declared it to be full of cucumbers.

"I'm glad you think so," said Sanyi.

The professor did not understand this response, but Sanyi explained that he was not making fun. It did not matter that they both knew the vegetables (fruit, the professor corrected him) were cucumbers, because all Sanyi needed was a signed attestation declaring the shipment an official variety of cucumbers and the professor would have a grateful friend in the customs service.

"Your flowchart is stupid," the professor said. "Go bring me the bag from my car." When Sanyi came back the professor dumped the bag out on the table and arranged his tools. Holding a cucumber he asked Sanyi what he knew about it and Sanyi had to admit he only knew that it was good in summer soup.

The professor shook his head. He wiped his glasses and started to talk. As he took measurements, he explained that cucumbers grew on vines and belonged to the same family as gourds, which meant they were related to melons, squash and pumpkins. "And other vegetables you will never ask me to drive out here to identify," he added. The Hungarian word comes from the Greek *aggouria*, like the German *gurke* and Russian *ogyrets*, while English took cucumber from the Latin *cucumis*. Their global popularity had little to do with their nutritive value, Sanyi learned. Cucumbers were not a particularly nutritious food, consisting of over 90% water, but they did go well in summer soups, the professor agreed.

Cucumbers probably originated in India, and the greatest genetic variety is still found north of the Bay of Bengal. How they got to Europe, and then to the rest of the world, is not particularly mysterious, even if the specifics remain unknown. If Alexander the Great did not bring them back with him, the Romans certainly did. Pliny writes that the emperor Tiberius ordered hothouses built so that he could have cucumbers year-round (they don't survive a frost.) Then they followed that empire to Gaul and beyond, and one of the colonial powers introduced them to the New World. China ignored all of this to concentrate on its own cucumber cultivation, and still produces the world's largest crop—over twenty million tons a year.

Modern cucumbers, the professor explained, were bred to reduce bitterness (in the early 20th century they were advertised as "burpless" because the bitter taste was thought to provoke gas) and increase their size. Smaller varieties remained for pickling, but the majority of the world's cucumbers now came from eight similar varieties.

"That's it," he concluded. "An idiotically simple fruit that we will always call a vegetable."

Sanyi admitted he did not really understand the difference.

"Vegetables are whatever the law says they are, it's an imprecise category. Some things like peas are technically vegetables only while unripe. Botanically, that is correct, as fruits are the ripened or fertilized seeds of plants. So these," the professor continued, waving a bitten cucumber at Sanyi, "are perfectly ordinary ovaries. I really can't imagine how your worksheet misses them."

Sanyi let the professor take a box of cucumbers as thanks and adjusted the official weight of the shipment accordingly. Including this payment and all the sampling that had been going on, the container's weight was down nearly twenty kilos. Still, he was glad that somebody was eating them, and he was even more relieved that his ordeal was over. He put the professor's handwritten statement in a transparent protective sheet on his desk. He did not want to spill coffee on it.

Sanyi spent the rest of the day typing up the professor's scrawl before he noticed that the form for botanical attestation required an active botanist with a certification number, not a retired one. He went home and lay down.

Day Six

Saturday August 17th, the weekend at last, but Sanyi could not bear relaxing at the bar with the cucumbers on his conscience. That morning he decided that the official organs of the state bureaucracy were not going to recognize the cucumbers, and perhaps they did not have to. He dialled Szeged as soon as he got to work.

"It's Szilágyi," he said.

"13975," Ildi answered. Ildi did not take days off.

"Right. The shipment is still unidentified."

"I congratulate you."

On the verge of giving up entirely, Sanyi recalled hearing a radio host discuss the European Union. A formal invitation for Hungary to join was a few months away (it would be made in December) but from Sanyi's perspective the process was as inexorable as it was mystifying. One could only be patient. Meanwhile there were trips to Brussels for officials in Budapest, training for senior regional officers, and supposedly random compliance inspections for the rest. Most importantly, however, reporters sometimes accompanied officials on these visits.

"I just heard from Nagylak that they had a surprise inspection with cameras and everything," Sanyi said. "What if they show up here and give a tour for Magyar TV? What'll happen when they find a container full of mouldy cucumbers, probably genetically modified, covered in god knows what Romanian pesticides? Shall I tell them not to worry, they are still in Romania?" He paused. "There's an orphanage nearby."

She was silent for a moment. "Wait," she said, and hung up.

Ten minutes later an order for the immediate destruction of a container of "unidentified vegetable matter" came through by fax, signed by the hurried hand of Anatoli Király. Sanyi grinned as he held the paper, still warm from the machine. Then he called a trucking company and told them to come immediately in case Ildi checked, and because he wanted to see the cucumbers vanish as soon as possible.

The next half hour was the happiest Sanyi had been all week, and then a familiar looking Renault pulled into the parking lot. It was Darius Corneliu, who was driving in Szeged now. Sanyi was too shocked to ask whether he had papers.

"I hate paperwork," Darius explained while the winch was pulling the container up onto his truck. "I thought, you know, things would probably sort themselves out." And he was glad they did. He gave Sanyi a box of cucumbers as a present and drove away.

***

ARNOLD'S COVE, NEWFOUNDLAND, CANADA, 1959

RE-CONFIGURATIONS: A TOWN IN NEWFOUNDLAND GROWS WHEN HOUSES ARE FLOATED IN FROM FAR-FLUNG OUTPORTS

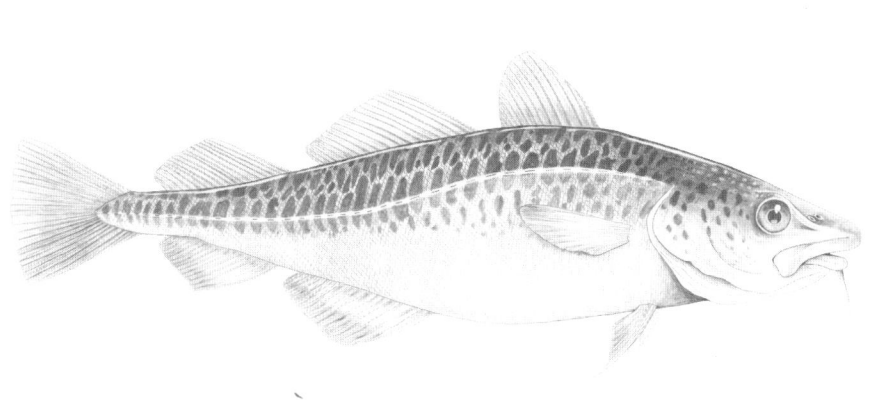

BY
MAUREEN POWER

From the kitchen window of Mary's place I watched Peter and Henry get our house on the floats. It wasn't a big house, even by St. Kyran's standards. Two stories; white-washed, with a green trim round the windows and door. We called it the green house. I had left the upstairs window open so that any water that got in would have a place to evaporate out of. I was watching as my curtains floated out and collapsed in the winds like a jellyfish lazing round the harbour. All day the men had worked to anchor the house, rolling it down slowly, steadily on logs to the waterfront before easing it up on the floatsold oil drums. It all looked so precarious. It looked like it would never work. But the resettlement was giving us each four hundred dollars to move into Arnold's Cove and that wasn't enough to build a new house so we are taking them with us.

Our house is like so many others. Not built into the ground but up on stilts, hidden behind a board to keep the cats and rats out, about a foot off the ground. This is done to get a level and to get some protection against the cold ground. A couple of years ago a travelling salesman came around selling insurance, but said that they wouldn't insure any house that didn't have a foundation. Some of the neighbours painted their board grey and called it cement in order to satisfy the insurance company. In the pictures you couldn't tell. We didn't see much point in insuring the house; it has already stood for a hundred years. If it burned down we'd just build again with the help of our family and neighbours.

Ours is white with green trim. The green house. There is a front door, that no one but the priest uses, that opens into a hallway. Off of the hallway is a parlour, again, only the priest uses the parlour. Only the finer things are in there. A sofa, chair, a small fireplace, and a couple of shelves with some ornaments on it that belonged to my mother. There is dark wallpaper on the top and dark wood on the bottom of the walls. Makes you feel a bit ill if you look at it too long. The family shroud is kept there. I leave it lying across the chair. I always hated going to a wake and the musty smell of the shroud would hit your nose. The mixture of death, decay, freshly washed body, and not so freshly washed mourning clothes was always enough to make me want to gag. Add the mothball reek of the shroud and I was done for. No, I kept the Ryan shroud in the parlour. I could always remove it before the priest came. It is a thing of beauty. Typically, in the old country, they were made of lace but since we have no lace around here it is made from a piece of linen with little flowers cut out all around one edge. The cut piece would drape over the face of the deceased.

At the end of the hallway is the kitchen that runs along the back of the house. Here is the heart of the house. The warmth of the stove in the far right corner. It is a fine stove. A No. 8 Favorite made in St. John's. Made of cast iron; it is a black beast. It is about five feet long, has six dampers and an oven that makes great bread. Not that I am one to brag but I do make the best bread in St. Kyran's.

There is a large table in the middle of the kitchen that I do all my work on and it is big enough to have twelve people sit at it at any time. A big, strong, heavy table; it looks as if it was built with the house. It actually came from a Portuguese ship that wrecked some time ago. There is also a rocking chair and a couch that sometimes Peter sleeps on when he is home. The walls have a paper on them that has little flowers on a yellow background. It makes me feel a little better during the ten months of winter. There is a Dixie potbelly stove that I can knit by late at night, opposite the couch and rocking chair. This saves spending the wood on the large stove. The two stoves keep this area of the house warm and inviting. The family lives in the kitchen. The kitchen has a porch off of it and the back door that everyone who isn't a visitor used. With the people, family and friends coming and going, I don't think the door is ever left alone long enough to really come to a close.

The porch is a pantry, a bit of a catch-all. Boots, mitts, and skates congregate there—testament to the multitudes that throng here. Upstairs there are three bedrooms. There is one at the top of the stairs over the kitchen. This is where the children like to sleep so they can eavesdrop when there are visitors. That way they get the bits of gossip going around. It is also the warmest room in the house. The first room in the hall is also partly over the kitchen. This is where my bedroom is, although the girls often sleep with me when Peter is gone out to sea. The front bedroom is for the boys. They can deal with the cold a bit better than the girls.

I love going down to the kitchen in the morning before anyone is up. I get up every morning before the sun, just me and the stove, and start the day by coaxing the embers from the night before back to life. It is a time for myself with my tasks set out for me, when I don't need to think or answer anyone's questions as you often do with a slew of children about. When I look out the window I know I am not alone in my ritual with the stove as I start to see smoke rise from other houses around the harbour. I have a basin on a stand by the window that overlooks the backyard. Back there I have a garden that is shared with my sisters, where we grow most of the vegetables that we eat throughout the year. There is also the root cellar off to the left built into the hill, which starts to slope dramatically up to the black spruce. The outhouse is in the back also.

When I look out of the upstairs window in the front of the house, I see the community through a clutter of seashells and bits of driftwood sculpted into grey serpents, and dried herbs tied to twine wrapped into the window frame. I can see the community, the way it hugs the shoreline like a crescent round the bay. The houses face the water and the backs face the hill. The hills rise up straight behind the sheds and houses in great veins of grey-red rock wrapped in lichens, scrub grasses and patchworks of spruce trees and alder brush so dense that to walk through them is like being whacked with a thousand switches all at once. Pride of place in St. Kyran's is the old church despite the fact that it trends toward St. Leonard. Four-storeys at its peak, with great window frames tapered to hook points at the top still rise into the sky but there's no glass in them today. When the weather is turning poorly the red granite stands out sharply, contrasting with the grey-black sandstone sent over from Ireland that buttresses the building to the shore. When it burned down in 1922 Father Fyme had a wooden church built. Even larger than the stone church it is, with the rectory attached by a walkway to keep the cold and wet away from Father. It also has its own wharf so that the dozen or so other communities around can come on Sundays. I don't know why, but it was always the ruins that caught my attention, perched up on the sloping meadow. All alone.

Ours was the first home to be taken up to Arnold's Cove. My sister Mary still lives in the family home next door, where she and I and our eight other siblings grew up. Six girls, four boys. The boys are all gone now, to the bottom of the sea or off to work the mines of Bell Island or Cape Breton. Never much of an option in St. Kyran's when there was more money to be made under the ground. Mother and father were buried behind the home in the family plot. Generations of us Ryans are buried here. But no more would we know it as home. Not with the opportunity afforded us. Still, I could see Mary crying on the shoreline, her heavy shoulders rocking.

I sighed, hands red and raw from a lifetime of chores gripping the steel ribbing of the washing tub. Feeling like I should go comfort Mary but knowing my words wouldn't mean anything to her, not now. Maybe later. Mary is a dreamer. Her heart and soul is in the old way of life. I couldn't help the tinge of excitement that coursed through me at the thought of moving out of here. Of all that awaits us in Arnold's Cove, of indoor plumbing, of not slopping water up from the brook for morning tea and washings, of electricity, streets with lights, a medical centre, and those "televisions" that the neighbours keep talking about. No, I am looking forward, not back like Mary. But I can't let it out. I must wait. Excitement bubbles inside me and I want to laugh out loud but to do so would mark me out. Everyone looks like they are here for a funeral. I cast my eyes down and avoid Mary. Perhaps they think I am too upset to comfort her? I may lose my own composure.

I gazed out at the men, busy preparing the house for tomorrow when they take her out on the water. Arnold's Cove wasn't far, a few hours by boat. The men busy lashing ropes, securing the float to shore and anchoring it against the spring winds. Peter jumping from boat to house to shore to boat, a cigarette shrouding his face in smoke that couldn't mask the smile that cut across his face. He too felt like me. When he is home and we are alone we talk about all the great things that are to be had in Arnold's Cove. He too is looking forward to getting on with it. He is hoping to get a job out of the fishery and off the water. Since the accident he has found it hard to fish.

I watched Peter come round the head of the bay in Madeline, *his trap skiff, and felt a cold shiver. I just knew something wasn't right. The* Madeline *looking for all the world as she did every day. It being into October month, Peter had taken two of our boys—Young Peter and Stephen—to fetch the spruce lengths that would be junked and fuel the fires through the coming winter. The men do this trip two, three, four times over to get enough wood. Madeline's gunwales were laden with spruce in ten foot lengths laid out as high as I am tall, so I couldn't even see Peter or the boys. But that just made me surer that something was gone wrong, that feeling of tragedy a knot in my stomach and I run out towards the wharf. Young Peter suddenly stood atop the pile then, waving his arms and confirming my feeling of dread.*

I barely even waited for the boat to nudge the wharf before leaping aboard, the smell of spruce laden with summer's warmth thick in my nose as I scrambled up the pile. There at the tiller was our boy Stephen and his father, looking ashen and holding his left hand, wrapped in his red flannel shirt, in his left. He smiled. "Shirt's ruined Mad. Gone and soiled it."

"What've ye done?" I pressed my hands on his face, cupping the narrow draw of his jaw bones, the feel of his breath on them. "What'd ye do to yer hand?" I felt like there was a bit of madness to him. Like he wasn't all there at that moment. Smiling and clutching his arm. Blood everywhere over the boys and Peter.

But Peter broke away and leaped to the wharf, steady going towards the stage. I trailed on behind, aware of Young Peter going off towards the rectory to get Father Fyme. I was begging for someone to tell me what was going on. Was Stephen that told me as we were chasing Peter to the stage.

"We were cutting away strappings with the hand axes and Young Peter was telling a story he'd heard from Ned at school about his father catching a moose out in the bay. And you know Peter's got the gift for a story. Captivated we was. I could close my eyes and see the terror on that poor moose's face at finding himself facing Tom Lannon with his rifle pointed his way, the very Angel of Death. Well, just at that moment we heard it." He went quiet, unsure how to continue. We were in the stage now. I looked over as Peter started to unwrap the shirt from his hand. It was then that I saw that Peter was missing four fingers on his left hand. Clear gone. He looked at us with a smile on his face and plunged his hand into the salt for curing the fish. I leaped towards him holding the arm that he had in the salt. He let out a sound that was unearthly. A yelp and howl. The salt on his stubs must have been agonizing. We all stood there, me clinging to his arm and Stephen standing back looking shocked with his mouth open and his long black hair dangling in his eyes. I am not sure how much time passed but after a while we all came to and left the stage and headed towards the church where we saw young Peter heading down the path with Father Fyme.

In the day's last light, with the gathering clouds of the first fall snow we buried his fingers in the churchyard under Father Fyme's directions, consecrated that they might rejoin Peter in heaven. As Father Fyme closed the service I saw a look in his eyes that glinted at some secret that only he knew. That somehow the loss of those fingers would bind us all to this community and him forever. I turned away from the church that night, the glowing hulk, picking my way home in a night as black as hell itself. I knew that now our lives on the edge would be harder than it was before. With mouths to feed we would have to do something. A one-handed fisherman is a rare beast and we would do what was best for us, whatever Father felt besides.

As the sun gave its last daylight from the sea I was suddenly mindful that I hadn't started dinner yet.

We were already in the process of resettlement when the accident happened. The community was still on the fence and we hadn't voted yet. We needed everyone to agree. We were ready to go but there were hangers on like Mary and her man Henry that wanted to talk endlessly, waxing on poetically about the loss of our lives but for us it was stay and starve or move and hope to get something that Peter could work at and we could support the family. If this opportunity hadn't come up I don't know what we would of done.

I remember when resettlement first came up. It was in the form of a letter sent out to all of us. It was sent out by Joey Smallwood.

"Ye won't believe this Mad," Peter said. This two years ago, in the dead of winter. The snows piled up round the house and the stove burning a cheery red, loaded up with birch junks. "Joey's gone and said that we—what was it now…"

He squinted down at a scrubby piece of paper, the skin round his eyes tight from years on the water. Peter wasn't much for reading. School was something he'd done between fishing season and he'd never seen the other side of grade three. I know. I did it with him before going on. But his pride wouldn't let him hand the paper over so we waited until he found it, his mouth working over the words silently.

"Here it is. 'It has long been felt by thoughtful people that the terribly scattered nature of our population has made it very expensive for the government to provide public services to all the people, such as post offices, telegraph offices, telephones, coastal boats, hospitals, roads,'" and he paused, his face crinkling up with the punchline and I smiled despite myself. "'And snow clearing!' The thought of it, Mad! The government is going to stop paying for clearing snow!"

We both laughed at the thought of the need to pay to clear snow. Sure, everyone just cleared the snow as they needed to! No one was paid for it! Must be a townie idea? But there was something in that typed statement from February 1957 that got me thinking that there might be life—a better life—beyond the limits of this place. That maybe our brood—Bridget, Colleen, Mary, Kathleen,

Peter, and Stephen—needn't work their hands raw and bodies ragged just to survive. That maybe there was something else, not yet defined but just beyond the horizon line of my thoughts. There were teachers, doctors, nurses, jobs that demanded schooling. More than my six years. I kept that typed letter folded up in the cupboard, behind the flour. Sometimes, between scrubbing the floors and hanging out the washing in the constant winds cutting down from the nor'east I'd slip inside, hands swollen and red from work and slip into the fantasy of that letter. Imagining a world where doctors worked in a building and didn't just show up when an illness got so far gone something close to a miracle was needed to mend body and soul together again. A world where Baby Margaret might have stayed with us. I felt selfish for wanting away, to something I didn't know. But that statement set in me a terrible loneliness, a forlornness from all this. Then suddenly, with Peter not being able to fish as well as before, here was our answer.

When we leave the last sight I shall have of this place will be the old church. It's the one part of this shore that I'll carry with me an' I never heard a mass said in its imposing hulk. It just feels like God was present, to have allowed something so majestic to have stood, even briefly, in a place so inhospitable to civilized life.

Looking around me now with the men working on the house I see Father Fyme. He's a stern, meagre man, spare of flesh. He was the spectre of a life I had always known, his visage the embodiment of spiritual and moral guidance against the chaos of the world that lurked round us. The aged Father Fyme, the look in his eye, the look of loss and pent up anger, his sermons of ruin and damnation have ruled this community for years. I grew up with the church on my back. Heaven forbid you didn't make mass or that you didn't give your tenth to the Church—after Gerald Lake snared his share at the general store. Sometimes I just wanted to keep our money, it was already so little and we were always behind paying back Mr. Lake. Father Fyme had been a thorn in the side of the whole resettlement, you ask me. I thought that we would never get a consensus with his hellfire and damnation sermons. Saying that we are doing God's work and that God wants us to stay here. God built our new church and we had to stay, as it is what He wanted us to do. Father Fyme just didn't want to leave his comfortable life here. In Arnold's Cove he won't be the only church in town. There are Anglicans, the Salvation Army, and Methodists to compete with. Here he rules the roost but his power will be lessened in Arnold's Cove. It also makes me wonder that if his hesitance to resettling was because in Arnold's Cove we would all have electricity and light, taking the power away from him.

There has never been electricity in St. Kyran's until Father Fyme arrived. He was born in the Netherlands and came to Newfoundland a young priest. When he built the new church he insisted on building a windmill to go along with it. He had installed lights in the church and the rectory powered by this windmill. It was quite a site for the people of St. Kyran's. The first night that it was up and running we all gathered at the church. I was only a child but I remember as we left the house the sight was amazing. The stained glass in the church glowed with this inner light. The whole building beamed lights of every colour across the harbour. The images of the saints and sinners came alive. When we got inside the sight was even more impressive. There were statues of St. Theresa, St. Patrick and, of course, the large painting of the Assumption above the altar. Well, the saints' halos glowed! They actually lit up. The painting of the Assumption over the altar was about twelve feet by eight feet and bathed in light. Father Fyme had the painting commissioned in Rome for the church. It depicts a life-size Virgin Mary on a cloud surrounded by angels. The Virgin is raising her hands and eyes to heaven as she is taken body and soul into heaven. The new church was a sight. And in the years to come it remained the only place with electricity. It was lit all night in all weather by the windmill. After the Second World War Father Fyme received a generator to run the lights in the church and his house.

The morning of our departure Mary was inconsolable. "Mad," she sobbed, eyes swollen and red. She collapsed in my arms but she didn't need to finish. Her whole life was here. She'd been the runt of the litter and leaving St. Kyran's, leaving Mom and Dad, leaving the church, was like chopping off her arm. "I can't," she managed in a sigh that rose into a low wail of sorrow and terror of the unknown. But we had decided and the cheques had been given out, were as good as spent. Henry wasn't going to stay behind if Peter left. A bond beyond brotherhood, born out of countless mornings looking after one another out in the boats held them together. "Can't imagine being 'ere without ye," was all Henry would say by manner of explanation when he told us he and Mary were coming too. They were the last members of the community to vote and they reluctantly voted for resettlement. Thankfully the priests weren't given a vote or we would have never left. Father Fyme was refusing to come down from his house. He was supposed to bless the house before we left. He was stubbornly praying in front of his altar, looking up at Our Lady as she rose to heaven body and soul. Perhaps he was hoping that the same would happen to him? We would get a blessing once we got into the new lots in Arnold's Cove. I have only heard about this from people coming and going lately but apparently they have lots set out for us in Arnold's Cove. The land is all split up evenly and we just haul our houses up out of the water and right onto the land. Nothing else needs to be done. They have poles that run electricity right to the house and they are ready to put running water in! I can't wait to see all the modern life.

It was time now. Time that we started hauling the house to our new home. I left the young children with family so that we can get settled and we will come back in a fortnight for them. Mary was coming with me to help me settle a bit. I think it also gave her strength to go through this with me first.

We travelled in Henry's skiff with our sister Cheryl's husband Ralph who would bring us to Arnold's Cove. To move the house, Peter borrowed a neighbour's speedboat as it had better pulling power. In the boat were Henry, Stephen, Young Peter, and Peter. The sky was light and grey, clouds skittering low with the gusts. I could smell snow in the air.

We got out in the boat looking back at the house on the shore with the lines and the men in the trap skiff ready to pull. Everyone in the community was there to see the house get hauled into the water. The shore was dotted. The men of the community were pushing the house as the speedboat revved up. There were logs laid down under the oil drums that the house was going to roll off of and into the water. With the pushing and hauling the house gave way within five minutes and in one loud splash it arrived on the water. It was such a funny sight, this house perched on the water that I started to laugh out loud. I covered my mouth to stifle the noise and glanced at Mary, who looked ashen faced and on the verge of tears. I quickly pulled myself together and held Mary's hand, the two of us watching the men, yelling soundlessly as the engines roared to life. The boat pulled taut with the load and I could see the house pull up behind us and then we were off, leaving St. Kyran's.

I couldn't help myself. I stood up and looked back, looking at the sweep of the community. The ruined church off to my left, snug against the rocky precipice that marked the end of St. Kyran's, as tall and majestic as anything I'd ever seen. My stomach leaped with excitement. Then I saw Father Fyme, hands by his sides, fists clenched, grey hair plumed above him. Watching the departure in a silent fury.

Just beyond the point I could feel the tenor of the water change, the way the organ in church will bring a chill to the back of my neck when the music changes. There was something powerful, unrestrained. The water was usually a bit choppier once you get out of the safety of the harbour but I felt it all the more as I turned and watched our house swaying back and forth in the waves. Its bobbing made it look like an unbalanced child when they were first walking, not quite sure if this feels right. My breath caught in my throat. Mary was staring hard too. Ralph was looking straight ahead, bent to the task at hand. He was setting the pace and it was slow and cautious. Our life was in that house, old and new. We were to hug the shore, only heading out when we had to go between two bodies of land. The Placentia Bay is full of islands and peninsulas. It should be easy to stay out of open water where the waves are hazardous and unpredictable. As the excitement faded and the roar of the engines drowned away even the sea, the smell of cigarette smoke and gasoline thick in our noses lulled us into a dreary resignation of the hours before us. Mary and I huddled close for warmth and comfort. The boats were putting along and the house was bobbing in the water but seemed no worse for wear. It was so heavy on the oil drums that it sat on the water right at the sill. You couldn't see the floats. I was preoccupied with thoughts of a new life mingled in with reminiscence of the old life. I was happy that Peter was getting out of the fishery. There was always something about the processing of fish that didn't sit well with me.

As a child I thought a fish looked like a fallen angel. The white wings of the meat splayed out on the dirty board, unrecognizable from the fish it used to be. I used to watch father and my uncles John and Peter split fish through a crack in the planks of the store. This before they all went on to work the Labrador. A revulsion close to physical illness would take hold of me but I'd be incapable of stopping, knowing that Ma would tan me arse for lallygagging but drawn to the ascension of fish into angel. The smell of cigarette smoke and brine and the gritty meal of men who've worked too hard for too long thick round the place—that too was part of the revulsion, the need to stay and watch.

One of the young lads from the community, usually a cousin, would be forking the fish from the boat onto the head of the stage. From there another lad would be putting the fish into reach of the men splitting. The table wasn't big but three people stood around it, two on one end of the long side and one across from them. In each long side there was a semicircle cut from the edge of the table and a piece of wood set back from this into the table. This steadied the fish during the splitting and it is also where the fish would be dropped down into a clean bucket. The first man, the cutthroat, would cut the fish from tail to gill and under the head. After this the fish was slid to the header who would crack the head off at the end of the table and remove the guts. From her the fish was pushed over to the splitter who would take the sound bone out in one stroke; the slightly curved splitting knife would go down one end of the fish's back and up the other, flinging the hard white bony sound bone up into the air and out a little window where the seagulls were waiting in anticipation for a meal. There was a piece of wood, the cleat, in front of the splitter here and a half-moon-shaped hole cut out of the table. The back of the fish would go against this piece of wood and the splitter would cut down the backbone on the right then back up on the left ending up with a fish that was flayed open. But you would only catch a glimpse before it was dropped down in the hole into a bucket of water hauled from the edge of the stage before splitting began. The sound bone would be thrown out a little eight by eight inch hole in the side of the wall next to the splitter. After a good day of splitting the seagulls would be there by the thousands eating the offal from the process. After the fish were split they were placed in the pounds for salting. Here the men would throw salt down and then layer fish, more salt, fish until the pounds were full. Here they were left to get a bit of water out of them and for the salt to get good and into the flesh so they wouldn't turn maggoty. After spending anywhere from a couple of days to a couple of weeks, depending on the weather, the fish would be laid out on the flakes to dry. This is where they really got the look of a fallen angel. Splayed out under the beating sun the white flesh of the split fish made me want to pay reverence. With thousands of fish spread out up and down the shore it looked like a massacre of the sacred. It is how I pictured the war between Michael and Satan in the bible. Fallen angels littering the shore.

An' somewhere I came onto the idea that I would save the fish, take them back to the sea and return them whole. The fish were a living gift from God that my father and uncles were destroying. I could save them by sending them back to the water before they became fallen.

Fishing was then an exhausting process. Up at three in the morn, out to sea by half past, the stuttering rhythm of the Acadia-engine labouring past the shoals woke us all up. The men would be back at eight-thirty, unloading fish in their plentitude upon the stage with prongs. It was on one such morning, my pail full of slops for the heap, that I made my mind up as fast as that, dropping the pail carelessly behind me and running as quickly and quietly as I could to father's stage. The men half dozing on the skiff, cigarettes dangling carelessly over skin weathered to leather. They'd only just finished unloading the boat and the stage was thick with cod, some as thick and tall as a man's leg. I got down on my hands and knees at the edge of the stage closest to the door and in one motion pushed all the fish I could back to the sea, surprised at the resistance, the weight. Surprised too at the heavy thump of their bodies against the water. In my mind they would have returned to the sea soundlessly, slipping past the fishers an' their devil-begotten tools like the angels they were. It was then that Uncle John, one eye leaking open sprang up.

"By Jeezus! Madeline!" he cried. He wasn't a big man but the shock of his bellow roused everyone awoke and in my terror of their reaction I tumbled after the fish into the water. The water off the stage was so cold that the minute I hit it all of the air got sucked out of my lungs and shock took over my body. I had no idea how to swim and the water was heavy with dead fish. I found myself fighting and flailing. Gasping for the surface. Sure that I was going to die, my last sight the waxy white of a cod fish limply falling to the seafloor.

After this I never felt the same about fishing. It was playing with God's intentions. Just like we were doing now. Tempting faith with floating our house, for it was some three hours into the trip when the wind picked up.

I noticed the sky starting to darken when we were passing by Little Brule on Merasheen Island over to Peaches Cove on the last run over fairly open water to Arnold's Cove. It had been overcast for a while now but the sky had changed to dark clouds and the winds were after picking up. I could see Peter and Henry talking over in the other boat. I wanted to know what they were saying. Mary was looking at the house then at the sky and back again. I could see her thinking what I was thinking, storm coming. I don't know what transpired on the other boat. It was probably a discussion over taking shelter in a harbour and run the risk of getting blown ashore there or trying to outrace the storm and get to Arnold's Cove and safety. Peter gave a hand signal to Ralph and we kept going.

It wasn't too far to Arnold's Cove. Far enough in a storm though. The rain started to spit down on us, great sheets of it that quickly soaked the woollen shawl Mary and I huddled beneath. The waves were gaining momentum. The trap skiff began to ride the waves, up and down. I couldn't help but look back at the house. Mary took my hand and we sat back facing the house, praying for it to be saved. Ralph staring straight ahead, jaw muscles clenched tight against the cold and the task of keeping the bow to the waves, keeping the lines taut and the house on the level. If we lost the house, we lost everything. Resettlement was one thing but we couldn't afford the building materials to build a new house in Arnold's Cove. It is a modern place. Peter needs to find a job. The rest of the houses in the community had to be moved yet. We have land waiting for us but without a house… The thoughts jumbled up in a quiet panic, like springtime ice, that settled over me in great spasms of shaking, my teeth chattering loudly and Mary beside me hugging me close, face awash in rain or tears—I couldn't tell which.

The boys were watching the house and checking the ropes that tethered it to the boat. Henry, who was driving, was looking round, trying to find a path through the storm that would get us safe to Arnold's Cove, knowing that a wrong move would mean the end. Everyone silent, nary a word spoken over the roar of the winds and the rush of the waves that were now battering at the boats and house. The men signalling back and forth to one another, a frantic debate over where to go as the storm swarmed in, sleet driving hard and cold into our frozen maws. Mary and I still as statues, pieces in a play holding our places until the curtain comes up. Then the storm settled in good and hard, the wind whistling along the water in a visible wave before buffeting into us, the ropes taut as we began to roll and pitch with the waves. Drenched in the cold, muscles set so tight they ached. I hugged Mary close now, cold and fearful as the waves broke over the bow. The boat set to rocking violently.

I could sense it before I saw it. That feeling that everything was coming undone. Ralph suddenly looking round with a wild start and I stood to see what he was looking at. *The Madeline* falling behind, a boat designed to weather the elements but not for speed. The ropes falling into the cold of the water and now trouble was upon us. Henry saw the danger, steered the speedboat away. I saw Peter grab him by the shoulder, pointing back at us. The house suddenly almost atop us before a wave carried it back and away, the ropes pulling house and skiff out to sea as the Acadia engine sputtered and coughed. Ralph's eyes nearly out of his head. Then just as suddenly the speedboat edged between *The Madeline* and the house, Peter holding the hand axe in his right hand, the axe that had taken his fingers. His eyes in mine, set and I knew what he had to do. Down came the axe even as a wave pitched the house up again, threatening to upend the boat into the dark roil of water below. Once more and the ropes coiled away, the house carried on the waves up and over. Waves tore at the bottom floor. I could see the ugly dark wallpaper as the front of the house was torn away. The back of the house, my kitchen, my stove, my heart seemed to fall off of the back of the house in a crash. It was probably the heaviness of the stove that caused the back to fall off so quickly. The Dixie stove that kept me warm while Peter was away, the No. 8 stove that kept our children warm and fed, gone. We hadn't taken the furniture out. It had all been moved to the top floor to keep it dry. Didn't matter now. I saw the bed fall out of the top bedroom I shared with my babies and husband. Within a minute or two the house was gone. There was nothing but debris scattering along the water. I felt like the wind had been taken out of my lungs. I felt as if I had been taken down with the house. The cold water hit my chest taking my breath, my skin felt like a thousand knives was digging into every limb on my body. The house was gone and with it a piece of me.

She was gone. Where the green house had been oil drums floated up. Henry had taken the speedboat away as Ralph frigged with the Acadia motor. Finally tearing my eyes away to look at Mary. Tears and rain and sleet mingling into a mask of agonized dread, her teeth biting down on her left fist, eyes raw and huge staring back at me. Then Peter was in the boat and he enveloped me in his arms as Young Peter threw a line to Ralph and…

When I came to I was in a house I had never been too before. I didn't recognize any voices but I did feel warm. I was lying on a day couch and there was a fire in a potbelly stove near me. I laid there for a long time thinking over what happened. Did it really happen? Maybe I had a fever and the house was fine and we were at some relative's in the bay. But deep down I knew. I knew that the house had gone, that we were homeless and that we were somewhere in a stranger's home.

"Can I get you a cup of tea?" I looked into the face of the woman who asked me, her brow furrowed lines of worry. A fisherman's wife right enough and she knew what the loss of a house meant.

"Yes, thank you," I said in a voice that I didn't recognize any more.

We were in Haystack on Merasheen Island. We spent the night bedded down in the kitchen as sleet slashed against the walls like bullets crackling over March ice. The stove roared red and still I was cold, huddled beneath the shawls and sweater. No one saying much. By morning a thin crust of snow enveloped the world and everyone agreed that we should go back to St. Kyran. There would be time later to go on to Arnold's Cove. I travelled with Peter and Henry in the speedboat, the others helping Ralph spring the Acadia to life. They'd meet us back in St. Kyran's. I had to go home. It wouldn't be until I saw the empty place where our family house once stood that I could start over.

We followed the same route out of Haystack and back to St. Kyran's, the seas oddly calmed. It seemed wrong to have had so much loss in such seas. I wanted them to be set on hell's fury, waves pitched in foaming white. Only then could the tragedy be real. Peter slowed down whereabouts we'd lost her, wanting to see of we could pick up any mementos of what we once had. None of us could talk to each other. We were silently making our way to the wreckage place. I just stayed looking back from the stern. I didn't want to look forward anymore. Henry and Peter were calling out to one another, hauling up different pieces of the house and then discarding them again. After about an hour, and only picking up shattered objects and pieces of the house, I heard Peter say that we were just going to head out again to St. Kyran's.

The boat started to pick up speed when I saw it. Floating on top of the water, fanned out across the top of the water, like an angel, was the family shroud.

"Stop!" I shouted. "Stop, stop!" The darkness of the water was in stark contrast to the white of the shroud, making the little cut-out flowers look as if they were of the darkest blue colour. I think Peter thought I was having a heart attack he leaped back to where I was in the stern. My finger crooked and raw with the cold; my lips curled round. As if in a dream I heard myself sobbing out, "Oh, oh, oh." Was then Peter saw the shroud. Henry grabbed the grappling rod and hooked the shroud. The shroud was laid on top of the water where the green house went down, the binding thread of the Ryan family to St. Kyran's.

I clutched the shroud the rest of the way home. It was damp and smelled like the water. It smelled better than the dead fish I fell in as a girl. It is funny how that moment popped up then, these moments of loss weaving themselves together into my conscious.

When we pulled into the bay where St. Kyran's was located, the church was ablaze with light. No one had heard about the accident in the community. Once people started to see our boat coming in they started to come out of the houses and down to the water to hear the reason why we were back. I didn't want to talk to anyone but by the time we pulled into the church wharf almost everyone was waiting for us, including Father Fyme.

"What happened? What are you doing back? Is everything alright?" I heard these questions but could not bear to say out loud what the awful truth was. It was all gone. Peter started to explain about the storm and the house going down. I just started walking up the wharf. Right at the end stood Father Fyme. Just as I was passing, he said as if he was on the pulpit, "I said no good would come of this! The Lord has given us this land and this water and we have turned our backs on it! No good will come of this! First it will be the houses, then it will be your Lord that you will lose. This will be the first of many to go." He looked vindicated, face upturned with some righteous victory and he glowered at us heading traitors before turning around and back up to his glowing fortress.

I felt defeated. It was over, we had betrayed some greater good and we would forever pay for it.

***

It has been five years on now since we moved to Arnold's Cove. Ours was the only house lost during the move. Just as well though. The land they gave to the people who floated their house came with stipulations. All the houses face the road now, not the water. No one has their own stage or store but fish out of the community wharf. Another one of Joey's ideas. And since we are the newcomers we are the furthest away from the wharf. Our family is nowhere near the rest of the people of St. Kyran's. Where we lost our house we also lost the right to the land. We had to start renting from a family who had moved to St. John's.

We live on an avenue called 4 Street. The house is nice, modern. It is one level with a small galley kitchen with the dining room off of it and the living room in front of the house open to the dining room. There is no formal room like the last house. If we had any treasures left they would have all been in the new living room with us. The shroud now is kept in a cedar trunk my sister gave me and stored in the basement. There are no more gatherings in the kitchen, there is barely enough room for me. My stove is electric so the cooking is easier. No wood to light or keep going, but it doesn't do the job of No. 8 Favorite. It is different to have to bring food out to another room to eat. And then another room to knit and talk. I feel like I miss most of what's going on. But there is a bathroom in the house and electricity. The house is heated with electricity. No need to cut or haul wood anymore. There is a television that we purchased with Peter's first pay cheque from his job with the railway. His new job is nothing exciting but you don't need two hands for issuing tickets and I know that he will be home sometime during the day.

We can't see the water from the house. If you look out the front window you see another house just like ours with a driveway and a shed. There are sidewalks so you don't get hit by a car. The whole place is planned and meant for railway workers. Apparently they have the same thing on the mainland, these arching streets with houses evenly laid out one by one. It is hard to get used to not seeing the ocean but we were lucky to get this place with all the people moving into Arnold's Cove. Places to stay are hard to find. Sometimes there are extended families all living under one roof, uncles, aunts, umpteen children, grandparents and great aunts and uncles. At least there are just us. And now we have a truck so it is only a five minute drive to see my sisters and their families.

It is strange to see all the houses from St. Kyran's in this new spot. They are all lined up in a neat row facing the roadway. Some were hauled across the street so they face the water but there is a road and another house before you reach it. There is no need for a root cellar anymore with the grocery store offering all different types of food all year around. People are building their houses back on stilts but the land is soft so the structure is not as strong. The city built up the land for the new houses not knowing that rock is where they came from. There are a number of sections to Arnold's Cove. There is the new section that we live in, the places for the resettled houses, the older area of town where the original people who settled Arnold's Cove live and Main Street where the shops and post office are. The hospital is over in Come By Chance and thankfully we haven't had to use it.

This is a new life we've come to and I wonder about it all sometimes. There was purpose in St. Kyran's that you can't find here with all these modern appliances. Work was endless, sure, but it wasn't the same as work here. There was a quality to it that resonated in the community, for everyone's well-being. It was a shared penance and we came to see it as part of the very fabric of our lives, as integral to who we are as the water we drank, the air we breathed and the rocks that supported our houses. You just did what you had to do in order to live. There was no moaning or discussing it. Now there's a car to drive places, a telephone, a working toilet and when we want heat, we just turn a knob. But when I want to see someone I've got to wait for Peter to get home from work to run me over. The kids are at school from eight thirty until three, but there's an idleness to their behaviour, a tendency to get up to no good that reminds me of Father Fyme at his most menacing. "The devil finds a place in idle hands and hearts!" he'd roared, and I see, at times, the embodiment of his direst warnings in the children. All of this has taken some time to get used to. I find it lonely but easier. I have gotten into the stories on the television, but I miss the stories of the people I know. Life here is more convenient. But is it the way I want to live my life?

***

NORTH CAROLINA, UNITED STATES, JANUARY 6TH, 1900

RETURNING TO A NEW LAND:
HOW THE ARCHITECTURE OF THE OLD SOUTH
MADE ITS WAY TO ARTHINGTON, LIBERIA

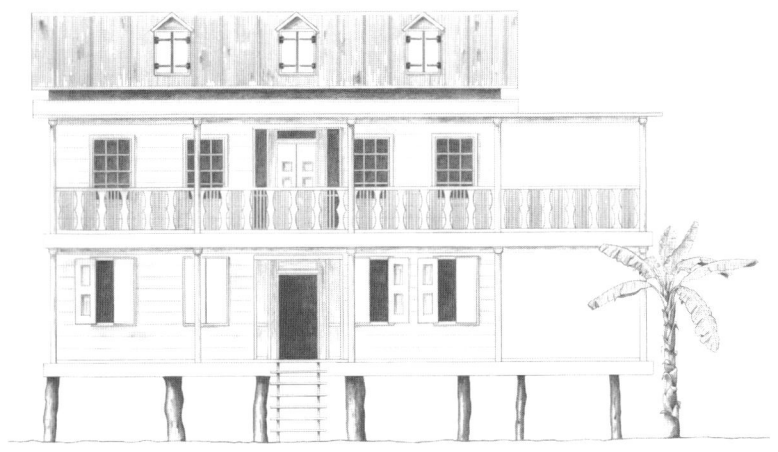

BY
BERNARD L. HERMAN

6 January 1900, North Carolina
Robert returned this afternoon, having made a trip to town, and collected the mail in the course of his usual errands. Sitting by the window writing on this gray winter day, a fire whispering in our old home's hearth, I glanced down the lane and observed as Robert, with his awkward gait, stepped across the frost-rutted garden and up the back stairs to the kitchen—a brown paper bundle tucked under his arm, mud and dead leaves on his boots. After a scuffle of feet on the floorboards, and a rap on the door, Robert entered the room bearing the parcel with its travel torn corners. "From your friend in Africa," he said, and left.

My dearest friend, how long has it been since last we exchanged letters? When you decamped for Liberia with the others from this neighbourhood, we pledged that correspondence would preserve our friendship, a friendship that had been sorely tested by the enduring habits and prejudices of this, our native country. And at first, our letters came and went, bearing my intelligence of family and friends left behind and your accounts of a new land and all that you intended to accomplish there. Slowly the pace of our exchange faltered until we lost connection. Thirty years, a lifetime—an ocean in itself, separate us. You decamped in the bitter years that followed the war, seeking a promised freedom that conquest and occupation failed to realize in practice. The prejudice of custom, they say, dies hard. Now, in the first grey days of the new century, I sit at my desk, the one where my father, your former master, kept his accounts of crops sown and provisions provided, your bundle open before me, reading all the letters I sent and that you saved—posted back to me with neither note nor explanation. I can only imagine the worst and wonder as to your health in that difficult and hopeful place. But why these letters were returned I do not know.

Reaching into the back of my writing stand drawer, I find a like bundle bound with ribbon and containing every correspondence you penned from the house you built in the settlement of Arthington up the St. Paul River. The two piles, side by side, unite as a single memorial to a conversation that has stuttered into silence. Reading these letters, yours and mine, today in this watery winter light, I marvel at your stories of the great labour invested in founding a new home on an alien shore, the tension between settler folk and native Kru and Vai that lingered unresolved, the relentless heat and privation that assailed your purpose of creating a nation that guaranteed the liberties denied you by law, custom, and the prejudice of this place. (How Father would sputter and scold, were he alive to read these words!) In all our correspondence, though, nothing aroused my imagination with so much force as your vivid renditions of the houses you and your neighbours built. Of particular interest was how these new settlements compared to what you all left behind. Scattered through your descriptions, these fragmented tales of house building helped me picture how you lived—and so, my beloved friend, in this last letter addressed to some future generation, a letter that shall never leave my desk, I try to weave together that vision of building Liberia, within the limits of my understanding.

Arthington, you wrote, was an inland settlement created in the years after the Southern defeat in equal measure by settlers from the sound country of North Carolina, the red clay hills of South Carolina, and the flat cotton lands of southern Georgia. Each contingent arrived in Monrovia as a group and under the direction of their leaders—a brickmaker and ministers—made arrangements for your move to the interior. You spoke of your slow progress up the St. Paul River, of how disease destroyed draft animals, and of your own mixed feelings about the natives of the country. Reading these tales of hardship, I at first saw stories of grand adventure, a noble ambition to conquer adversity. In their re-reading, though, your letters reveal that making a civilized and Christian home in a strange land was arduous labour that both wearied and elevated the spirit. "People at home," you mused, "delude themselves that we have returned to Africa, but this not so. I was born and reared in North Carolina, as were my parents. I am an American, as are we all, striving for independence in this foreign land. Ours is not a tale of homecoming, but rather a new adventure in which the colour of our skin and the denial of our abilities no longer impedes rightful advancement."

"Dear Friend," you wrote in subsequent correspondence shortly after your arrival, "I will briefly relate the state of the first houses built in this place in order that you might ascertain the nature and degree of our progress. Monrovia, the capital city, is marked by a great variety in its dwellings, the best built of brick and standing two-stories tall with their gables to the street. I've not had much experience with city residences, but acquaintances assure me that this is the style of building in Charleston, South Carolina. The most pitiful of homes are frame affairs scrapped together from wood. Time and climate conspire against the longevity of ruder dwellings and we do not expect them to endure much beyond ten years. For those few seasons, the poorer quality homes are soon in want of constant attention and repair. We esteem these first cabins only as a necessary first step on a journey toward the realization of the finer houses we intend to build for ourselves. A poor house offers a daily reminder that the anticipated progress of our situation will be achieved only by dint of hard work and divine providence." The houses I found most intriguing, though, were those you described in the backcountry up the St. Paul River on your way to Arthington.

"People speak of the first houses with an earnest sense of progress. Their settler dwellings were often rough affairs and their predicted demise through rot and insect encouraged a happy and optimistic view of the future condition of those first families and their descendents. Built of wood—some frame, some log—these earliest accommodations stood but a single story tall on blocks of wood to get them off the ground and raise them above the threat of the scourges that undermine and devour buildings from the bottom up. The interior arrangements vary from one to four rooms augmented with a loft under a steep roof, a front piazza, and a shed across the back. Cooking is conducted in a separate building, oftentimes little more than a thatched shed supported on poles. Glass for windows was in short supply, thus simple shutters covered the openings, leaving the inhabitants to constantly re-assess the lesser of two evils. The admission of breezes came attended with voracious insects that seemed to suck the marrow from our bones. Respite from their bite and sting came at the price of choking heat and floods of sweat. The coarse settler houses and their like have, over the years, become more and more the shelter of a poorer class of people. Their example is one I would avoid."

Reading these words, I look out the window and see the old kitchen in back of our house where our beloved Sissy laboured, sweating over pot and griddle for our culinary pleasure, and where she rested late at night on her pallet in the corner by the chimney. How like it is to the rude yet hopeful cottages you described. Perched on wood blocks, roughly framed, shuttered windows without glass—the irony of it all gives me pause. You relate how those first houses in your African home offered hope, yet here in your old neighbourhood, I see them as offering nothing but an increasingly relic reminder of all that was denied.

Your observations on the houses people desired, gleaned from your neighbours and new countrymen, surprised me much. I cannot invoke the passions that darkened Mr. R.M.'s expression when he shared with you his frustration on the cost and difficulty of building the house he believed so strongly should be his by right. Like so many, he began with a house intended to suffice until he could raise one better. That he could not build the house he would have for less than double the cost of the same accommodations in the United States caused me to start in amazement. Your relation of his situation proved my presumption of easy and universal advancement for the settlers, a view encouraged by other reports, to be false. Yet, your letters invariably convey notes of hope and progress.

"My Old Friend," you penned in a lengthy letter crowded with detail and bright enthusiasm, "the building of houses in the settlements along the St. Paul River proceeds at a dizzying pace. Enterprising fellows from across the 'old country' apply the skills forced upon them under the former regime to new projects of their own device. Free men now, they turn their hands with invigorated industry to the making of brick from native clay and the preparation of scantlings from trees felled on their own ground. Much of the sawyer's work is done by hand with timber laid across trestles and sawbucks piled together from felled timber or over pits excavated for the purpose. No matter the heat and labour, there is joy in this work and the pride of progress and property made visible on every hand. Among us are some with talent enough for the fine task of sawing fancy work. The best of our labours appears almost alive, dancing with scrolls and figures. A house, no matter how grand in size, without ornament cannot fully demonstrate the delicacy of our sensibilities and taste. I will describe in another letter a singular house that is an epitome of our advancement."

And, so you did.

"The finest house I have seen is that newly raised by the enterprising P. family. Brave and magnificent in every regard, it stands for all that we have achieved here and all that was denied at home. I lack the fineness of hand to send you sketches of what I esteem a mansion, but I hope my words will suffice to draw a picture in your mind. Like the very grandest residences in this country, whether of wood or brick, the house rises bravely two full stories high—an impression of height made greater by the piles that hold the structure above the ground and the neat windows that pierce the roof. Sawn boards, such as encase your own dwelling, seal the house without. Like boards, well planed, placed on end and butted hard against each other, close the inside. I understand from several neighbours that this practice follows the style of many American places where the want of plaster encouraged this mode of finishing the inside of houses. My new friend, Mr. J. from Georgia, assures me that this is the style of even the best houses in his former home, and that when finished with whitewash and paint they are as fine to the eye as any plaster. Panels pierced in fantastic patterns of waving plants, stars, hearts, fans, and even angels admit and circulate the air even as they delight the eye. Across the front of the house, a grand piazza stretches with pretty work in the railings and eaves. Sheltered by deep eaves, the upper gallery provides a place where the family, their intimates, and privileged visitors may sit or repose in whatever breeze might be stirring and regard from their elevated station whatever events transpire without. I have attempted a draught in words that limns the interior arrangements so that you may determine for yourself the elegant and commodious prospect of our advancement offered by this fine residence. The P.'s house is as good as any as ever I saw in the old neighbourhood."

The word sketch you penned describes a house of the kind I associate with the best families here: "A visitor ascends a low flight of steps, no more than five or six, and steps onto the piazza that stretches the length of the dwelling. A few quick strides convey him through double doors and into a broad entry. As in the finest houses in my former home, the entry runs the depth of the house offering a pair of rooms on either side of its course. The better room, what you might term a parlour, stands away from the stair, to the right of the entry, and is marked by broad opening that offers something of a vista of the dwelling's interior appointments. The parlour and its counterpart, a somewhat lesser sitting room, across the entry, are well-lit and ventilated—complete with sash windows acquired and installed at considerable effort and expense. Every other chamber in the lower story has but one such opening, but even so the use of glass makes them better by far than the custom of simply shuttered windows. A smaller room stands behind the finest apartment and serves the purpose of a private chamber. Across the entry, three rooms extend from the front of the house back in diminishing quality of finish and purpose. You will not be surprised when I tell you that the oppressive heat renders fireplaces and chimneys unnecessary, but requires pierced panels above the doors to effect the free circulation of air through the house. A covered area at the back of the house spans the open area between two work rooms, offering protection from rain and sun."

"Such a house," you wrote, "mirrors the polite manners and elegance of society I associate with the most refined sensibilities in our old neighbourhood—and illuminate our capacity to express a delicacy of feeling second-to-none and the envy of all." You were astute in your assessment of quality and refinement. Even in the hard times that have troubled our society and economy, the old mansions still mark the zenith of our long established plantations. Without effort, I can enumerate and remind you of a dozen fine houses of the class the P. family erected for themselves in their new African home—all the seats of the old slaveholding estates and not a one inhabited by persons of colour in a capacity greater than that of servant. That degree of architectural accomplishment in the Liberian backcountry is truly a marvel, one that realizes a degree of aspiration that few of the ancient class of masters and mistresses here could envision. Seeing their former bondsmen forever as their social inferiors, they could not grasp the extent and meaning of your achievement. The houses erected by you and your countrymen prove them wrong, but I wonder how many of the ancient class or their descendants could comprehend those African plantations as more than imitation. Here those houses are increasingly monuments to a relic past; in Liberia they herald liberty and prosperity for those who can afford the luxury of such building.

As encouraging as your account of the P.'s house and others like it in the settlements strung along the St. Pauls River were, it seems there were many others that were not so fine. In one letter, you report that some in the Arthington settlement had yet to raise a dwelling of the better sort. These residents sheltered in houses one-story in height and but one or two rooms in compass. As demand dictated, these poorer families encumbered their dwellings with sheds and additions of every size, cobbled together with whatever materials came to hand. Some of these "thrown together" residences became so caught up in their many additions that it was scarcely possible to discover where the house began and where it ended. "In the waning years of this century," you wrote, "it seems more and more that only the fortunate have found the means to build the houses they desired. As we strive to increase our wealth through the cultivation of coffee and other produce for market, we find ourselves in a difficult situation. Labour here is scarce, and the native people exhibit scant inclination to enter our employ—not that we have the resources to entice them to do so. Because our produce brings too little in the market place, we have not much hope of correcting this situation. There are those who conclude that they cannot achieve a finer house and that custom and trade will always hold them back. There are those who have come to see the foundation of their sojourn in this country not as liberty, but as banishment. There are those who protest that they were better off in their old home and would return if they could. I am not of this mind and will remain true to the purpose that brought me here."

And so it seems your words revealed a situation, not unlike our own here at home, where those with the means to commission a grand house and display their enduring reputation in wood and brick were precious few in number. The greater commonality of settlers might build houses they could call their own, but the obvious inferiority of their quality was apparent to all, and their accommodations suffered by comparison to the better sort, marking their continued dominion by those of means. "Still," you noted, "even the poorest settler house stands far above the habitations found in many native villages. Built of mud, thatched with fronds, round with bare ground all around, these dwellings make visible the gross lack of civility and sensibility that philanthropy, providence and our own history would have us correct by example."

Following a series of travels that carried you to a number of settlements up and down the coast, you wrote, "You ask about the houses we have built for ourselves and I have obliged you with accounts of residences that range in quality from the finest to those that can be judged only as indifferent. What I have not shared with you are houses of a different sort—the churches that occupy a prominent place in our towns. On a recent journey down the St. Paul River to the communities at the mouth of the St. John River, I had opportunity to observe a number of churches. Many settlers, as I remarked in an earlier account, arrived as congregations and among their first endeavors was the establishment of churches. The denominations are those we have at home, chiefly Methodist, Baptist, Protestant Episcopal—and families worship freely in the churches built by others. There is talk among the Baptists in Arthington of planning for a new masonry church with a bell tower and sheltered porch—but work has not yet begun."

"Leaving Arthington, we stopped in Clay-Ashland. The Baptist Church there follows close on the arrangements of the plain churches and meetinghouses that we knew in our neighbourhood. (I am reminded that I always sat in the gallery consigned to the place set aside for my race while you took your place with your people below.) Two flights of steps lead to two separate doors and each of these doors opens onto an aisle that leads to the front of the church. The congregation, seated in rows of pews, faces the minister who preaches from a lectern behind a kneeling rail. Vigorous singing punctuates the oratory and many call out in response to the preacher's exhortations. Service is dignified and spirited—and nowhere am I reminded more of home than in the churches we have built for ourselves. The Presbyterian Church in Clay-Ashland is a more humble affair, built for a more modest congregation. Very simple in aspect, this brick meetinghouse is the plainest I saw, with no relief in its outward show more than its whitewashed foundation."

"We visited similar churches along the St. Paul throughout our journey, but for me the most striking outside the capital city were in the settlements of Edina, Hartford, and Fortsville. Edina lies nearest the coast on the north shore of the St. John River and it is not unexpected that this place should have the most elegant house of worship. Like the great majority of churches here and at home it presents a gabled front to the street and an interior scheme like the one I saw in the Baptist church in Clay-Ashland. A portico carried on four whitewashed columns and whitewashed buttresses down the red brick length of the building gives an impressive effect. The Hartford Church, like the Edina Church, ministers to the Baptists. Built of brick this pretty building is distinguished by a bell tower topped by a metal weathervane in the form of a fish. The plainest of the three is the Methodist Church in Fortsville. Positioned on a little rise, the Fortsville building is more meetinghouse than church, with little outward show beyond its whitewashed front and neat door and windows. The Methodists here rejected the prideful show of a steeple and bell, electing instead to place their bell in a little open wood structure to one side of the churchyard. I attended a service in every one of these places and in them found the familiar comforts of my one true God and his only Son. In prayer and song each congregation carried me to a land that knows neither the distance of oceans nor the prejudices of place."

"Since I last wrote to you of the churches along the St. John River and in my own district," you wrote subsequently, "I have been to Royesville where the Baptists have built themselves a pretty little meetinghouse in the plain style of those I attended in Clay-Ashland and Fortsville. The distinctions between places that we note in the United States are not so apparent here, at least in the style of churches and houses. There is a kind of comfort for me in the recognition that our buildings reflect our larger status as 'Liberian' and transcend our particular origins in the United States. Our buildings, manifest in our churches, speak to the larger faith and optimism that joins us in this place—our new home so far away."

As our epistolary conversation stretched through the years with ever diminishing frequency, I meditated on each new account you offered, striving to grasp the vagaries of your fortunes. Even as your words enriched my comprehension of your situation, they left me pondering. Nothing surprised me more, though, than a letter containing a small engraving neatly cut from a popular periodical of uncertain date and title. Your accompanying correspondence addressed only your family situation and your then current anxiety that one of your children might marry a native—much to the objection of you and your wife. Your efforts at Christianizing and civilizing the indigenous people had never been intended to bring about a marital union. But, it was the picture that caught my fancy.

Although you provided no clue as to the origins of the engraving, it struck me as one that might be discovered in the pages of *Harper's New Monthly Magazine* or something of the like kind. The scene depicted is on the coast where a broad road curves between two great houses and down to a still bay where a small sailing craft makes its way. The horse and oxen on the road tell me that invention colours the content of the picture—you have taught me that much. What holds my eye, though, is the plantation in the distance. A mansion with two-storied verandas, front and back, occupies the space between bay and what I suspect are coffee groves stretching into the surrounding countryside. This is a settler house of the best quality—the seat perhaps of a planter and merchant grandly positioned between farm and sea. Behind the mansion house, a row of six small cottages set eave-to-eave stretches to the picture's edge, leaving the impression that there may well be more. The uniform appearance of these buildings, their alignment in a row, immediately evoked an association with the "streets" once a fixture on only the very largest plantations. I know not the truth of this depiction, but the enduring impression is one of housing provisioned for workers. A seventh building occupies a position at the head of the row and closest to the principle dwelling. Its position and the presence of a chimney in one gable suggest that this building worked as the kitchen and it corresponds closely to your description of the placement and appearance of the stone kitchen behind the president's house in Monrovia. I did not linger over this picture at the time, but now it imposes itself on my consciousness. If a house serves as a portrait of its builders and occupants giving the viewer the measure of the subject's character and sensibility, then what character does this picture make visible? This single image, folded into your letter without comment or clue, the only picture ever consigned to me other than those painted by your eloquence, has rendered all I thought I knew of your Liberian career uncertain.

When we stood so many years ago at the point where our lane met the public road, I asked you what you had chosen to take on your journey. "I have packed but few essentials," you replied. "I have a Bible and the few clothes that I can call my own. You have given me an allowance" (far too stingy I reflect now reading these letters in this dimming room), "and the gift of reading and writing." You paused (I remember this with great vividness) and toed the edge of a wheel trace where it curved from the lane into the road and trailed away, "and I have the sum of knowledge that all the experience and memory of living in this place and these times has given me. That knowing will shape my comportment and destiny as surely as conviction and faith." Your words perplexed me, and I ascribed them at the time to the emotions that governed your departure. This winter evening, your letters and mine before me and the picture, part real, part fiction, unfolded on the blotter, I revisit your words.

There is no innocence in the possession of knowledge. We can never entirely absolve ourselves from the injustices and cruelties we inflict on others, nor can we be free of those inflicted on us. Rereading the letter that accompanied the picture, I grasp at this late hour the struggle in your heart as you sought to reconcile your child's romantic affections against your own prejudices. You could not admit your feelings in words and so you sent the engraving to do that work. The plantation house with its attendant dwellings assigned to those who worked for and under its authority resonates with the customs and practices of this place. The view is not about the replication of buildings, although that is what some viewers might assume, if they thought about such things at all. I estimate now that the view is a window into your deepest feelings. I cannot guess if the picture before me illustrated the steeling of your resolve that settler and native would not mix—or if an awareness that "the sum of knowledge" revealed to you a deeper personal conflict. Did the achievement manifest in the buildings within the image signify liberation and attainment for some and the subjection of others? And, at what cost to the heart and spirit? Who can know the answers to such questions?

As I fold the picture back into its letter and the letter back into its bundle, the arrogance of my own interest in your adventures in Liberia measured out in your accounts of houses becomes palpable to me. My fascination with your architectural progress and that of your neighbours stemmed from a hidden interest in something else far more elusive than I recognized. I read your letters in the embrace of this house and marvelled at your fortitude and progress. In retrospect, I realise that my estimation and indeed the opinion of all who looked upon Liberia as the validation of a belief in your capacity for progress relied on the degree to which you could create a "home" in a new land. The houses you built manifest your accomplishments. The arrangement the P. family's elegant house, with its fanciful appointments, the constellation of church and meetinghouse, the modest residences of families less successful in the enterprise of establishing a new country but in marked contrast to the huts of the natives—all of these and more are the epitome of your understanding of your old home and all that its buildings entailed. Yes, you carried knowledge with you—but it entailed much more than the understanding of design and how houses are built. The knowledge you carried grew from your understanding of the order of our society and how our houses and other buildings made that order visible. I fear you knew us better than we did ourselves and in the end you could foresee the inequities as well as the iniquities of what the settlers erected. Still, you persevered and hope, more than anxiety, fills the pages

I have ribboned together and packed away for posterity. I add to the collection this letter to you, my absent friend, in the hope not that you will ever read it, but that I have obtained some small degree of the deeper haunting ironies of this place.

I detect Robert's coming in the passage and hasten to pack these letters away. His arrival means supper and I catch the scent of Sissy's granddaughter's stewed chicken and dumplings. Robert, ever practical, has no patience with my musings and meditations on distant lands. His attention dwells on the tasks at hand. The roof, he says with his usual matter-of-factness, leaks and demands repair lest seeping rainwater threaten the integrity of the very timbers that support this house. What shall I do should my own house built by my foreparents rot, weaken, and fall? What memory will I carry forward then? What house would I build?

***

THE SEASIDE, ENGLAND, JULY 20TH, 1969

OH BUNGALOW, BORN BY THE BAY OF BENGAL, YOU CONQUERED AN EMPIRE—AND THEN THE WORLD—REDEFINING SUCCESS EVERY STEP OF THE WAY!

BY
DAVID HOWES

Grey skies again today. I suppose one can't expect too much in the way of fine weather at an English seaside resort in July. No one's outside anyway, they're all gathered around the television in the lounge, watching the Americans land on the moon. I'd rather sit in my room and watch the sea, watch the waves, always moving restlessly.

I was talking with Mrs. Rawlins in the lounge yesterday and she mentioned that she liked the name of our hotel, "The Bungalow Hotel." "It's so comfortable sounding," she said. "It gives you a feeling of being at home and away on vacation at the same time." It would give me a feeling of being at home too if it were anything like the bungalow in India I grew up in.

This place is just a three-storey building with William Morris wallpaper and 1930s furniture. The bungalow I grew up in in Lahore was a large, flat-roofed house with a wide veranda all around, set inside a walled compound filled with tropical plants. That was a real bungalow.

Of course, the original bungalows, I suppose, were the ones built by the native Indians for themselves before the English came. Those were thatched huts with an overhanging roof. That kind of house was called a *bangala*, meaning that it came from Bengal. The kind of bungalow my family lived in might have been based on native forms of architecture, but it was definitely a colonial creation: an Indian dwelling suitable for Englishmen.

Our bungalow was not a hut, but it was simple; one-storey with rooms for entertaining and rooms for sleeping. The surrounding compound provided space for a garden and for servants' quarters but most importantly it allowed the house to be well-ventilated. In such a hot climate we were grateful for whatever breeze came our way. That's why the house didn't have hallways, to keep the air flowing from room to room. On particularly hot days the servants would be kept busy splashing water on the window and door screens to cool the air as it blew in. The screens were made from bamboo, which made the air passing through fragrant. When I think of our bungalow I remember that smell.

I spent much of my time playing on the veranda, watched over by my Ayah, as Indian nannies were called. I remember there was a snake that lived under that veranda and sometimes it would stretch out its shiny head and watch me, not do anything, just watch. My Ayah was scared that snake would bite me but I knew it wouldn't, we lived on peaceful terms with each other. The shade provided by the veranda helped cool the air around the house and make it more bearable inside, but I always preferred to be outside anyway.

Inside the house was a piano, brought from England by my mother, which I was expected to play for half an hour every day. I think my mother thought of piano practice as a way to keep me from becoming too "native." We lived surrounded by Indian servants, servants to clean, to cook, to garden, to fetch and carry... It didn't bother me but I think it worried my parents. The number of servants combined with the open design of the bungalow didn't really allow for much personal privacy. The heat seemed to bring us even closer together, all stewing, as it were, in the same hot, moist air. Whenever my parents met with their friends there would be talk about native revolts and uprisings. The feeling was that what happened outside in the city might happen inside in the bungalow. Each bungalow was imagined to be like a miniature empire, teeming with useful but potentially rebellious natives. Each bungalow had to be firmly ruled by its English master. How Father took that mission to heart!

Aside from the piano, the rest of our furniture consisted of Indian copies of copies of European originals. My mother held them in contempt for their "inferior workmanship," but I liked their slightly crooked lines and unpolished finish. All the furniture in my grandmother's house back in England seemed too smooth and shiny and slippery by contrast. Nothing to hold on to. As a special sign of high status we had a porcelain bathtub, imported from England as a gift from my father to my mother. Of course, it still had to be filled by servants carrying heated water in old kerosene tins brought all the way from the kitchen out back. The kitchen was separate from the house. It was located near the servants' quarters, so that the bungalow wouldn't be affected by the heat and odours of cooking.

My bedroom was at the back of the house. The walls were thin and I would lie in bed at night, feeling the breeze blowing in through the mosquito curtains and hearing my parents talking. My mother would come in wearing a floating, lacy dress and kiss me goodnight before going out to a party. Then I would fall asleep to the sound of the jackals calling somewhere outside the compound.

Though I thought of the bungalow as our property it was, in fact, rented. Almost all the homes occupied by the English were rented since people always expected to be moving on after a few years. Our bungalow was actually owned by a wealthy Indian businessman. It, like all the other bungalows in the city, had been built by local Indians using the same materials, brick and wood and clay tiles and lime plaster, and based on the same design. There seemed to be no point in catering to personal tastes when people came and went so frequently.

Mind you, there were bungalows and there were bungalows. Ours was a substantial house because Father was a senior administrator. A low-ranking official, however, might only have a little four-roomed bungalow with odds and ends for furnishings and walls that were whitewashed instead of painted. Though such distinctions mattered, they didn't seem to matter quite as much in India as they would have in England. If you were short on cutlery for a party, for example, one of your guests might have a servant bring along an extra supply. No one really seemed to mind such things. I think there was a feeling among the English that they were all making do together in this foreign wilderness in which they happened to find themselves.

When I left India to go to school in England I thought I'd left bungalows behind forever. I knew they'd built bungalows for Europeans in Africa. "The Indian bungalow is the one perfect house for all tropical countries," some supposed expert said. So up went the bungalows in the Gold Coast and in Nigeria and in Kenya. My brother Tom, who was a District Commissioner in Kenya, had a very handsome bungalow there, judging from the photos he sent us. It rested on pillars, which raised it a good eight feet off the ground to protect against the "exhalations of the earth" that were supposed to cause malarial fever. The way it was situated in that European enclave on the hill outside of town meant that it commanded a magnificent view, but Tom said it was for "hygienic" reasons, the supposed dangers of contagion from mixing with the native Africans in their village compounds, that he built there. He called his house "detached."

Well, bungalows in Africa are one thing but I couldn't see why anyone would want one in England, which must be one of the least tropical places in the world. The typical English home for me was my grandmother's Victorian villa. It was very upright: three storeys plus an attic, ten-foot ceilings, two sets of stairs (one for the servants). And it had so many divisions: the front hallway, the sitting room, the study, the basement, the upstairs hallways, the master bedroom, the girl's bedroom, the boy's bedroom, the nursery. Every room had its own fireplace, so there were lots of chimneys jutting out of the roof. And there was the gingerbread, so intricate, so much work to carve, so distinctive!

After the Great War, however, bungalows, or what were called bungalows, started springing up all over England. They had nothing to do with being good housing for a tropical climate. They were thought of as modern and economical. A bungalow was really just a small, square, one-storey house, like a child's building block. You didn't need any servants if you lived in a house like that. And, as I recall, servants were getting harder and harder to find before the War, never mind after. I suppose for many people, people like Mrs. Rawlins, who grew up in one of those boxy post-war bungalows, a bungalow does mean home. An English home at that, though not much of one. In India a bungalow was an important residence, it meant something to live in a bungalow there. It still does I understand. Here it just seems to mean cheap housing.

Though, now that I think about it, I realize there's more to it than that. One of the reasons for the spread of bungalows in England was that they were seen as more natural, more informal and more open to the outdoors than traditional English housing, such as villas and townhouses. Just as life in India could feel more informal and more natural than life back home. I suppose people wanted some of that in England. That's why bungalows became so popular as vacation homes. It was supposed to be the free and easy life. But when they migrated from the edges of the sea to the edges of the city, and were all massed together on street after street, all identical and with hardly any space in between, the sense of freedom became a sense of entrapment.

Where the bungalow is really popular now is in the United States. Somehow it came to stand for everything people there wanted: freedom, closeness to nature, efficiency, modern progress and, of course, low cost. My daughter Nora tells me there's even a place in California called "Bungalow Heaven."

Nora should know because her second husband builds bungalows—whole communities of them—in California. In fact, that's how Nora met Bill: "Bungalow Bill," I call him, like that song they play on the radio. He was building a house for Nora and her first husband Ted, and their two teenage girls. Then when Ted left Nora to go to India to meditate with the Maharishi like the Beatles, Nora was left with the girls, the bungalow and its builder. I went to their wedding last year, and stayed with them in their new house. It has one and a half storeys, overhanging eaves, and shrubs planted along the front. No servants' quarters, but a big garage for their automobile. Lower ceilings than I was used to, and not much to look at inside. I couldn't get over the kitchen, though, with all its cabinets and gadgets—including a machine for washing dishes! The family even eats right in the kitchen. The rest of the time they're in what they call the "living room" watching television.

While I was staying with Nora and her family, I had quite a few conversations with Bill about his bungalows—and the girls joined in too, particularly Nora's eldest, Melanie, who is reading Sociology at Berkeley and has her own ideas about how people ought to live.

Bill thinks he knows what a real bungalow is: "It's an All-American house, originally from California." When I protested that the bungalow originated in India he said that might well be, but it was "perfected" in California, and that's the model that spread from West to East across the U.S., to Canada, Australia, New Zealand, and even the U.K. back in the 1920s. "The bungalow embodied the Californian Dream, and it is the epitome of convenience and efficiency."

This "Californian Dream," he explained, had to do with a youthful, informal, outdoorsy lifestyle. The first "California bungalows" were summer houses. Their wilderness situation and their low silhouette contrasted with the uprightness of the Victorian villa, while the open interior of the bungalow did away with all the divisions of the Victorian house, and the stuffy social conventions that went with them, making for a "cosier" family life, or so Bill claimed: "Just look at the low roofline of a bungalow, how it radiates cosiness; think how it blends in with nature, instead of trying to dominate the countryside like some castle on top of a hill."

How I bristled at that last swipe, directed at some imaginary Englishman (whose "home is his castle," as the saying goes). But I had to forgive Bill all his not so subtle swipes at the British, for I could tell that he was actually reacting against his own Puritanical heritage. One visit to swinging London would cure him of the idea that the British remain locked in the Victorian era.

It was at this point in our conversation that Melanie intervened to point out that the rows upon rows of bungalows in the suburbs around Los Angeles do not blend in with nature, they obliterate it; that suburban sprawl has resulted in suburbanites having to spend more and more hours on the freeway commuting, which is anything but convenient, not to mention polluting; and, that people may once have found the California climate refreshing and wanted to be outdoors, but now they just sit in front of their air conditioners watching television, completely cut off from the natural world. "Air conditioners are not cool," she said, as if she wished they didn't have one. I don't think we would have refused them back in the old days in India.

And, Melanie continued, the isolation from nature is matched by the social isolation of the nuclear family secluded within the "privacy" of its own home. Contrary to what all the women's magazines say, home life for the housewife is not "relaxed, informal, and efficient"; rather, Melanie averred, it is filled with repetition, boredom and despair—an endless round of cooking, changing diapers, looking after "little ones" and trying to please one's husband. You could tell Melanie would have none of this. That's what comes of doing away with servants, I thought: my mother would never have deigned to do such work.

But the worst thing, according to Melanie, was the conformity, the way everyone aspired after the same possessions, the same "markers" of middle class social status. Americans had become far too "other directed" in the words of one of her profs, and the sameness was stultifying, as in the words of that 1962 song Pete Seeger sang, "Little Boxes."

Little boxes on the hillside
Little boxes made of ticky tacky
Little boxes on the hillside
Little boxes all the same

"But they're not all the same!" Bill exploded. "I sit down with every one of my clients the same way I sat down with your mother." Melanie rolled her eyes. Bill carried on: "We go over the plans, particularly those for the kitchen, and make adjustments, within limits, of course. Every bungalow I build is unique in some way, even if the walls and everything are prefabricated and the appliances all mass-produced. But that's progress! And that's the beauty of it: the bungalow almost builds itself it can be assembled so quickly—a matter of weeks —and, with all the labour-saving devices available nowadays, what more could a housewife want?"

I was swayed by Bill's argument about the technological efficiency of the modern kitchen, until Melanie shot back: "How about a different division of labour? And, how about a life?" What Melanie had in mind was Dads shouldering some of the load, and Moms having their own jobs outside the home. She also pointed out that all the so-called labour-saving devices weren't much good if they didn't allow women to leave the house.

Bill sputtered on about how the bungalow encourages individuality because its style is so flexible, and how it supports democracy too, because everyone is on the same level! This provoked Cathy, Nora's youngest, to bring up her plight as a teenager. Her room was only big enough to study and to sleep in. There was no space in the house for her to have her friends in (by which she meant no space where she was not under the watchful eye of her mother). There was no place in the endless winding streets of Downsview (the name of their subdivision) for young people to get together outside either. "But what about all the playgrounds?" her stepfather responded. Now it was Cathy's turn to roll her eyes. (There seemed to be a lot of that going on in this household.) Obviously, Downsview had been planned for families with very young children and this had resulted in most young people feeling left out.

"The bungalow is clearly totally 'dysfunctional,' and so is Downsview," Melanie opined. Bill gasped. Perhaps he didn't know what "dysfunctional" meant. I don't think I do either, but it certainly does sound bad.

"There is a solution, though," Melanie proclaimed brightly. "This is America and we should do like our fellow Americans–Latin Americans, that is. Ever notice how from Mexico to the southernmost tip of Argentina, all the towns are laid out around a central plaza? The plaza is a place where everybody congregates, even teenagers. And the houses are laid out the same way. They are patio houses, which are like bungalows in that they are usually low, one-storey buildings, but the reverse of bungalows in the way they bring the outdoors indoors by having a patio at the centre, while distributing the rooms around the outer wall. The way the rooms all open onto the patio makes the house cosy, while the garden at the centre makes the house cool and, best of all, you are never cut off from the sky because there is no roof over the patio. You're not cut off from other family either. The patio house easily accommodates extended families, since it is like a commune to begin with."

I saw what Melanie was saying, but I couldn't help feeling that had it not been for the disappearance of the veranda the bungalow could have remained a far more "functional" dwelling (to use Melanie's language).

On another occasion I took this matter up with Bill. I said that I didn't think the houses he built could really be called bungalows because, while they were simple, single-storey, single-family dwellings with extended eaves and open interiors, they lacked a veranda. He quoted me a line from some builder's book he had on hand: "Although the bungalow has a number of distinguishing characteristics, none of them is so important as to be indispensable." The veranda was one of these, he said, or rather, in the U.S.A. it had been replaced by the porch. Before World War II, I learned, most houses had a front porch and a broad stretch of front lawn. The porch was a place for entertaining and for talking to neighbours as they strolled by on a summer evening. After World War II, most people wanted their porch to be at the back of the house, overlooking a garden, and the front porch was replaced by a garage to house the indispensable automobile. The increased traffic and the decline of the evening stroll were further reasons for doing away with verandas or porches, though Bill had found that many of his clients still wanted to put in a bay window. That permitted them to watch without having to hear or smell their neighbours.

In any event, Bill said, the new buzzword among builders is "ranch house." A ranch house is really the same as a bungalow, he confided. But people think ranch house sounds more distinguished, so I build them a bungalow and tell them it's a ranch house.

One time when Bill (diehard salesman that he is) was going on about how perfect the bungalow is as a "starter home" for newlyweds eager to "move up" from an apartment in the city to a (cheap) house in the suburbs, where they can raise their children in "wholesome surroundings," I pointed out that it made a good "finisher home" too. Seniors appreciate bungalows because there are no stairs and everything is in reach. It was the first time anything I said gave Bill pause. "Now why didn't I think of that," he said, and instantly began sketching a vision of a new subdivision called "Pleasant View" full of "specialty bungalows for old folks." It had to be a new subdivision, he thought, because you don't want to mix old people with young families, and it would probably have to be in some other state, like Florida, because of California's youthful image, but what a great idea! Personally, I found the name sounded too much like a cemetery, and I think the generations should be integrated, not segregated, so I was not impressed.

Sitting here in "The Bungalow Hotel," I have to wonder: Is the bungalow intrinsically flawed, the way Melanie seemed to think? That question begs the question of what a bungalow is, exactly. Colonial residence or single-family dwelling? Vacation house or suburban house? Starter home or finisher home? If it is all these things and more, then perhaps it is the ultimate multipurpose dwelling, good for everyone, everywhere. And if that's the case, it must be because it was a hybrid to begin with, a mixture of England and India.

I hear a lot of noise coming from the lounge downstairs. The Americans must have landed on the moon. They'll soon be wanting bungalows there too, I suppose. Well, I'd better go and have a look. I like to move with the times.

***

IROQUOIS, ONTARIO, CANADA, OCTOBER 30TH, 1967

ON THE MOVE OF IROQUOIS, ONTARIO: HOW CHOOSING A SITE TO THE EAST OFFERS AN OPPORTUNITY FOR FUTURISTIC LIVING

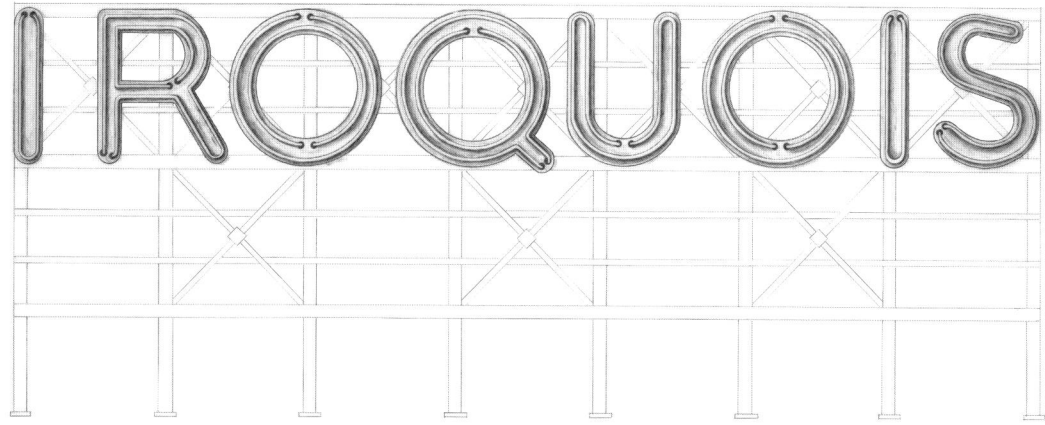

BY
PETER SEALY

"Why don't we pull over here? Yes, pull off here, now. Please." Wells Coates' words, which he mumbled with a strange urgency, caused me to brake quickly. Unsure why, I moved the car over to the exit from the highway.

"You know, I haven't been back here since they sent me that telegram to let me go. It was such a long time ago."

"Here?" I replied, unsure if he meant the acres of farmland rolling down to the water, or this place in particular. I assumed "they" were his ancestors; earlier he had told me that his great-grandfather had settled in Prescott; his Mother's family, the Wintemutes, were Loyalists who had crossed over from Vermont not far from here.

"Yes, here." There was a hint of nervous anger in his voice; something I hadn't heard at all during the days we had spent together in Montreal. There, he had been almost euphoric both in his praise and his criticism as we visited the Expo, which had showcased so many of his ideas. "You know, I don't think I'll ever get over this place."

His words hung in the air as we turned towards a smallish town, set back from the water. The late October sunshine fell on a series of houses a short distance away, some old, some new.

"Should we find a place to have lunch?" I asked tentatively, although it was surely too early, and I had planned for us to reach Kingston before we would take a break.

"No. Stop here, please. I don't know if I will be able to, but I want to tell you about this place. About what they... about what I could have built here."

I pulled over to the side of the road, and Coates started talking. He was always talking; when we were visiting the final days of Expo, he was always explaining this or that, and telling us what Canada could do. Here it was different. Wells Coates, architect and planner, among so many other things, was sharing with me all the pain of his greatest disappointment. Before World War II he had been one of leading Modernists in England, with his office in London. All the great architects (Walter Gropius, Marcel Breuer, László Moholy-Nagy, and later Jim Stirling) had lived in the Isokon Flats, which he had designed, on Lawn Road Flats in Hampstead. Agatha Christie had stayed there during the war; Arnold Deutsch, the Soviet spy who had recruited the Cambridge Five, lived in Flat no. 7.

"After the war, nothing seemed possible in England. When we were demobilized, we came out knowing there was so much work to do, and we of the Modern architectural school wanted a real chance to do it, without old men's nonsense interfering. I had so many projects but none of them went through: mass-produced low-cost housing, a hotel in Kent, cinemas in Scotland... the only thing I managed to have built was the Telekinema for the Festival of Britain in 1951."

Despite his good reputation among the architects of the day, who recognized his role in the fight to introduce Modern architecture to Britain in the 1930s, the post-war work he had hoped for in the U.K. never materialized. Part of this was due to the austerity of the time, but part was due to Coates' inability to get along with his clients. He was a man of integrity, serious and devoted, but he was known for having a horribly vain and arrogant manner, inflexible in the extreme. The problem with Wells Coates, and especially for all his projects as an architect, was his inability to suffer fools, or anyone whom he perceived to be lacking in the sort of imagination that propelled him in his endeavours.

"I had to look elsewhere to realize my ambitions. There was so much silliness in Britain, everything was so hard, with the rationing and the small bureaucrats running things in the most dismal way. They were trying to build New Towns everywhere, which were often pointless and of no economic necessity, when it really made sense to do them here in Canada, and in Australia and New Zealand. When I came out here in 1951, I really thought that Canada was set for a new classical era in architecture. Not just to produce singular buildings in the Modern style; that could be done anywhere. What Canada could do was to apply coordinated planning so that Modern architecture could reach its full potential and social responsibility."

The frenzied passion in Coates' voice as he explained why he had set his sights on Canada told me that he was back in 1951.

"I found out about this place when I was visiting to work on a plan for a New Town in Kitimat, British Columbia, which was being planned for Alcan. I was trying to push them away from the old idea of a company town—a factory surrounded by dwellings—into a true planned community, with a diversity of industry, housing and recreation. I contacted people from Iroquois, and convinced them to let me serve as their consultant. I was amazed by what was possible in Canada. All my plans were being dashed in Britain at the time, and I knew that this was my chance to come back to my country and to prove my ideas. Not for a sailboat or a kitchen, or even a building, but for an entire New Town. What was needed was the opportunity for industry and people to leave Britain and set themselves up abroad. I was going to do a city planned on the best principles, to do right for the people here, and to show the world what Canada's future would be."

***

Iroquois. That was the name of the small town where we were now pulled over to the side of Carman Road. A golf course and a small airport divided the town from the shore of the St. Lawrence River; now more a lake, thanks to the large dam visible in the distance. Almost thirteen years had passed since the day Wells Coates had last set foot in Iroquois, a few weeks before the townsfolk had finally rejected his plans for their village. The course of his life had taken him from Japan, where he was born and lived as a child, to Canada, where he studied before moving to Europe, then back to Canada, and then again to England. Iroquois, Ontario, had been a small town with a population of 1,000 or so people, who worked mostly for the Caldwell Linen Mill. That this place would have provided Coates with his greatest opportunity seemed strange, except that Coates was proudly Canadian, and he did feel that his family belonged to the area. He had set his sights on his homeland, in which he had hardly lived, jumping at the opportunity he felt had been waiting for him. Above all, in 1952 Iroquois was a place in search of an architect.

The town of Iroquois lies on the Upper St. Lawrence River, between Kingston, at the foot of the Great Lakes, and Montreal, from whence the Lower St. Lawrence flows into the Gulf and then out to the Atlantic Ocean. The riverbed changes depth suddenly many times in the sector around Iroquois, creating the International Rapids, which before canals were built in the middle of the 19th century left this part of the St. Lawrence navigable only to canoes and flat-bottomed *bateaux*. In the 16th and 17th centuries, trade and war alternated in the valley of the Upper St. Lawrence between the surrounding peoples: the Iroquois nations to the south, the Hurons to the west, the Algonquins to the north, the French to the east. It was just a little upriver from the site where the town of Iroquois was later built that the French made their last, heroic effort to defend the approaches to Montreal from the English in 1760.

The town of Iroquois took its name from the nearby Point Iroquois jutting into the river, site of a favoured camping ground for the Iroquois Nations. This protected a small bay, beside which the first European settlers, Loyalists from New York with names such as Carman, Coons, Ault and Brouse, started establishing their new homes in 1784. They built a mill, and then a wharf to supply timber to the small steamers that were beginning to ply the river. The town grew slowly until the opening of the Galop Canal across Point Iroquois in 1847 led to the opening of new mills. The Grand Trunk Railway, linking Montreal and Toronto, was built through Iroquois in 1854, solidifying the town's position of regional importance.

Incorporated in 1875, the town came to be known as the "Limestone Village" because of the material used for most of its buildings. Iroquois had a population of near 2,000 people in 1879, and it was an established centre for shipping agricultural produce from the region, as well as for local crafts and industries. In 1897, the Galop Canal was improved; a new lock, constructed to a length of 800 feet, was the largest in Canada at the time. In the 20th century the Caldwells opened their linen factory; by the 1950s, the Caldwell Linen Mill was the largest employer in Iroquois. However, the town's development had by then been stymied for quite some time, and its population was stuck at 1,100. Iroquois was a town that's economy depended on its position on the river; it was this very position which now put the town at risk. After over a half-century of speculation, the plans for the construction of the St. Lawrence Seaway were then on the verge of approval.

Despite the construction of the Galop and other local canals, the International Rapids were essentially a bottleneck in the St. Lawrence–Great Lakes system of waterways. Navigation was limited to boats with a draft of 14 feet. The idea of opening the Upper St. Lawrence to ocean-going navigation dated from the end of the 19th century. In 1932, the St. Lawrence Deep Waterway Treaty was negotiated, following proposals made by a Joint Board of Engineers, which called for a 27 foot channel for navigation and full development of hydro-electric power from two dams. The U.S. Senate blocked the treaty in 1934, one of many signs of hesitation on the part of the United States, where interests from the Atlantic seaboard worked to block a project supported mostly by Midwestern industry and agriculture. The idea was revived during the war, only to be blocked again by the U.S. Senate in 1952, leading to Canadian proposals to go ahead without American cooperation. However, this proved unnecessary, as the final approval from all sides was obtained in 1953. Construction of the Seaway began in the summer of 1954; over the course of 2,350 miles and a change in elevation of 602 feet from Lake Superior to the Atlantic Ocean, the Seaway would be brought about through channels, locks, hydro-electric dams, and artificial lakes.

Throughout this half-century of planning and debate, the people of Iroquois lived with this prospect hanging over their heads. Simply put, in order to carry out these plans, the level of the river would have to be raised, so as to submerge the rapids and also towns such as Iroquois, Ingleside, Long Sault, Mille Roches, and Moulinette. Why was there so much desperation to go ahead with the Seaway? I think there were two main reasons, one to do with nation-building, the other to do with pure economic interest. The Seaway was the final chapter in a vision that had sustained Canada from the 19th century, one based upon the opening up of an "empty" country to immigration and international commerce. Conversely, there was a feeling in the Upper St. Lawrence of having been bypassed, left behind as industry had spread out across Canada, and it was hoped that the Seaway, and the power it would generate, could arrest this decline. It was estimated that the hydro-electric capacity of the St. Lawrence River could be increased by 2.2 million horsepower thanks to the project. The price to pay for this electricity would be the loss of 15,000 acres of land (on the Canadian side) and the displacement of 6,500 people, not to mention a cost to the Canadian government of over 300 million dollars.

Although I remembered the Royal Visit of 1959, when Queen Elizabeth had joined President Eisenhower aboard the Royal Yacht *Britannia* to open the Seaway, I hadn't known anything at all about Iroquois or the St. Lawrence Valley until Coates started talking that day. He had rushed over the history of the area, leaving me to fill in the gaps later by reading old newspapers and magazines. However, he did explain the crux of the matter. Since Iroquois was going to be flooded, not only for navigation on the river but also in the name of power generation, responsibility for "rehabilitating" (a term which he detested) the people to be displaced resided with the Hydro-Electric Power Commission of Ontario. Faced with so much uncertainty, and unsure what the government planners would offer them, the people of Iroquois decided to seize control of matters and find an architect to plan for them a New Town. Eventually they had been forced to choose between the vision of Wells Coates and the reality of what Hydro was willing to offer.

"First of all, I knew that this problem offered a magnificent opportunity for regional planning on a scale which Canada needed above all else to realize. Modern architecture requires more than isolated buildings; communities must be planned as a whole."

Wells Coates began to explain his plan for Iroquois. His words poured forth with meticulous detail as he recited ideas surely committed to memory through hours of lengthy meetings, presentations, and endless correspondence on the matter. At first all had gone well for him in Iroquois. The townspeople adopted his planning proposals, and even the Ontario government seemed happy to have a distinguished figure such as Wells Coates planning the future of the St. Lawrence Valley. Briefly, Wells Coates' plan proposed to use Iroquois as an opportunity for realizing his ideas, at every scale, from regional development to housing design. For this village of 1,100 inhabitants, Wells Coates proposed a New Town, which would later grow to house 30,000 or 40,000 people, most of them emigrants from Great Britain. The New Iroquois would use its geographic position on the Seaway, close to Montreal, Ottawa and Toronto, not to mention the United States, to attract business and industry from Britain and Canada. For the site of the New Town, Coates had proposed to move slightly to the east from the old Iroquois. New Iroquois would occupy a larger territory, stretching from Carman Road, where we sat and talked that day and which reached down to the (submerged) site of the old village, almost all the way to Morrisburg in the east.

"The site was crucial; it had to be suitable not only for present-day considerations but also admirably placed for the needs of the future. As planners we were trained to think for the future, and prophesy and plan for its necessities. The site I chose for Iroquois was ideal: it had commanding natural beauty, islands and small harbours on the new lake, good drainage from a gentle, rolling land. There would be space for expansion, both for industry and for tourism, as the new town would grow. Hydro's chosen site, just above the old town, was all wrong; their "Hydroquois" was in the wrong place from the industrialists' point of view, wrong from the businessman's point of view, and it was throwing away the chance to attract tourists. What opportunity did their plan leave Iroquois to survive as a community, to grow, and to enrich itself? As you can see, not much. By moving east, as opposed to merely back, the town would have found itself again on the water, with the railways and highways shifted so as to be behind the town, not cutting through it, where Hydro's plan had placed them. Then, unlike what Hydro was proposing, all the functions of the town would have been carefully arranged and divided into separate sectors for living and work, as well as leisure and recreation, which were to be linked throughout by a system of communications."

Crucial to Wells Coates' ideas of Modern planning, as he repeated endlessly, were the divisions of those four functions. Before the War, he had helped to establish these principles in Europe, along with Le Corbusier and the other great pioneers of Modernism. Their manifesto for urbanism, the *Athens Charter*, had now been tried and tested for almost two decades, and Wells Coates believed that most of the major problems had been discovered and worked out.

"The New Iroquois would have ably arranged these four functions, which would have radiated from the centre, or as I termed it, the *Heart* of Iroquois. This would have been set on an island next to the harbour that would have been created by the flooding of the Nash Creek area, to the east of the old village. All the central activities of the village were to have been placed here: the first churches, the local shops and the community hall, surrounded by parking lots and parkland, with rock outcrops and fine trees—an area for the recreation of mind, body and spirit. I proposed that all the present Iroquois residents, if they so desired, could have been relocated on this island with water on three sides, not miles away where Hydro put them. I would have personally dealt with the requirements of each family, and had made provision for different housing types, from single-family units to low-rental apartments."

***

Although Coates stressed relentlessly the opportunity that their forced move presented the people of Iroquois—never questioning the reasons for the Seaway, or the damage it would cause—in his description I found a remarkable sympathy for the villagers. It was his desire, expressed with care and empathy, to use planning and architecture to take them to a better situation.

"From this central island, a single-span pre-stressed concrete bridge, of great beauty, would have led to the west across a *Children's Island* for recreation, to reach a third island, the only part of the old Iroquois village to remain unflooded. This would have been the *Sanctuary*, which would have commemorated the Old Iroquois with a monument, a chapel, and a cemetery. In the other direction, this bridge would have lead from the *Heart* eastward across the harbour to a promontory with the commercial centre, the town hall, the hospital, and the recreation centre. Here would have been the second neighbourhood for the new town, where new residents would have moved before they settled into houses in one of the "neighbourships" I proposed to the north. Together, all of this would have been the centre of the New Iroquois. The principle in planning such a centre is growth from the *Heart* outward in an organic process, so that any time in during the history of the development of the town, the places would have looked right, without vast open spaces or deserts left for many years between sectors. Then, spanning out from the *Heart* and linking the town with its own components and the outer world, would have been a system of communications, respecting a hierarchy of circulation. First, the expressways: the 401 between Montreal and Toronto above the new town, and then an international link, which would have run across the new Iroquois Dam to the United States. Then, the parkways, highways, and roadways would have provided the links between sectors, while driveways would have served neighbourly groups of dwellings. Finally, walkways and pathways would have provided routes for pedestrians and children."

Coates went on, explaining all the ideas he had to provide for moving traffic across the main roadways without using overpasses or underpasses. His solution would have created special "pens" that could have contained service stations, local shops, and even community amenities. I didn't quite understand how this would have worked, and so prodded him to explain his ideas for arranging the new housing areas of Iroquois into what he called "neighbourships."

"What was most important was the way the housing sectors were to be organized. Here you had a town of 1,000 people, looking to grow into a city of 40,000 or 50,000. The housing sections for the new Iroquois would have comprised an entirely new conception of neighbourhood-unit planning. Each of these neighbourships would have provided for a mixture of single-family dwellings, low-rental terrace units, and apartment blocks with elevators. The dimensions for the neighbourships were taken first from the farms, which the United Empire Loyalists were given when they arrived here in the 18th century. They were arranged in long strips leading to the Great River. There were around 2,000 feet, or three farms each, between the parallel roads, which run to the river and divide the site for the new town: Carman, Gravel, Parlow, Flagg. Inside these strips, the oval driveways were to be arranged across a width of 1,500 feet, leaving a green belt between each neighbourship. No neighbourship would have been alike—except in the general road pattern which I had proposed. Inside the neighbourship, smaller groups of 12 to 20 dwelling units would have been grouped around their own driveway. An average of 1,000 persons, approximately the original population of Iroquois, would have lived in each neighbourship, six of which would form a neighbourhood unit. This was a human type of layout. Each group of dwellings would have formed a special unit of neighbourliness: each neighbourship was a size that could be comprehended; even each neighbourhood, with around 6,000 people, was not too large for everyone to know more or less who lived where. All the houses would have been properly oriented in terms of sun and view, and given people the feeling of living in the country, yet close by to a thriving town and a very specific part of it."

"For the specific housing types, I wanted to use my ideas for prefabricated Room Unit production, on which I had begun to work in 1947. Just at the time I was involved in making my plan for Iroquois, I was also redesigning my Room Unit housing system to make it as flexible as possible. Equipment units, such as kitchens and bathrooms, would be prefabricated, while the other part, the living area for each Room Unit, would be shipped as a flat kit. From there, I began to work, just as Le Corbusier did with his *Unités d'Habitation*, on a three-two arrangement in sections. I wanted Iroquois to be a flagship for this sort of modular design in Canada, and I had hoped to establish a Room Unit production factory at the Iroquois New Town. However, I knew the residents were impatient, since Hydro was showing them copybook drawings of what their new houses would look like, or else offering to move their existing buildings, while I was concentrating on getting the planning, getting the systems right."

Wells Coates had planned for Iroquois' growth in stages, from the relocation of the original residents to the arrival of the first newcomers, which would bring Iroquois' population to 6,000 or 8,000 within five or six years. Then a second stage would soon follow: a decade of rapid expansion to reach 20,000 inhabitants. The final stage, long and unpredictable, would have seen the population rise again to 30,000 or 40,000 persons. By now Coates had convinced me, despite all the evidence in front of my eyes, that his plan for Iroquois had been serious and meticulous, and not some capricious figment of imagination. However, the whole project had hung in the balance of whether or not he could find the industry to invest in the construction of the New Town, and convince the residents of the plausibility of his plan.

"I knew that if Iroquois couldn't attract industry to itself during and after its relocation, then Iroquois would always remain a village, and never grow into a town or city as the residents desired. For Iroquois to become a fine community with a real chance to enlarge and enrich itself, my plan offered all the attractions that industry would require: proper communication by sea, road, rail and air close at hand; port facilities with rail spurs for those certain types of industry which would need them; and finally, adequate facilities and amenities for housing and recreation for their workers, in a growing and constantly enriching community, offering a wide variety of employment to the growing generation."

Coates had worked at first with a syndicate in London and then on his own to attract interest from British industries: shipbuilders, chemicals firms, manufacturers for the Canadian market and for export. In the end, it was the lack of firm commitments which the town used as its reasoning in the fall of 1954, when they accepted Hydro's plans for compensation and a move northward. It was the Caldwell Linen Mill, Iroquois' principal employer, who first accepted Hydro's deal, with the rest following. And so, Iroquois remained a small village, on a new site removed from the water. Maybe Coates' plan never had a chance once Hydro became involved, or maybe the people of Iroquois had lost their nerve and missed out on a brilliant opportunity. Moving Old Iroquois began in the fall of 1955 and continued right up until the floodwaters arrived in the old village on July 1, 1958. Many of the houses were moved to the new village; others went to become part of the heritage park at Upper Canada Village. A New Iroquois was built, not at all as Wells Coates had intended. On her tour in 1959, to open the Seaway, the Queen had stopped to visit the new shopping plaza.

"Iroquois had before itself one of the greatest opportunities to show its vision and its will. History is marked by a succession of lost opportunities, and this was one of them. When the city of London was destroyed by fire in 1666, two basic plans for the rebuilding were prepared in a few days—much as I worked to prepare plans for Iroquois in such a short span of time—and presented to the King: one by Sir John Evelyn, and the other, more famous plan, by Sir Christopher Wren. Both of these, though supported by the King and his councillors and advisors, were eventually turned down by the shopkeepers, merchants, and burghers of the City of London. They all desired to be relocated about where they had been located before. The chance to change the face of London was lost for nearly three hundred years: Hitler's bombing provided another chance, which the City of London accepted, at least in part. What I planned for Iroquois was, of course, a great deal smaller than the City of London, but it was equal to the importance of the history of our times, of Canada. Iroquois could have become a prototype for the 20th century Canadian city, expressing our boldness, our confidence in the future, our capacity to do big things, not only in terms of billions of dollars of natural resources to sell to the world, but also in terms of humanity, of a better life for our children and those who would come after them. I never apologized for putting the case for Iroquois in those terms, and I am no less convinced today that this was a site, unequalled in any country, for development into a lively and vigorous community, and an example of what could have been done by cooperation between all persons for the betterment of all."

Exhausted, his message complete, Coates' voice tailed off into silence as a light rain began to fall. There were many titles which were applied to Wells Coates: designer, architect, planner, engineer. After those few days with him, I had come to realize that they all held the same meaning. He was meticulous in arranging his life, and the lives of others as well. His career had been built upon bringing Modernism into vogue, from the arrangement of a room to the plan of a city. Even today, I still don't know what to think of what Coates told me. Despite the force and detail of his argument, I have no idea whether his plans were feasible, or how to judge that question. Perhaps Iroquois New Town would have been the shining beacon for Canada's centennial celebrations. Or perhaps it would have been a white elephant. I didn't doubt Coates' sympathy for the townspeople, but who can say that the ambition of his design would have soothed the pain of the loss of their homes and the village they had always known. I don't know. I suppose, to find out we would have had to get out of the car and speak to people. But Coates couldn't bring himself to do that.

"Let's go."

With those words Coates broke our silence, and I hurriedly manoeuvred us back on to the highway. I caught his eyes in the mirror, furtively looking backwards towards the town that should have been booming that summer, his plans reaching their full fruition.

Coates' energy and his good humour returned as we moved further away from Iroquois, and he was soon back making his usual comments, and telling me stories of his childhood in Japan and his adventures riding out West in the 1920s. By the time his flight was about to leave Toronto for Vancouver, he was all talk of new projects and possibilities, with nary a word on all the disappointments that had marked his career. When we had visited the Expo in Montreal, I had asked him how he felt seeing such a celebration of Modern architecture and Modern ideals. While he was very generous towards the work being done in Montreal and across Canada at the time, I could feel that he was disappointed. Outwardly, his criticism was that such single buildings lacked the cohesiveness which only proper planning, carried out with brilliance and imagination, as opposed to banality, could bring. Inwardly, I imagine he was disappointed not to have been the leader of this great age for architecture in Canada.

Postscript: In reality, Wells Coates wasn't with me on that drive back from seeing the Expo. Nor was he there as I wandered through the pavilions on that final weekend in October, for the had died in 1958. I had known him previously, when he was living in Vancouver. He had told me all about his plans for Iroquois and his frustration at their ultimate rejection. I had proposed that we make a visit to so that he could show me his proposed site—but there was no way he would go there at that time, not with the bulldozers at work on Hydro's plan, not to see the place of his ambitions used to reconstruct a small town.

Before he died, he had given me a copy of typewritten notes for a presentation he had given to the people of Iroquois, back when he had been their "pilot" guiding them through the storm. There was such a force, an optimism in the words that he had used as he fought for his dream, that I couldn't help but think that maybe he could have done it after all. What made the sharpest impression upon me was the one part of his scheme, which I have transcribed here:

26. The first building

Your consultant has carefully considered this matter from many aspects and sought a solution which would be at once practical, economic and spectacular. In the development of a new town, and towards its final stages, it becomes an economic proposition to build "high blocks" for offices, consulting rooms, hotel-apartment and apartment accommodations. It is proposed for the new Iroquois that, instead of constructing such a building in a final phase of development, to give scale to the whole architectural conception: THAT THE VERY FIRST BUILDING IN THE NEW TOWN SHALL BE A SEVENTEEN OR TWENTY-STOREY HIGH BLOCK

...

27. Effect of First Building will be spectacular

...

This first building will have at its penthouse level a large neon sign spelling out "I R O Q U O I S" for all the world to see and then to commend the spirit of old Iroquois, rising so proudly above the ashes of the village. In a splendid 20th century conception it is your consultant's firm belief that this building will be a veritable signpost and signal to attract people, firms, industries and cultural institutions towards the new Iroquois – and right from the commencement of the operation.

As I drove that day, I couldn't help but think of Coates, and I felt his presence with me in the car as we neared Iroquois. I pulled off the highway, and spent an hour remembering his words, which were still vivid in my mind. After all, he had once told me it would be a long time before he could imagine going back...

I could only wonder if Habitat and Buckminster Fuller's dome might very well have paled in comparison to the Iroquois sign as symbols of postwar Canada. Coates' plan for Iroquois had used its Modern principles to merge sympathetically two experiences, both of which were at the heart of his persona: that of the local, living in his or her ancestral place, and that of the emigrant, looking to find a way to integrate in a new situation. He had hoped that his Iroquois New Town would leave the original townspeople of Iroquois, the British emigrants and, perhaps above all, himself in a place where they could feel they belonged.

***

LOIRE ESTUARY, FRANCE, MAY 5TH, 2008

DEADLY RE-EVALUATION: WHEN THE IBIS, ONCE SACRED IN EGYPT, BECAME AN ALIEN MENACE IN FRANCE

BY
ANDERS BELL

The sky was cloudless through both the windscreen and the rear-view mirror, but Charles could not shake the feeling that a storm was brewing. Every time the mercury dropped his mood would do the same without fail. Yet today, it seemed his internal barometer was malfunctioning; the horizon was clear, the trees were still.

Perhaps it had something to do with the Sacred Ibis.

Charles Carnot had left his driveway at number 3 rue Hermès in Carquefou early in the morning. He had driven along the E60 then turned onto the N171 at Savenay. A half hour drive along the north shore of the Loire Estuary had taken him through St-Nazaire to the regional park at Brière.

The park was busier than usual for the time of day. Several groups of men milled around wearing orange safety vests marked ONCFS (Office national de la chasse et de la faune sauvage). Charles had donned his own similarly-hued vest and attached himself to one of the groups. Unlike the others in his party, he was unarmed. He was there to observe and to assist in any way that he could, but mostly he was there to learn; something he began doing almost immediately as shots began to ring out across the marsh.

Charles' group came upon a solitary Sacred Ibis and, without pause, an agent took aim and fired. Charles was not sure if he was more surprised by the speed at which everything had occurred or by the fact that the bird had made no effort to escape. It had observed their approach and seemed curious at the noise of the gunfire, it was otherwise altogether unmoved by what was happening around it. Unlike Charles, who found it all quite horrific and had to keep telling himself why this was happening... why this had to happen. Despite his self-assurances, the sight of the rust red wound blossoming between the bird's soot black neck and the chalky white plumage of its body was not an image he would soon forget.

The agent had gone off after another bird and had left him to deal with the disposal of the carcass. Charles noticed a band on the dead bird's leg as he carried his burden to a nearby cream-coloured van. A young woman, who looked about as unhappy as Charles felt, stood behind a large trestle table covered in assorted papers and measurement devices. She took the bird gently from Charles' arms, where he had been cradling it, and placed it onto the table. She removed and inspected the band, then leafed through a register until she found what she was looking for; inscribing a small cross next to one of the numbers on a list headed "Lac de Grand-Lieu." Charles knew the place. He had visited once with his parents and the lake had been teeming with many different species of birds. He was pretty sure he remembered seeing Sacred Ibis there.

The woman weighed and measured the bird, then proceeded to fold back its long black neck onto its white body between the wings and put it into a container along with several other birds, which was then in turn placed into the dark cargo space of the van. A long white tail feather remained upon the scale. The woman sighed. So did Charles.

After several hours and many more dead birds, it was time for Charles to leave the gruesome spectacle at the park. He had learned a lot about this aspect of the agency's work. He had also learned a lot about himself, or at least he had asked himself a lot of questions that morning—few of which he was able to answer.

He had also managed to learn the name of the woman at the trestle table. Diane. Like him, it had been her first experience of a cull. They had arranged to meet again. However, Charles had to admit to himself that the circumstances of their first encounter were a little inauspicious.

Charles began the drive back towards Nantes. His day wasn't over yet and he wondered if it would get worse before it got better. He had been given a task that could either be a formality or could lead to a long and perhaps acrimonious debate. A private landowner had requested a visit from a member of the ONCFS before he would give his permission for agents to shoot the pair of Sacred Ibis that lived on the lake adjoining his property. Charles had been given the task. He was new and no one else wanted it.

The owner's house was near the village of Maupertuis and wouldn't take him far off his route back to the office in Nantes. The owner, a certain Dr. Aurélien Carassius, was a retired academic of sorts. Charles had spoken to him briefly on the phone and confirmed that he would be there in slightly less than an hour. Perhaps it would all go smoothly and he would be back in Nantes by two. He switched the radio on and after skipping through a few presets he settled on Radio France Bleu, where a current affairs program was just beginning. A familiar story began to be outlined by the presenter, it seemed there was no escape from the Sacred Ibis today. He could have changed the channel, but he resisted the temptation. He might hear something that would prove useful should his discussion with the lake owner take a confrontational turn.

"The Sacred Ibis, a large white-bodied bird with a slender black neck and head, has become a common sight in our marshes and wetlands in recent years. These gregarious birds are often found in large groups or colonies around nesting sites. Their usual diet consists of insects, fish, molluscs and crustaceans, but they are omnivorous and opportunistic feeders and have been known to also feed on small mammals and bird eggs. It is, to some degree, due to the latter that the Sacred Ibis has been vilified of late, getting naturalists up in arms about the need to protect France's native bird populations from this invasive species. At the same time an equal movement to protect and save the Ibis has been growing in voice and support. Both sides make good arguments, but despite a seeming impasse between the differing polls, a cull of the Sacred Ibis has been ordered and has indeed now begun

in the Loire-Atlantique region. Today, we endeavour to bring the facts of the case into the open.

I recently met with members from both sides to discuss the fate of the Sacred Ibis and we shall begin with Dr. Louise Apollin, from the Invasive Population Unit, a part of the French National Institute for Agronomic Research, who I interviewed last week.

Dr. Apollin, can you please give our listeners a summary of the history of the Sacred Ibis and its presence here in the Loire region?"

"Certainly. The Sacred Ibis, as its binomial name, Threskiornis Aethiopicus, makes clear, is not native to France. It first appeared on our shores in the 19th century as a living souvenir from the Orient to bolster private collections around the country. Some birds are known to have escaped and there are several reports of birds living successfully in the wild. However, these were all solitary birds, and lived out their existence alone or perhaps among colonies of other waders. In any case, they did not procreate and it is only in more recent times, due to changes in zoo-keeping practices, that pairs of birds have begun to live and to breed outside the confines of their enclosures. While some birds continued to return to their nests within the parks, others chose to literally spread their wings and find other suitable habitats nearby. One of our local parks at Branféré, in the Morbihan region, imported 20 Sacred Ibis from Kenya between 1975 and 1980, and added to their stock again in 1987 with another 10 birds. By 1990 the park had 150 pairs living within its boundaries and, at the same time, Sacred Ibis began to be sighted as far away from the park as Ancenis, a good 90km away. In 1991, the first known successful nest site was discovered outside a protected habitat and the same site registered successful reproduction in 1993. A little more than ten years later, a study estimated the wild population of Sacred Ibis to have grown to between 3,000 and 5,000 individuals and it is thought to be increasing rapidly."

"Is there no way that the number of birds could be managed without resorting to a total cull? Is the proposed action in any way related to the Sacred Ibis' alleged fondness for bird eggs?"

"Well, the decision to cull the Sacred Ibis was the result of a long period of research and discussion among biologists, local authorities, farmers and other concerned parties. During this process it has been our policy to continually monitor the populations of Sacred Ibis, as well as the locations of their colonies and nesting sites. Recently several reports began to surface stating that the Sacred Ibis had been observed feeding upon the eggs of native birds, such as the Sandwich Tern. On at least three occasions they were also sighted raiding the nests of Black Terns and Whiskered Terns. Reports of predation of other birds, such as Mallards, Black-winged Stilts and Lapwings, have also been recorded. Most disturbingly, in April 2005, a pair of Sacred

Ibis were seen at the nesting site of a colony of the endangered Roseate Tern. Fortunately, this was before the Terns had begun to lay their eggs. Finally, in addition to the danger posed to other birds, the presence of the Sacred Ibis may also threaten the populations of newts and other amphibians, as well as various water-borne insects that form an important part of the food chain in the ecosystem of this region. Of course, it must also be remembered that the Sacred Ibis is not a native water bird species in France. It is thus subject to the African-Eurasian Waterbird Agreement, a United Nations environmental treaty which applies to the European Union and which France has ratified… One moment, I have the document here with me… [sound of papers rustling]

'The parties shall prohibit the deliberate introduction of non-native waterbird species into the environment and take all appropriate measures to prevent the unintentional release of such species if this introduction would prejudice the conservation status of wild flora and fauna; when non-native waterbird species have already been introduced, the Parties shall take all appropriate measures to prevent these species from becoming a potential threat to indigenous species.'

This alone is enough to justify the eradication of the Sacred Ibis colonies. We must also take into consideration the fact that the omnivorous nature of the bird often leads it to feed at human dumping sites and even rubbish bins near fast food establishments. This has been suggested as posing an epidemiological risk to both animals and humans who come into contact with the birds. Action was deemed absolutely necessary, not only to protect the biodiversity of our native wildlife, but also to uphold our obligations under European law in preventing this African bird from colonizing the continent."

"So this week the prefects of the Loire-Atlantique, Morbihan and Vendée regions issued the orders to begin a cull of the bird. Who will be conducting the cull and how will it proceed?"

"The cull is being conducted by agents from the National Game and Wildlife Agency assisted by deputized officers from the parks where the Sacred Ibis nest. The method used for the cull is small-calibre rifle fire. At the same time, any eggs that are found will be sterilized to prevent hatching. These methods, rather than poison or trapping, minimize collateral danger to domestic wildlife."

"Thank you Dr. Apollin."

"For another side to the story we spoke to Mr. Régis Théberge who is a member of 'Save the Ibis,' a grass roots organization who have opposed the cull from the very beginning.

Mr. Théberge, the prevailing reasons often cited for the necessity of the cull are the apparent danger posed by the Sacred Ibis to the biodiversity of this region and the non-native 'invasive' status of the bird. How do you respond to these arguments?"

"First of all, may I say how sad we are that a cull has once more been enacted, despite our continued support and presentation of evidence in defence of this beautiful bird. The Sacred Ibis may indeed only have been present on French soil since the 19th century, but it does belong here. It is listed among the bird species that make up the inhabitants of the wider ecological zone, of which France is a part, known as the Palaearctic. Further to which, the Sacred Ibis itself has been listed as a protected European bird by the Berne Convention of 1979 and is among the pages of the current edition of the official inventory of French birds."

"But what about the evidence showing the Sacred Ibis feeding on the eggs of native birds, such as the Sandwich Tern? Does that not concern you?"

"Well, aside from the fact that the Sacred Ibis is not doing anything that other birds, or should I say other French birds, do all the time. I have not seen any studies showing more than hypothetical dangers. Tern colonies are known to fluctuate in numbers and were doing so long before the arrival of the Sacred Ibis on these shores. They build their nests on the ground and are thus subject to the predation of any one of a number of species. Other than the occasional photograph, there is absolutely no conclusive evidence that in all the cases reported that it was indeed the work of Sacred Ibis rather than that of a French animal, such as the red fox."

"And the risk of them spreading disease?"

"The notion that the birds could potentially spread disease because of what they eat is nothing but a distraction. A simple warning probably intended to get the public on-side, but one that could just as easily be applied to seagulls, crows, and pigeons; none of whom I believe are currently being threatened with a cull of any sort. Secondly, a lot of paranoia about the Sacred Ibis stems from the outbreak of mad cow disease in this country just after the millennium. A reputation has lingered on despite the eradication of that disease and the lack of any link between it and the bird."

"So where do you go from here?"

"We will continue to lobby the prefects of the three regions that have enacted the cull. We have the support of many of the local population, who have even taken to calling the bird the 'Brittany Ibis'. With their support we intend to carry on the fight until the future of the Sacred Ibis has been secured. For we believe that one day the birds may even become an attraction, bringing tourists to the region."

"But what if your efforts prove to be in vain and the drive to eradicate the Sacred Ibis from the region continues to prevail? Do you believe that there are alternatives to its destruction? For example, what about the proposed idea to round up the Sacred Ibis population and send it back to Egypt where they used to be so prevalent?"

"Well, obviously I don't think our efforts will be in vain. But in answer *to your question, the fact is that the idea of repatriating the birds is nothing but a rather romantic fantasy. The simple truth is that the birds currently living in France were not brought here from Egypt; indeed they were not brought here at all in most cases. The current generation of birds were born in France and have only known this environment. It is highly doubtful that any of the birds would even survive such a transition. Lastly, the same reasons being touted as grounds for culling the bird here in France can be used equally from the Egyptian point of view. The French Sacred Ibis could be carrying parasites or disease from this country that could wreak havoc among the current denizens of the Nile—why should there be one rule applying in France but not in Egypt?"*

He pulled into a short gravel track which led up to what must have once been a windmill, but now the building had been repurposed into a house and was flanked by more recent additions. On his right-hand side Charles saw a small lake. He did not need to look hard to see the pair of Sacred Ibis, their black and white forms stood out against the mixed green palette of the lake and the surrounding trees.

As soon as Charles stepped out of the car he was greeted effusively by the owner, who had obviously been waiting for him. The retired professor seemed overtly happy to see him. Possibly a good sign, thought Charles.

"Welcome, welcome, please do come in. I've been looking forward to your visit. Are you hungry? Would you like a drink? A coffee perhaps?"

After he had recovered from the sudden warmth of his welcome, Charles accepted the offer of a coffee and was then left alone in a hallway, his host having disappeared, presumably, into the kitchen.

"Make yourself comfortable in the study, I shan't be long," said a disembodied voice.

Charles had no idea which of the doors led to the study, so he decided to try each one in turn. His first attempt led to a narrow escape from a cluttered broom cupboard, but he was luckier on his second try. The door opened into a medium-sized room filled from floor to ceiling with books and papers, often in precarious looking piles. In some cases, Charles noticed, the piles themselves were serving as semi-permanent supports for bookshelves, with a reasonable degree of success.

"Sorry for the mess," said Charles' host on arrival, "I'm afraid I am rather partial to it." He picked up a pile of papers from a chair that Charles had not previously known was there and motioned for him to sit down. "Now where were we?"

Charles found the warmth and peculiarity of his host endearing, but he knew he couldn't relax. This was official business and the issue of culling animals on private property was thorny at best.

"We haven't really begun yet," said Charles. "To be honest, I am not at all sure why you requested to meet with an ONCFS representative."

"I received this form in the mail about the Sacred Ibis nesting at the lake," said Dr. Carassius, motioning with the stapled pages at the lake that could be observed, partially, through the mostly obscured window.

"Have you signed it?" asked Charles tentatively. One could always hope.

"No." Came the unhoped-for response. Then after a brief pause the professor continued. "It is your intention to cull all of the Sacred Ibis in the Loire-Atlantique region, correct?"

"That is the intention of the ONCFS, yes," affirmed Charles, but he added, "It was a decision reached by a committee of experts and following the publication of a study into the case of the Sacred Ibis and its effect in the region."

"Very well," said Dr. Carassius. "I just want to make sure that you know everything before you proceed."

"What do you mean everything?" said Charles, somewhat intrigued. "We have been studying the Ibis for quite some time I can assure you."

"I don't mean since it has been in this region," said the professor, "the Ibis had a fascinating history in Ancient Egypt long before it graced our shores."

"What does that have to do with anything?" said Charles.

"Why, it has everything to do with everything," replied the professor. "Listen, what if I told you that this history of the Ibis has a profound cultural connection to France and her people?"

"I would be interested in what you have to say," allowed Charles, for he was interested. But then he remembered his employer and he added, "However, I don't see why any of this is of any concern to the ONCFS."

"Allow me to show you," said the professor. Without waiting for an acquiescence from Charles, Dr. Carassius got up and headed for one of the overloaded bookshelves. After a moment's gaze he extracted a heavy leather-bound volume and laid it upon the desk. Before he opened the enormous tome, he picked up the pile of papers occupying the needed space on the desk and dropped it upon the floor with a resounding thud. He really seemed to have a flair for the dramatic, Charles thought to himself.

"Do you know what this is?" said the professor pointing to one of the plates.

Charles saw a scene laid out before him, showing an enthroned deity standing before several animal-headed figures and a large set of scales. It looked Egyptian, but he had no idea what it was. The professor pointed to one of the animal-headed figures, who Charles noticed appeared to be writing something on a board and whose head possessed the eyes and beak of a rather familiar bird. There it was again.

"Ibis-headed Thoth!" announced the professor, delivering the line as if he was acting in a play where the audience were sitting a long way from the stage.

Charles began to wonder if Dr. Carassius' performance had been rehearsed.

"What you see here is a scene called the "weighing of the heart," a vignette from the Egyptian Book of the Dead. The god Thoth is shown recording the weight of the heart of the deceased, which can be seen on the scales. Thoth, or Tehuty as he was known then, was one of the most popular and, at various times, also the most powerful of the Ancient Egyptian gods. At one point the Egyptian myth of creation was adapted to include him as the creator. In this version Thoth, in the form of a Sacred Ibis no less, laid an egg from which Ra, the sun god, was born. Another myth credits Thoth with autogenesis, creating himself through the power of words. He was also known as the moon god, a role he inherited from Horus, whose eyes were said to be the sun and the moon. Some have said that Thoth got this mandate from his connection to Sacred Ibis, whose curved beak can be seen to resemble the crescent of the waxing moon. But there were other reasons as you'll see. Thoth was credited with the invention of writing, medicine, magic, religious lore and sometimes even music… one could say he represented culture or learning in general."

The professor paused to let the last line sink in.

"Thoth had one more extremely important role in Egyptian mythology. The scene that you see here is, as I mentioned, from the Egyptian Book of the Dead, a funerary text designed to help the recently, and need I say wealthy, deceased gain access to the afterlife. As you can see, he stands, stylus in hand, ready to record the result of the weighing of the deceased's heart against the feather of Ma'at, the symbol of order or, in this case, simply what was "right." If the heart weighs more or less than the feather, then it is eaten by the chimeric beast, part lion, part hippopotamus and part crocodile, seen here waiting patiently, like a dog for table scraps. The soul of the deceased would then be condemned to non-existence."

Charles listened as the professor continued his lecture. This was all fascinating he thought, but what did this have to do with the cull? Perhaps if they had been considering similar action in Egypt then this kind of intangible cultural heritage may have been used to save the bird, but this was all moot in France, especially since the cull had already begun. Eventually Charles had to cut in.

"I'm sorry to interrupt, but you still haven't explained what any of this has to do with France other than there may be a few representations of Ibis in the collections of the Louvre. If anything, the value that the Egyptians placed in the bird just confirms that the Sacred Ibis would be better off in Egypt."

"Actually that's not true. For one thing, the Sacred Ibis died out in Egypt in the 19th century," said the professor.

"What?" Said Charles.

"Yes, I'm afraid so. No one knows why exactly it happened, but it was probably due to human encroachment in some way. Using the river banks for industry and the like." He paused, stuck in mid-thought. "Actually, that reminds me of something once told to me by a rather well-to-do Egyptian lady at a conference somewhere or other. She was quite vehement in her opinion that the Sacred Ibis had left Egypt of its own accord for the simple reason that the Egyptian people had ceased to revere and care for them as they once had in ancient times. Moreover, she maintained that the modern human population occupying the bird's former habitat along the banks of the Nile no longer remembered the names of any of the birds living among them. They were all just "birds.""

"Is this true?" asked Charles.

"Well, I can't really vouch for her opinion about the ornithological knowledge of modern Nile-dwellers, but she was most definitely wrong in thinking that the Sacred Ibis had it easy in ancient times."

"What do you mean?" said Charles, intrigued.

"I'm getting to that," replied the professor. He paused to recollect his thoughts for a moment and then as if remembering his lines, he asked. "Tell me, what do you know about mummification?"

"It's how the Ancient Egyptians preserved their dead," said Charles.

"Well, there's a lot more to it than that, but I suppose that's about the long and the short of it. Did you know that they mummified animals too?"

Charles thought back to his last visit to the Louvre. He had to think back a long way, but he remembered something about cats being mummified and said as much.

"Ah yes," said Dr. Carassius with a twinkle in his eye, "but not just because they were beloved family pets." Another pause, followed by another question. "So, which animal do you think was mummified the most in Ancient Egypt?"

Charles shrugged even though he knew quite well what was coming.

"...The Sacred Ibis!" Dr. Carassius was rolling again, his voice loud enough to reach the cheap seats. "And in such numbers... thousands... millions... uncountable; entire cemeteries full of them during the Ptolemaic period."

The professor continued. "Each bird was usually shaped into a more compact form before rigor mortis set in. The head and the neck were folded together and attached to the back between the wings; the legs were tucked into the body. Then it was usually dipped in resin before being wrapped, often in intricate patterns, with white linen strips. Finally the whole was placed inside an earthen jar or in certain cases in golden ibis-shaped sarcophagi, depending on the wealth of the donor—a rather lengthy and expensive funeral for a bird, don't you think?"

Charles agreed.

"Well, they were rather special. In fact, the birds were often buried with messages for the dead, or with prayers or requests for aid from the gods. Entire farms were needed to keep up with demand."

"I see," said Charles, and then paused. Earlier, he had wanted to get his form signed and get out as quickly as possible, but now he could not help but feel more than a little curiosity at the professor's stories. Might as well hear him out he thought. "So…" he said, "why the Sacred Ibis?"

"Well," said Charles' host with the hint of a smile, "you are not the first Frenchman to ask that very question."

Here we go again, thought Charles to himself, wondering how he was following the same script as the professor.

Dr. Carassius returned once more to one of the bookcases and retrieved another volume. Charles noticed that this book was bound identically to the one he had been shown earlier and must be from some sort of series. The professor opened the book to an exquisitely drawn plate showing two birds, a Bald Ibis on the left and a Sacred Ibis on the right, with a stone tablet with a hieroglyphic inscription at its feet.

"What does it say?" said Charles, pointing to the inscription.

"Not much I am afraid, a sort of abecedarium showing glyphs for water, land, the horned viper *Cerastes cerastes*, and the Sacred Ibis. Interesting, but not why I am showing you this. Look at the name written here."

Dr. Carassius pointed to the top left of the image, where Charles could make out the characters, which he read out to the professor.

"*Zoologie : Oiseaux par J. C. Savigny.*" The name didn't ring any bells.

"Marie Jules-César Lelorgne de Savigny to be precise!" came the triumphant cry from the professor. The bells no longer needed to be rung.

"Do you know who he was?" said Dr. Carassius.

When Charles replied in the negative, the professor gave Charles a disapproving look, but continued.

"He was one of the savants who travelled with Napoleon on the great expedition to Egypt in 1798, landing at Alexandria in July of that year. Napoleon brought 36,000 soldiers of various stripes with him, to push out the ruling Mamelukes, and 151 academics from various disciplines to recreate the wonders of France in the new colony. They were known as the Commission of Sciences and Arts, the first time such a group had ever accompanied a military expedition. They included mathematicians, men of letters, economists, architects, antiquarians, mineralogists, chemists, geographers, engineers, and of course botanists and zoologists; among which was the young man whose name you see here. Their job was to set up an outpost of French civilization as I mentioned, but they had a second task, that of amassing every grain of knowledge that was to be had from this unexplored colony in order to share it with the French population on their return. The book you are holding in your hands and the other volume I have shown you today carry within their pages the knowledge and illustrations garnered by those experts and are the legacy of that expedition."

The professor returned the books to the shelf and looked at Charles, gauging his reaction. "What do you think?" he asked.

"You are saying that France and Egypt have historical cultural ties, the ibis is an Egyptian bird, ergo, we must save the ibis. Is that what you are trying to tell me? Sounds like rather false logic to me." Charles was beginning to get tired of the questions.

"No, no, that would be silly. Listen, de Savigny did not stop with his work in *Description de l'Égypte*. He had a very long and successful career and one of his most celebrated works is all about our friend the Sacred Ibis."

The professor handed another, this time much smaller, book to Charles, who opened it and read the title on the frontispiece. *Histoire naturelle et mythologique de l'ibis*. He skimmed a few pages and looked blankly at the professor.

"Probably best that I give you a summary," he said before continuing.

The look Charles gave the professor signalled that he was right.

"It all begins with Herodotus and a few other early historians such as Pliny, Aelian and the like, have you read their work?"

"Er... No, sorry," said Charles.

"No need to apologize. I wouldn't bother actually, unless you are in need of something to read on the beach." The professor then continued, "Pliny's overrated, Aelian's a bit of a windbag and Herodotus... well, he's Herodotus. The so-called father of history, but more commonly referred to as the father of lies."

"I see," said Charles, striking the names off the reading list he had just mentally written.

"The problem with these ancient historians is one that affects writers even today," continued the professor. "They were lazy and had a habit of using secondhand information from a selection of unreliable sources."

"An Egyptian guy in a pub told me, so it must be true."

"Exactly!" Said the professor.

"So, all of these writers mention the Ibis at one time or another in their histories, but the most famous passages are those of Herodotus, who goes on at some length about the bird. He describes the Egyptian reverence for the Ibis as being due to the bird's enmity for snakes and the fact that it was known to devour the latter in great numbers, including a mythical winged viper that apparently attempted to invade Egypt at one time. Thus the bird was elevated to god-like status for protecting the people from this menace. It would not be the first time that an ability of benefit to mankind would elevate an animal to symbolic or even god-like status. However, in the case of the Sacred Ibis, this ability just simply isn't anatomically possible."

"What do you mean?" asked Charles.

"Well, our man de Savigny had wanted to verify Herodotus' statements and so dissected several Sacred Ibis specimens on his trip. However, he found their stomachs to contain nothing even remotely serpent-like, just molluscs and crustaceans. Exactly the kind of food you would expect to find in the stomach contents of any wading bird. Moreover, the beak of the Ibis is not designed to spear fast-moving snakes, but is instead suited to sifting through muddy river bottoms for their customary diet."

"So, if they didn't protect the land from snakes, then why were the Ancient Egyptians so keen on them?"

"Well," the professor replied, "de Savigny did have a go at trying to get to the bottom of this mystery and I think he is probably pretty close to the truth although we shall never know for sure. He started from the fact that the Sacred Ibis was a migratory bird in Egypt. After spending the dry season further south in the Horn of Africa, it would arrive during the season of *Akhet*; the period when the Nile would burst its banks and provide life-giving waters to the flood plains that lie on either side of the great river. As the level of the river rose it would drive away venomous snakes, such as the horned viper, who prefer the drier climate of the desert. Thus the coming of the birds each year was linked with both the fertility of the land and with a diminution of serpents. One can see how the Sacred Ibis could easily become semiotized and how it could become so important to the Ancient Egyptians."

The professor leafed absent-mindedly through the pages of the book in his hands. He stopped at an illustrated page and gazed at the drawing for a few seconds. When he spoke again his suddenly hushed voice seemed almost conspiratorial, as if he did not want the walls to know what he had to say.

"Between you and me, I think the Sacred Ibis had a symbolic value for de Savigny too. I think he saw parallels between his mission of bringing the knowledge and culture of Egypt back to France and the idea of the Sacred Ibis bringing the life-giving flood waters of the Nile to the Egyptians each year."

With that, Dr. Carassius closed the book and put it down on the desk. His eyes lingered for a moment where it lay; then, after a moment, he reached for the permission form now partially hidden beneath various books and, to Charles' amazement, he picked up a pen and signed and dated the appropriate page.

"What are you doing?" asked Charles. Then thinking that one question was not enough to get the answers he needed, he added two more. "Why did you sign? What was the point of all of this?" He was both gesticulating wildly and on the point of asking another question when Dr. Carassius stopped him.

"I have done what I set out to do," he said.

"But all the stories? The lectures? The questions?" Despite having got what he wanted, Charles felt cheated somehow. "Don't you care about the Sacred Ibis? About *your* Sacred Ibis?" Charles motioned towards the window.

"Of course I care! Especially about them." The professor stood up and moved as close to the window as the piles of books on the floor would allow. "Leukos and Melanos. They've been with me for three years now... but I am also aware of the larger picture. Even if, as I believe, this cull is happening because of decisions based on faulty data, that doesn't change the fact that legally it has every right to happen. The risks posed by the introduction of the Sacred Ibis into France are significant, and although one could argue that one species pushing out or even wiping out another is natural selection and that trying to preserve the status quo is a rather old fashioned point of view, one mustn't forget that the Sacred Ibis did not arrive in France through a natural migration. We brought it here, and while it is terrible that we shall now kill thousands of innocent birds to make up for our own mistake, it is a necessary sacrifice."

"I understand," said Charles, "but that doesn't explain why you told all of this to me."

"For the simple and selfish reason that I had no one else to tell," said Dr. Carassius. "I live alone and don't get out much these days. The arrival of the permission form gave me the idea. Obviously I had no idea who they would send, but I figured that no matter who arrived, they would at least know about the current state of affairs and I could fill in the rest."

"I am not sure what to say," said Charles. "What am I supposed to do with this story?"

"You can do whatever you wish," replied Dr. Carassius with a smile, "but I rather hope that you will be kind enough to pass the story on to someone else."

***

BARRE, VERMONT, UNITED STATES, 1900–2000

EXPATRIATE EXPERTISE: WHEN THE ARRIVAL OF SKILLED ITALIAN WORKERS TRANSFORMED THE VERMONT GRANITE INDUSTRY

BY
ILARIA BRANCOLI BUSDRAGHI

I am the grandchild of a stoneworker from Northern Italy; I live in Barre, Vermont, where most of my family has been living for over a hundred years. We moved here from Baveno, a small town in Piedmont: my grandfather came first in 1886, my grandmother, my father and his sisters followed two years later. My grandfather died of silicosis when he was 42; I never met him, but I grew up hearing my grandmother telling the story of his life, his work, and of the Italians in Barre, of how it was when they arrived, and what they brought with them. My grandmother's tales often begin with one date, November 28th, 1900, the day when the Socialist Labor Hall in Barre opened its doors. That building is still standing today and, like the men who built it, it has had an adventurous life. I will retell that story as if we were there on that opening day, celebrating with my grandparents and the Italian community.

It is November 28th, 1900, and today the Socialist Labor Hall opens its doors here in Barre, Vermont, the "Granite Capital of the World" as it is often called. Built on Granite Street by Italian stoneworkers in their free time, it has a straightforward design: a brick building, in the front its main volume, two-storeys high and with a flat roof; in the back a second volume, only one-storey high, with a gambrel roof. The red brick façade is simple: seven windows on the top floor, six windows and the central entryway, reached by climbing eight stone steps, on the bottom, and with windowsills carved from Barre's granite. Right above the main door, a detail prominently declares the belief of the Italian community in a political ideal: a medallion, carved by sculptor Egidio Dunghi, depicts an arm bearing a hammer and the initials S.L.P, the symbol and the initials of the Socialist Labor Party, respectively.

The building does not correspond to any specific architectural style, but its functional, utilitarian design reflects the purpose for which the structure is destined: an assembly hall. Most of the space of the main volume is occupied by a large room, forty-eight by eighty-three feet, with maple flooring, and plaster walls and ceiling. The walls are decorated with a simple scheme: a blue-grey pattern on the dado, brown on the chair rail, and a grained finish on the plaster part of the post. Just above the dado and below the beam on the post are stencils applied in gold finish. A mirrored chandelier hangs from the ceiling.

The enthusiasm of the Italian community in Barre for the construction, completion, and opening of the Labor Hall is great. Seven hundred Italians participate in festivities for the inauguration; Camillo Cianfarra, editor of the socialist publication *Il Proletario*, travels to Barre from New York and delivers a speech entitled "What is Socialism?" After the speech, all the participants dance until dawn to the rhythms of the Transatlantic Band.

Camillo Cianfarra's response to the building is euphoric and inspired. "What at first will seem impossible," he writes when he returns to New York, "is a *fait accompli*, as the Hall stands now in Granite Street, a superb and masterly synthesis of the collective effort of workers united and guided by the ray of an idea like ours. To many, perhaps, this Hall will mean nothing, for many others it will be the subject of jokes; but for me, when I saw it for the first time, it spoke a language full of wisdom." As such, the Socialist Labor Hall is the materialization of the desire to have a place that, within the texture and the landscape of Barre, expresses identity: it tangibly shows who the Italians are, and what they can do. There is much more to the Labor Hall than meets the eye: the forms may be simple, as are the materials, but the ideals that inspired it are prominently manifested for all to see. Through the architecture and all the activities that find a space in that structure, the Italian community clearly announces: "This is who we are, and this is what we do." The Socialist Labor Hall is at the same time the point of arrival after a long journey and the starting point for more travelling.

The story of the Italian stoneworkers in Barre starts a little less than twenty years before, in the 1880s, when the first migrants arrive from Italy. At first the men come alone; thanks to the improved safety and better prices of the transatlantic crossing, they can and want to take advantage of the higher wages that the stone industry in Vermont pays, and then return to Italy. Already in 1884, however, Edgar Baratta applies for U.S. citizenship in Montpelier, the first of the Italian migrants to do so. What started as a temporary migration turns for many into one that is long-term, if not permanent. As all migrants, they and their families have to deal with all the many different ways, big and small, in which the migration experience is uprooting. They find help and solace, however, both in what they find in Barre and in all that they bring with them from Italy.

Originating from Lombardy and Piedmont in northwestern Italy, and from the area around Carrara in northern Tuscany, these stoneworkers have not come to Vermont looking for jobs as unskilled workers. They are not the stereotypical Italian migrants, but are instead artisans and artists, highly skilled stoneworkers whose professional expertise has been carried over through many generations. They are here because of their long connection with the stone, be it granite or marble, because for centuries they have been extracting, cutting, and transforming stone into artefacts. Vermont's booming stone industry has the technology to extract and cut the marble and granite; it is, in fact, ahead of Italy from this point of view. What it needs is the artistic skills that the Italian stoneworkers have.

The story that took these men and their families to Vermont, a place—at that point all but unknown in Italy—started a long time ago and, as all good stories, it has many characters and story lines: emperors, famous sculptors, travelling workers, guilds, unions. I will tell you that tale by taking you further back in time.

Piedmont and Lombardy have had a long tradition of migration: since the 13th century from these two regions, and especially from the pre-alpine valleys, specialized workers from the same family, village or region have established migratory itineraries, as they seasonally migrated south into the Italian peninsula, to Central and Northern Europe, and to the Mediterranean basin. Alongside silk workers, chimney sweeps, and animal tamers, there were also many stoneworkers. In those valleys the granite and marble quarries provided alternatives to the meagre agricultural economy that the rough and hard soil of hills and mountains allowed. The workers could market abroad the skills they had learned at home and they travelled as far as Saint Petersburg in Russia and various cities in the Ottoman Empire. Besides the skills of their hands, this long experience of migration provided a crucial knowledge: working the same trade and very often being part of the same family created a tight web of relationships that made it possible for these workers to gain a measure of control over the job market. Through the centuries they have created the maps, both geographical and mental, the know-how, the confidence, and the network of relations and information that are now, in the 1880s, invaluable for those who decide to migrate, this time crossing the Atlantic.

As for the northern part of Tuscany, it is also an area from where skilled workers have been migrating for centuries. Already in the 17th century figurine makers from Barga and organ players from Lucca could be found in Saint Petersburg, New York, and Buenos Aires. As for the marble, in the area of Carrara marble has been extracted for nearly two millennia, since the early days of the Roman Empire. It is here that Julius Caesar first extracted marble to rebuild Rome, and from here came most of the stone that Michelangelo used for his sculptures. Specialized quarrying, cutting, carving, and sculpting skills have been passed on from fathers to sons. Working marble has always been physically taxing and dangerous, and in the 19th century the technology has not changed much and every step of the process brings with it enormous risks for the workers. Once a massive block of marble has been detached from the bedrock with treacherous and labour-intensive effort, transporting it down the steep mountains to the valley below is no easy endeavour: the slab slowly glides down the debris-covered slope, rolling on logs that the workers keep on shifting in front of the moving block. Once they reach the bottom, the men load the marble on ox-drawn carts. In spite of the risks connected with quarrying and working marble, the stoneworkers in this region are more rooted in the territory and, as a result, migration is a less established strategy for economic survival.

Because of this long history, for all these stoneworkers—those from Piedmont and Lombardy, and those from Tuscany—the sense of the value of their skills is almost instinctive, and results in a collective history and identity that have been strengthened since the Middle Ages by the membership in professional organizations—guilds at first and labour unions later. Guilds and unions are not only important for each individual member, they also have an important social role: solidarity provides these workers with a security net, both from an economic and from a cultural point of view. The membership in labour organizations also means that the stoneworkers, unlike the vast majority of Italians, are actively involved in politics. As a result, at the end of the 19th century, Carrara is one of the most important centres of Italian anarchism and the anarchist ideals are generated by and have spread among its marble workers. The stoneworkers from Piedmont and Lombardy, too, are politically involved. While some are anarchists, they are for the most part socialists, and for them participation in the political life of the valleys plays an important role in their decision to migrate. One of the tangible outcomes of the stoneworkers' political activism is the publication of newspapers in which, in articles and letters, they can find a wealth of information about the emigration experience. These publications' pages deal with every aspect of the passage across the Atlantic and of the new life in America: how to travel, where to find a job and a house.

When these Italian granite and marble workers move to Vermont, they bring with them, together with their specialized skills that are the primary reason for their migration, strong cultural values and radical political ideals. The combination of identity and solidarity is an essential element during the migration and settlement experience, and provides them with a great source of strength.

In these same years, developments take place in Vermont and in the United States that create the demand for these skilled stoneworkers. The end of the Civil War in 1865 has marked the beginning of an intense phase of urbanization and of public commissions for a large number of federal buildings: court houses, monuments, administrative offices. The private sector follows suit, with the construction of banks, libraries, theatres, and railroad stations. New cities are created and existing ones are rejuvenated and expanded. Thanks in large part to the rapid growth of the railway system, the use of materials like marble and granite in great quantities becomes feasible and is indeed often favoured for such commissions. Solid, dignified and fireproof, marble and granite are chosen also for their association with ancient Greece, symbol of democracy, and with the Roman Empire, symbol of power: the new public buildings, in their monumentality and permanence, better represent the values and the power of the young United States.

Naturally, Vermont's granite has been used in many different ways for a long time, for arrowheads, stone axes, buildings, cemeteries, and streets. The native Abenaki's Coos Trail goes through the region of central Vermont, long before the opening of the first quarries they were using the granite outcrops of Barre that are most easily accessible. Later the first settlers use the stone for mills, window and door frames, doorsteps, mantels, and tombstones. In 1815 the first quarry opens on Millstone Hill, overlooking the town of Barre. The granite extracted from these early quarries is of high quality: it contains very little iron, so it remains clear of stains even when exposed to water or the elements for a long time. When the time comes to build the Vermont State House in Montpelier in the 1830s, the builders chose stone from Millstone Hill, as well as other quarries, such as Cobble Hill.

There is ample space for Vermont's young stone industry to grow by adding more complex and artistic carving and sculpting to the quarrying of the stone itself, but in the 1850s many obstacles still stand in the way. The quarries are still relatively remote, far from the large urban centres of the United States, and moving the stone is dangerous and labour-intensive: the blocks of granite are moved by ox teams, at a pace as slow as four miles per week. For the larger blocks they wait for winter when the use of sleighs allows for faster transports. This operation is such a risky endeavour that, at the time of the building of the Vermont State House, some people say that Barre's granite will never be used again for big structures, a prediction that proves wrong. Instead, more commissions follow, like the paving of the streets of Troy in New York State, but it is not until the completion of a railway link in 1875 that the granite industry really takes off. With Vermont now connected to the rest of the country, the transportation problem is solved. Barre thus becomes more accessible for the skilled workers that the expanding industry needs. Shortly thereafter the so-called "Sky Route" connects the top of Millstone Hill with the carving sheds in the town of Barre, and train engines now replace oxen and horses.

What is still missing, in fact, is a specialized workforce that can, on paper and in stone, bring the granite carving industry past the simple door frames and steps, and stretch its reach beyond regional boundaries. The recruitment of skilled workers happens in several ways: publications such as *The Granite Cutters Journal* list the available jobs, information about them travels across the ocean by way of letters and articles, and the American Emigration Company employs workers on behalf of American enterprises.

Our travel from 1900 back to the 13th century is coming to an end but before we get to the Italians, I have to tell you about the Scottish, the first to migrate to Barre in 1880. They are mostly from the region of Aberdeen in Northern Scotland, where the granite business in these same years is going through a serious crisis that has made work more difficult to find, pushed wages lower, and rendered work conditions stricter. Some of these workmen are cutters and sculptors, but for the most part they are skilled quarry men. They have a strong unionist tradition: Aberdeen is one of the most unionized communities in the United Kingdom and, once in Vermont, they immediately become proactive members of the Granite Cutters National Union (G.C.N.U.). Barre's local section of the G.C.N.U. will be organized in 1886 and in 1900—when Scottish and Italians have combined forces—it will become the largest in the United States, with more than a thousand members.

The Scottish are the driving force behind the reorganization of the granite business: instead of one overarching owner holding a monopoly on production, a myriad of small privately owned sheds emerge—in the 1890s there are more than one hundred—where what counts above all is the individual skill in working the stone. In workshops of all sizes, the issues of national identity, work, and politics are closely intertwined; creating among the workers of all different countries a connection that surpasses the sharing of a nationality.

This professional and ideological situation is very compatible for the Italians who start arriving in the mid 1880s, either directly from Italy or after working in quarry towns in other parts of the United States. Many arrive from Proctor, Vermont, the centre of the marble industry. While marble is a much softer stone than granite, switching from marble to granite proves not too difficult. My grandfather is one of these men: he comes to Barre from Proctor in 1890, looking for a place where, together with his skills, he can also bring his political ideals. He likes what he finds. In Barre the workplace is diversified and open; the expression of one's political views and the participation in unions is not restricted as it is in many other places, but is instead expected and even encouraged. The Italian stone workers who arrive in Barre are socialists and anarchists, and in this town they find ample space to express their opinions. And they do so with energy and conviction, through their work, in their lifestyle, and also by means of the institutions they create and the townscape to which they contribute.

Their first contribution is, of course, their skilled work, their ability to design and realize major projects around the country: memorials, such as the John D. Rockefeller monument in Cleveland, soldiers' monuments and mausoleums; and civic buildings like, among many others, the city hall in Chicago, the train stations in Memphis and Washington, D.C., the Wisconsin state capitol, the National Museum in Washington, and the Western Union Telegraph building in New York. I have always thought it somehow ironic that men known for and proud of being socialists and anarchists used their creativity and skill and put their health at risk to create works that, for the most part, celebrate the political and economic establishment. Pride in their work, however, is also an essential element of who they are, and the possibilities that Barre offers keep on attracting them here.

The town of Barre, in fact, is growing fast: for the first eighty years of the 19th century it has been a village of 2,000. In 1890, 6,800 people live here. In the last twelve years alone, 625 houses have been built, an average growth of one house per week. Barre in these years has, not surprisingly, all the characteristic of a boomtown: fast and disorderly growth because of the sudden increase of the population; lack of building regulations; real estate speculation; neighbourhoods only partially provided with electricity, water, roads; and a severe lack of schools. The situation, however, improves rapidly. The Italian neighbourhood grows in the northern part of the city, the North End. The Italians live near each other; their professional high status and identity, their common origin, language and even dialect, and their political ideals strengthen their sense of community. As much as possible they try to replicate what they have left in Italy. Rice, polenta, and pasta are the basic staples on their tables—in Barre as well as in Italy. Vegetables and grapes grow in the small gardens in front of the houses; mushrooms put to dry in the sun become part of the urban landscape. They pool resources and make wine and grappa at home. Imported ingredients to prepare Italian dishes can also be bought in the stores that many Italians, often from the same regions as the stoneworkers, are opening in Barre.

On Sundays the Italian community gets together in Dewey Park, along the river between Barre and Montpelier, for big community picnics with food, games, music, songs, and dances. They bring wine, polenta, and big pots of braised chick-en. After eating, fathers, mothers, and children dance to the music of accordions, and sing old Italian folk songs and the famous opera arias that they all know. Music is an important element in the life of the Italians in Barre. The presence of the Italian community is one of the reasons of the success of the Barre Opera House. After a devastating fire, the Opera House is rebuilt and reopened. With its imposing presence right in the centre of town, it is one of the reminders of the great prosperity of the city. Many Italian theatre and opera companies, including one formed by the Italian community, perform here and, in this way too, the immigrants try to recreate, in the middle of Vermont, the familiar physical and cultural landscape of the home country. Beside offering space for theatre performances, the Opera House also functions as a community site where current topics and politics are discussed: the famous socialist Eugene Debs speaks here, for example, as does anarchist Emma Goldman.

The Italian immigrants create various associations for mutual help and recreation, such as the Mutual Aid Society, the Italian Pleasure Club, the Columbus Band, and the Italian Athletic Club. Amidst all this, the Socialist Labor Hall becomes the centre of the Italian community. It is a place that is the expression of the ideals that the migrants have brought with them from their homeland and, at the same time, a door open towards their new country, and towards migrants of different origins. The Labor Hall provides a space for social gatherings and cultural functions, and for political debate. The activities that take place at the hall are varied and not limited to the Italian community, as some events from 1901 indicate: on February 11th the program announces a "mass meeting to see about putting up candidates for municipal office. Socialist Labor Party Mayoral candidate, John Anderson." On March 5th, there is a "mass meeting with Philip Halvosa speaking on 'Class Conscience: United International Action by the Workers of the World.'" On June 9th "over a hundred members of the Italian colony attend ball and dramatic entertainment." On August 16th, a "dance raised money for benefit of 'the families of the strikers at Berra, Italy.'" Local, national and international events, be they cultural or political, all find a place under the roof of Barre's Socialist Labor Hall.

The Labor Hall's big room on the ground floor is always full of activities, such as with weddings, card-games, English language lessons, study circles, theatre and musical productions, and sporting events. There are weekly balls: my grandmother remembers dancing in the big room with the other women and the children, while the men are in one of the smaller rooms discussing politics and current events, playing cards, and drinking the wine that reminds them of Italy.

Also in 1901, the Union Co-Operative Store opens in the basement of the Labor Hall, and a bakery where an Italian-style brick oven is installed as well. The store has its own monetary currency: coins depicting the arm and hammer of the Socialist Labor Party. Its statutes specify that, should the co-operative close down, title would go to the city of Barre. The municipality, however, would have to give it back if a new co-operative pledges to use it for Italian producers, consumers, and workers, or to transform it into either lodging for the poor or a hospital.

The ideals of solidarity that are the foundation of the Socialist Labor Hall are apparent at every turn, whether one is entering the co-operative store or going to the weekend dances. Most of the dances are organized to raise funds for the families of the many stonecutters who die of silicosis, the result of inhaling stone dust and a true plague in Barre, where it is estimated that more than 80% of stoneworkers die of that disease. Paradoxically, the very quality that make Barre's granite so valuable and sought after also causes the death of so many of the men who work in the sheds: granite can be beautifully polished, but in doing so, especially now that the men work with pneumatic tools, an extremely fine dust develops and minuscule particles of silica invade the stonecarvers' lungs. The lungs subsequently fill with fluids, leading ultimately to a slow and painful death by suffocation.

In Italy, in fact, silicosis does not have such a massive impact because the stone carvers work in open sheds where the air freely circulates, but this is not possible in Barre where, in the winter, temperatures at times reach minus 30 degrees Fahrenheit. Here in Vermont's climate, architecture and technological advancements combine to play an unforgiving role; in the last few years stonecutters and carvers have started using pneumatic power tools. While these certainly allow working more efficiently, they also produce more and finer dust. A white fog blocks the view from one end of a carving shed to the other, covering everything and everybody in a layer of fine stone dust. When the blowing of the whistle signals the end of the workday, the men that come out of the sheds are like ghosts, covered from head to toe by silica dust.

The impact of this deadly disease is such that it spills over from the families of the stoneworkers into the fabric and economy of the town. A number of streets in Barre are called *strada delle vedove* (street of the widows). Many women are left with children and without a reliable source of income. A popular solution to this problem is for these widows to take in stoneworkers and offer them room and board. Between 1880 and 1910, no less than an impressive 45 to 51% of women in Barre choose to do so. Out of economic desperation many women also operate speakeasies from their homes, an illegal business, as Barre is officially a dry community during much of this time. Not surprisingly, many of these widows are routinely arrested. Their names, as recorded in the court documents, are almost all Italian. The local branch of the Granite Cutters National Union, made stronger by the cooperation of Italian and Scottish stoneworkers, also helps the widows of the deceased shed workers. Its meeting place is the Socialist Labor Hall.

The Labor Hall's big room is also the stage for heated debates between socialists and anarchists. Many illustrious guests participate: Luigi Galleani whose presence in Barre at the beginning of the 20th century makes it the epicentre of anarchism in the United States, Emma Goldman, Eugene Debs, Joseph Ettor and Arturo Giovannitti, Bill Haywood, Ann Burlak, among many others.

In these many debates oratory is the weapon of choice, with one important exception. On October 3rd, 1903, the socialist Giacinto Menotti Serrati, director of *Il Proletario*, is to give a speech on the differences between socialism and anarchism. For a while now from the pages of *Il Proletario* he has been fuelling a sharp ideological polemic with the anarchists that he calls forgers and liars. The socialists in Barre hear rumours that the anarchists intend to disrupt Serrati's speech, and even before he arrives in the building the tension runs high. On that day, Alessandro Garetto, a fervent socialist, goes to the Labor Hall to prepare it for the evening. He carries a handgun out of precaution. When people start trickling in, a group of anarchists blocks the way to Garetto and a brawl ensues. In the confusion that follows, two shots are fired from Garetto's pistol. One of these bullets hits Elia Corti, a highly regarded and respected anarchist who, according to some witnesses, is trying to calm the situation. Before they take him to the hospital in nearby Montpelier, Corti formally recognizes Garetto as the man who has just shot him. Corti dies in the hospital thirty hours later, to the chagrin of the entire community. No less than two hundred people attend his funeral.

In the twelve years that he has lived in Barre, Elia Corti has earned the respect of the whole community through the quality of his work and his great personal skills. He first works ten years for the Barclay Bros., one of the big granite companies in Barre; for them he carves the highly admired four panels on the pedestal of the statue of Robert Burns, the great Scottish poet, in downtown Barre, working with another Italian stoneworker, Sam Novelli, who sculpts the statue. After creating this monument, Corti and Novelli's reputation is strong, and they decide to create their own small but respected company. A fervent anarchist, Corti has a gift as a mediator, a position that allows him to resolve many controversies in the sheds, both between colleagues, and between employers and employees. He is an important reference point for the first generation of Italian stonecutters, but he has gained the respect of the entire community in Barre. In the traditional photo that all the immigrants have taken of themselves and their family to send back to the old country, Corti looks young—he is thirty-four when he is shot—and well-established. He is accompanied by his wife and their two young daughters. All are elegantly dressed, comfortably sitting in front of a painted background that evokes a sober prosperity. Corti's gaze is engaging, serious, and self-confident, indicative of a man fully at ease in his new world.

As is the custom among Barre's stonecutters, when Corti dies his family, friends, and colleagues work together on his funerary monument. Abramo Ghigli, a known sculptor in Barre, makes the drawings; Elia's brother Guglielmo and brother-in-law John Comi carve it. Made of one single piece of granite, the monument shows Corti life-size, again elegantly dressed, in a pensive pose, seated in front of a rock, with his left hand resting on a broken column. No detail is missing, from the crease in his trousers and tie, to the buttonholes of his jacket. At the foot of the broken column lie the tools of his work. Corti's monument is erected in the Hope Cemetery, the final resting place of most of Barre's stonecutters, where American granite and Italian artistry seamlessly merge in the many figural memorials, forming a genre of tombs that is nearly unique in North America.

The Socialist Labor Hall is the stage on which many community histories take place and unfold, and it is also the place that symbolizes the connection with like-minded workers in other parts of the country. On January 12th, 1912, the textile workers of Lawrence, Massachusetts, start the so-called "Bread and Roses Strike" that soon turns into one of the bitterest confrontations between employers and employees that the North-East of the United States has ever seen. Lawrence is the centre of the American Woolen Company, one of the largest textile companies in the country, employing 30,000 workers from all over the world: Italians, who make up the largest percentage of workers, Germans, French-Canadians, Poles, Lithuanians, Belgians, Syrians, Greeks, Russians, and Turks—a true mosaic of immigrants. In response to a new law that reduces the workweek for women and children from 56 to 54 hours, the American Woolen Company lowers their wages by thirty-two cents, the equivalent of the price of three loaves of bread. The day the workers discover the reduction, they leave the textile mills, and within a week 20,000 have walked out. The tension rises and violence escalates, but in spite of intimidations by the employer and the authorities, arrests and clashes with local militia and state police, the strike continues for many weeks. As a result, the situation for the families of the strikers becomes extremely hard and dangerous. In Barre, ten committees that coordinate help for the strikers are formed. In a reunion at the Socialist Labor Hall, the Italian stoneworkers decide to pay for some of the "Lawrence children" to come to Barre. On February 17th, thirty-five children between four and fourteen years of age arrive; they all wear pins that identify them as either a Lawrence boy or girl. They are immediately brought to the Labor Hall where portraits of Karl Marx now hang on either side of the stage. The large hall is crowded and a big banquet takes place. Local physicians examine all the children who are then photographed. These images are sold as postcards to raise funds for the strikers. Local families house the children, and storeowners donate bread, milk, fruit, and sweets. At Barre's Opera House, the local company performs an Italian piece titled *Gente Onesta* (Honest People). Tickets sell for thirty-five cents and the event raises about a hundred dollars, a sum that goes in its entirety to the strikers in Lawrence.

One of the big events that every year takes place in the Labor Hall is the *Primo Maggio*—the First of May, a celebratory holiday that everyone in Barre knows as the Italian Labour Day and that unites Italian communities worldwide. The *Barre Evening Telegram* publishes notices both in Italian and in English to invite all to attend and participate. Debates, fairs, balls, and plays are organized; the celebrations start in the Labor Hall with speeches and the enactment of *Il Primo Maggio*, a popular play by anarchist playwright Pietro Gori, and continue in the streets of the town with a festive parade accompanied by a marching band.

It is events such as these that underscore the fundamental difference between Barre, the centre of Vermont's granite industry, on one hand, and Proctor, the centre of the state's marble industry, on the other. Separated by the Green Mountains, the two towns are not geographically distant. Both, moreover, are booming towns thanks to the rapidly growing stone industry—granite for Barre and marble for Proctor. At the same time, they could hardly be more different: east of the mountains there is Barre, with its autonomous granite sheds, big and small, and its heated passion for politics; forty-seven miles away, west of the mountains, in Proctor, is the Vermont Marble Company, the sole owner of virtually all Vermont marble. Redfield Proctor, a native Vermonter, is the ambitious founder of the company. He has not only created a flourishing industry; he has also wanted to create a society—and a workplace—free of passions and conflicts, and to shape the lives of his employees. The Vermont Marble Company rents and sells houses to its employees, and runs a cooperative store and the Redfield Proctor hospital. Harmony in the workplace and in town is what Mr. Proctor wants and claims to have achieved. As a result, for the stoneworker in Proctor there is a high price to pay; involvement in and discussion of politics are not allowed. The by-laws of the Recreation Club, inaugurated in Proctor on May 1st, 1909, state that the association is dedicated solely to entertainment: it organizes parties, concerts, and shows of various kinds but the discussion of work and politics is strictly and explicitly barred. The contrast with what happens in Barre on the very same day, May 1st, could not be stronger.

The activities held at the Socialist Labor Hall in Barre display the ideals of community and solidarity among the Italian immigrants. For people like my grandparents, who have moved to a new country so different and so far away from their hometown, that building and all that happens in it constitutes a bridge that keeps them closely connected to the world they have left and, at the same time, helps them to make the new world more their own. In fact, through how they use the Labor Hall, they demonstrate cultural and ideological values that go well beyond the local Italian community, making them part of a larger context. The activities at the Labor Hall do not eliminate the hardships of emigration. Through their work and their initiatives, however, the Italian stoneworkers are able, already at an early stage in their integration, to play an important and proactive role in Barre's professional and social life. Shared ideals and values, a strong work ethic, and highly specialized skills bring down the barriers between the various nationalities. For uprooted migrants far from their homeland this is no minor achievement, one in which the Socialist Labor Hall plays a crucial role. As one stoneworker puts it, that building and what it represents help them to keep body and soul together while getting used to a strange, cold place.

Over the years the Socialist Labor Hall follows the ups and downs of the granite business and of political movements that are increasingly perceived as too radical, starting after the First World War and the first Red Scare. Before long, there is no more space for socialists, anarchists, communists, and many of them are arrested and deported. The Socialist Labor Hall ceases to exist as such in 1936, when it is auctioned off and bought by the Washington Fruit Company that uses it as a warehouse. Over the years the building is owned and used by different businesses and gradually falls into disrepair.

What follows next, however, is once again an exceptional story of a community that comes together to salvage a piece of its own heritage, turning the now defunct Socialist Labor Hall into a vital and lively space for social and cultural activities of all kinds.

On October 4th, 1994, Karen Lane, the director of the Aldrich Public Library in Barre, who has done extensive research on the history of the Labor Hall, receives a phone call announcing that dozens of boxes filled with papers are being transported from the old Socialist Labor Hall to a far away landfill. Despite a rush to the landfill, Karen Lane is not able to save the documents, but the outrage that ensues over such a loss brings together the whole local community with the goal of saving and restoring the Hall. Monthly workdays and fundraising events are organized, and people from all venues participate. As in 1900, the unions proactively take part in this effort: the Granite Workers Association, the International Brotherhood of Electrical Workers, the United Association of Plumbers and Pipe Fitters, all donate money and labour. On May 16th, 2000, the National Park Service of the United States designates the

Hall as a National Historic Landmark for the role it has played in the history of Italian anarchism and militant unionism in the United States. It is one of only a handful of historic landmarks commemorating anarchism or socialism in the entire United States.

On September 12th, 2000, Labour Day, the Socialist Labor Hall reopens its doors with another grand celebration and with food, music, traditional labour songs, and many speeches. While it still needs work, the hall is once again a centre for the entire community of Barre. That night, George Clain —the president of the International Brotherhood of Electrical Workers, Local 300—declares: "You step in there and there is something that tells you where you are. You can feel it, a magnetism, a power that moves you forward. This is where I ought to be. It's like going home."

***

THE BACK-AND-FORTH CYCLE:
HOW TEMPORARY SENEGALESE WORKERS LIVE ON THE EDGES OF ITALIAN SOCIETY AND RAPIDLY TRANSFORM THE BUILT ENVIRONMENT BACK HOME

BY
IAN CHODIKOFF

Planting the Seed

Mamadou Ndiaye was never afraid of hard work. A good student, the young Senegalese always found a way to pay for things that he wanted in life. Born in Pikine, an informal settlement established just outside Dakar in the early 1950s—which has since grown to a population of well over 800,000 people—Mamadou was always able to see the bigger picture of the world in which he grew up, a world that extended beyond Senegal, and a world that included it.

As a teenager in the mid-1990s, Mamadou began to notice some of the older kids in their twenties drive around Pikine in fancy used cars imported from Europe. Some of the cars still had European plates on them, while others were adorned with colourful bumper stickers broadcasting political slogans or businesses with telephone numbers of far-away places. The kids driving these cars were very proud of what they did—many of them were seen as resourceful for having made the journey to Europe to work. The burgeoning desire to work abroad filled Mamadou's thoughts. At night, he would fall asleep dreaming of Europe as he'd stare at the dog-eared and fading images of Senegalese and Italian football stars taped to his bedroom wall.

Mamadou knew that he wasn't alone in his dream of working in Europe. Every week, he would read or hear about various success stories of young Africans making their fortunes abroad. There were even music videos on television that depicted the lives of the thousands of transnational migrants, mostly men, who were beginning to travel to Europe in search of fame and fortune. Mamadou's older sister grew angry at these people who seemed to lack a commitment to their native country by working abroad. She would argue regularly with her parents and friends about what she saw as a growing phenomenon that was a potential social and economic detriment to the future health of Senegal. But even Mamadou's sister realized that this was an unstoppable global trend, repeated in dozens of countries around the world—nations that continue to be the source of the estimated 200 million transnational migrants at work today, somewhere on the planet.

Through various media, including regular radio and television interviews, the cultural influences tempting young Senegalese men to seek work in Italy and achieve their "transnational dreams" remained persistent. It is therefore not so surprising that the thousands of small groups of Senegalese transnationals operating in European cities had an impact on the livelihood and patterns of urbanization in Senegalese cities, mostly through the amount of money being transferred back to their families.

As the adventures of Mamadou illustrate, there are positive side-effects to transnational migration. The specific dynamics in which the Senegalese continue to stick together, and how their ethnic or cultural ties continue to flourish, are very encouraging, despite the cultural homogenization of global consumer culture. In the case of the Senegalese, their cultural links are preserved by high levels of social capital which continue to exist across geographic boundaries—knowing who your friends are and trusting those who share similar cultural roots is crucial, especially in a world containing infinite social networks, many of them incomprehensible to the outsider. For the roughly 100,000 young men who have left Senegal and continue to work in Europe, maintaining a strong connection to their friends and family back home is critical for their ongoing emotional and economic survival abroad.

Young men like Mamadou don't philosophize about being a "transnational migrant"—a term used to define a 21st century migrant's cultural, economic, political and social experiences of living in a "host" country (i.e. Italy) with an ongoing connection to their "home" country (i.e. Senegal). Men like Mamadou just want to work abroad to earn their keep. The current form of transnational migration between Senegal and Italy began in the mid-1980s. Most of the immigrants travelling to Italy were Muslim, of Wolof background, and affiliated to some degree with the Murides—an important Sufi Islam brotherhood centred in Senegal. Working largely within the informal economy, these migrants reside in Europe on a temporary basis while regularly sending money back to their families. Comprising roughly half of Senegal's GNP, men like Mamadou (only a small percentage of Senegalese who work in Europe are women) have undeniably shaped the new transnational spaces of Senegal. For the many Senegalese who lack economic opportunities at home, transnational migration provides a necessary means of generating income for their future. Just like a typical, young, ambitious North American twenty-something, these young men simply want to build a better future for themselves and their families.

Making the Decision
Mamadou Ndiaye's decision to make the journey to Italy officially began in 1999, when the 23-year-old from Pikine hopped onto a tiny, packed bus destined for the Muride-run Marché Sandaga in Central Dakar to buy cheap prescription drugs for his father's diabetes. Mamadou's story is not unlike the other men his age who live in Dakar or the surrounding cities like Pikine, Guediawaye, Rufisque, Bargny, or Keur Massar. Known as the Cap Vert peninsula, the region is home to roughly half of the country's estimated 13 million people. As the middle child, Mamadou has been assuming a large role in his family for a number of years. His oldest brother has been working in Gabon for nearly a decade and his older sister married a doctor in Thiès seven years ago. With two younger brothers and a mother much older and frailer than her 55 years, Mamadou was wise well beyond his years.

Riding the crowded bus out of Pikine, the driver picked up a few more passengers in the adjacent settlements of Les Parcelles Assainies. Operated by the Muride Islamic brotherhood based in the holy city of Touba, the distinctive blue and yellow buses are either decorated with images of the Touba mosque or have the names or images of Muride religious leaders painted on them. The buses can be seen almost everywhere and their presence keeps people moving efficiently as Senegal lacks any kind of light rail transit and the public bus system is under-served and unreliable.

When Mamadou returned home from Marché Sandaga with his father's medication around eight o'clock that evening, he decided to think seriously about becoming a *modou-modou*—the Muride term for a transnational worker. Like everyone else his age, he had many friends who either worked in Italy, or had brothers who did. He called up his uncle and asked if he could take him out to a local *dibiterie* for a couple of kilos of barbecued goat served up with some onions and a baguette—the place was not much more than an open fire pit with a couple of benches set up in a makeshift structure beside the road. He wanted his uncle to help him get a plane ticket and visa for Italy so that he could begin to map out a future for himself—a future that would one day include a home and a beautiful wife. Working with the UNACOIS (Union Nationale des Commerçants et Industriels du Sénégal), his uncle had developed important connections over the years and was fairly confident that he could hook his nephew up with the necessary papers, a place to stay, and a job. After the discussion over goat meat, it was decided that his uncle would loan him money for a plane ticket, and give him a thousand dollars to get him started. Four months later, Mamadou had his bags packed for Rome.

Senegal is roughly 94% Muslim, but is tolerant of other religious affiliations even though Islam permeates everyday life. Although the Murides comprise over 25% of the Muslim population, their influence is felt everywhere. Not only do they control a large and ubiquitous private bus system, but they also control significant components of the country's shipping and commerce while continuing to exert a degree of influence over government policy. And while there are other Islamic Brotherhoods who exert a considerable amount of influence, there is stability, peace and equilibrium in the country—President Abdoulaye Wade visits the Muride leaders in the religious centre of Touba regularly in an effort to maintain the delicate balance of the secular state. Touba has emerged in the middle of a desert with a Moorish-inspired religious campus at its heart. It exists as a Mecca for the Murides and it is here where people want to be born, live and die. At least a three-hour drive east of Dakar, Touba is a holy city with no hotels, one restaurant and where most women will choose to wear long skirts and head coverings.

Aware of the long-term benefits of being associated with the Murides (i.e. job prospects, business and cultural connections), Mamadou's uncle devoted his youth to the brotherhood while giving the organization money throughout his adult life. He was a successful merchant who used to be in the groundnut business and managed to build a modest three-bedroom house for himself and his family on land given to him by the Grand Khalif in the late 1970s, when Touba occupied little more than 500 hectares with a population of less than 50,000 people. Today, the rapidly expanding city has an estimated population of around 500,000 people and continues to accept those who dream of living in the holy city. Mamadou had impressed his uncle with his desire to earn money abroad and his commitment to the hard-working Muride ethic. He felt blessed to be given an opportunity to work in Italy.

Arriving in Italy: Act One
Arriving at Rome's Fiumicino airport, Mamadou was tired and overwhelmed. Presenting his tourist visa, return ticket, and an address and phone number where he would be staying, the officials didn't give him a second thought—this was pre-9/11 and the world was a very different place. Once past customs, he went to a pay phone and called a number provided by his uncle. From the airport, he hopped onto a train headed to Rome Termini in the centre of town, arriving just after 10 p.m. Two Senegalese men were waiting for him—one of whom was busy on his cell phone. Little did he know that these men would become his new roommates. When he arrived at a nine-storey apartment building in the suburbs of Rome, he almost thought that he was back in Senegal. The building was almost entirely rented to Senegalese who shared apartments with up to eight men per unit—and where one person would take turns cooking for the others. Mamadou was lucky: he was living in a larger one-bedroom apartment with a total of four other men. Most of the men worked in the informal sector, selling all kinds of merchandise. Occasionally, someone would find a factory job, preferring the steady income and modest benefits over the mentally and physically demanding challenges of selling merchandise on the street.

It didn't take Mamadou very long to settle into his new life. He even got used to the fact that his apartment reeked of body odour due to the tight quarters and constant coming and going of roommates and visitors. Piled up against the walls were sacks of rice, flour, cooking oil and laundry, not to mention the mattresses and sheets that would be set up across the floor at night.

Before Mamadou began his business day, the first thing he'd do would be to visit the Chinese wholesalers who would provide him with blue garbage bags of sunglasses, CDs or imitation luxury handbags. His responsibility was to sell the goods by day's end and bring back any unsold merchandise. The Chinese would take a significant cut, leaving Mamadou with the remaining cash. It would take some time for him to develop his negotiating skills with the Chinese to get a better commission from his earnings. Most mornings, Mamadou would work the tourist areas or the subway stations where there would be a lot of commuter traffic—places where he could quickly vanish if the police appeared. Typical of many Senegalese sellers, he would lay out his merchandise on blankets or makeshift stands made of cardboard and duct tape that could be easily folded up and hauled away at a moment's notice, once a scout alerted everyone to the presence of police. Relying on the support of other Senegalese had its advantages. Other nationalities had tried to work in Italy—transnational migrants from places like Cameroon, Bangladesh or the Philippines—but these people didn't enjoy the extensive support networks of the Senegalese community, nor did they exhibit the patience and quiet demeanour required for a job that demanded long hours and inevitably included regular harassment by passersby and local officials.

Mamadou's existence on the street in Italy underscores the fact that what we see in our everyday world only represents a small percentage of the reality that surrounds us. In our contemporary cities, there are many aspects to our daily lives that exist beyond our level of comprehension—we walk by Mamadou on the street, uninterested in the fake Prada bags that he has neatly arranged on a blanket. His life remains invisible to us and his motives remain hidden. The contemporary city, much like the life of Mamadou, is increasingly intertwined with layers of globalization that extend well beyond the manufacture, marketing and desire to consume recognizable brands such as Chanel, Nike or Louis Vuitton.

Every two weeks, Mamadou would call home and speak to his family. On the rare occasion that he would call his uncle, the discussion would invariably include his dream of owning a home in Touba, or his ability to donate some of his earnings to the Murides to support their *daaras*, or small religious schools that operated throughout the country, mostly inside rooming houses and apartment buildings. Despite the fact that specialty food and beauty shops catering to the Senegalese were operating in many Italian cities, or that Internet cafés where immigrants from around the world would congregate had flourished, the Senegalese in Italy made very little urban impact on where they lived other than evolving the presence of informal markets that have existed for centuries.

The last week of every month, Mamadou would send money back to Senegal via Western Union, paying their exorbitant fees that practically amounted to paying a private tax to a multinational corporation rather than to the Senegalese government. Sending money back was a matter of pride and kept him motivated. Everything sent to his family was well spent—the house would always need repairs, new clothes would need to be bought—but most of the remittances were being spent on building a new family home in

Pikine that would have a modern shower and kitchen.

Whenever he made a money transfer, Mamadou would e-mail his 20-year-old brother Zal, who would then use the codes that his older brother sent him to claim the money at the Western Union outlet next to his favourite Internet café around the corner from his house in Pikine. Cashing the money at the bank, the funds would be quickly spent on building materials purchased from the many construction material shops and depots set up along the major roads. Zal would arrange for bags of cement to arrive at the construction site while cheap reinforcing bar was purchased wherever they could get the best price. Deliveries would arrive on donkey carts driven by 15-year-old kids. Cement blocks would be made by hand with cement mixers on site and the whole front of the property would often be seen with dozens of blocks drying in the sun. Buying rebar was a bit trickier, as some of the cheaper reinforcing rods were far too brittle. Once the concrete blocks were put into place, the house would be parged with cement and readied for the application of tiles from Italy or Spain that could easily keep off the dust and dirt. With the exception of the 250 architects in Senegal, who mostly worked on resort properties or large commercial developments, building standards remained primitive, which may explain why the standard designs for most of the new single-family residential construction were so uniform.

The cycle of sending money back to Senegal every month was paying dividends. Mamadou was garnering increased respect from his family. Even Ousmane, his precocious 14-year-old brother, was taking an active role in the construction process despite his father's half-hearted pleas to stay in school. With his Nokia cell phone, Ousmane would take pictures of the construction site and e-mail his older brother the images, sometimes including a few silly poses for the camera. His brother's pictures made Mamadou homesick, yet motivated him to keep working hard for the sake of his family.

It took about a year to finish the house. The pace of construction was directly proportionate to Mamadou's money transfers. With the house complete, Mamadou was eager to fly back to Senegal to see what he had accomplished. Over the next six months, he began saving up for a cheap ticket to Dakar along with a little nest egg. Buying a last-minute ticket just in time for the Grand Magal in February—the annual Murides festival that takes place in Touba—Mamadou made the return trip.

Coming Home for the First Time
After two years away, Mamadou stepped off the plane in Dakar. Eager to reacquaint himself with old friends, most of whom stayed behind to look for what precious little employment opportunities there were, some of Mamadou's friends were jealous of his experience in Italy and what he was able to achieve—a new home, some property, and respect.

Not everyone who wanted to travel abroad was so fortunate. For those who couldn't afford a plane ticket, or who couldn't get a visa, there was the option of travelling overland through Mauritania, or taking the riskier journey by pirogue. Traditional flat-bottom fishing boats, pirogues were used out of desperation by those who foolishly paid a handsome price to travel with up to 30 other men to Spain or Italy with the hope of seeking asylum and eventually finding work in Europe. The pirogues rarely made it to their destination. It was a dangerous game of Russian roulette and Mamadou was horrified to find out that two of his friends died the previous summer when their pirogue destined for Lampedusa, an island off the coast of Sicily, capsized after only two days at sea. All 25 men drowned, leaving the families devastated. Many of the men couldn't swim and those that could never stood a chance in the cold Atlantic waters. Occasionally a pirogue would make it to Europe. If the Senegalese were lucky, they'd be picked up by the Spanish or Italian coast guard and brought in questioning at a refugee camp. There, the men would pretend to be fleeing a hostile nation—even though Senegal certainly didn't qualify as a nation with an oppressive government.

Accomplishing the goal of building a home, Mamadou was now interested in getting married and starting a family. Working in Italy allowed him to save up enough money for a small dowry and have some money left over for a wedding. Mamadou's uncle introduced him to a handful of suitable women and it didn't take long before a decision was made—he chose to marry a beautiful woman by the name of Fanta that April. A couple of weeks later, Fanta moved into the new family home that Mamadou's money had built over the past year. His life in Pikine seemed full of hope and happiness.

His parents and two little brothers moved into the ground floor of the new house. Mamadou and Fanta lived in an apartment upstairs that had its own washroom and separate entrance. The roof was used to dry the laundry and made a great place to have late-night tea. The house was clad in shiny white ceramic tiles with an odd baby-blue patterning intended to resemble marble. The front of the house was decorated with two simple Italianate arches. Mamadou found it to be quite beautiful, as he had spent his life in one-storey homes, with the exception of his Italian apartment. Every morning, he would take his sweet tea, baguette and cheese out onto the roof where he would watch the donkey carts move through the neighbourhood, sounding their distinctive horns. A few streets in the densely populated neighbourhood were paved, most were still of hard-packed dirt. The occasional street lamp illuminated sections of the neighbourhood at night but the area remained mostly tranquil and dark. With all the remittances coming into the country from transnationals like Mamadou, the government saw very little of the money in the form of income tax. Therefore, it was a challenge for the state to find the money to build the necessary roads, streetlights and sewers for the rapidly expanding Cap Vert region.

Mamadou's interest in real-estate development began as soon as he moved into his new house. He started to think about how he wanted to build a larger home for himself, or even a small apartment building where the first floor could be rented to an appliance shop that could sell used freezers and washing machines from Italy. Over the past couple of years, the fever of real-estate speculation had descended upon Senegal with vigour. When Mamadou first left for Italy, the government was pretty successful in making sure that there were enough affordable housing and subsidized units available. Today, subsidized housing was either rented out at market rates or sold on the open market, furthering the rising cost of real estate. People would invest in several properties, only to flip them. The prices would continue to rise and because everybody has an uncle that could find a way to put a down payment on a property, the process continued unabated. The country's delicate socioeconomic and urban fabric was changing. A variant of North American suburbanization and income inequality had begun to take root in Senegal with no known outcome over the long term.

With all the land speculation and building, urban sprawl of the Cap Vert region was noticeable. Not only was getting around the city increasingly difficult, but the amount of agricultural land was rapidly disappearing and being replaced with privately financed or state-sponsored development. Where neighbours once built small additions to their houses every year, they were now completing buildings in a few months. An increasingly confident class of Senegalese developers were building turnkey operations—four, five, six or more housing units at a time. The market was becoming more sophisticated, with state-run banks falling behind in terms of offering affordable or accessible mortgages. Outside Dakar, speculative developments continued to pop up everywhere and anywhere: row houses, semi-detached housing and other types of developments that only a few kinds of Senegalese could afford were being built by increasingly confident and risk-taking developers.

Still dreaming of becoming a developer, Mamadou discovered that the banks in Senegal are generally not very interested in helping people like him start up new businesses. Typically, the banks are reluctant or incapable of taking on any risk associated with lending money to individuals like Mamadou. Interestingly enough, an increasing number of foreign banks can be seen operating in Senegal—institutions with roots in Morocco, Tunisia, Lebanon or Egypt. These banks were willing to take on more risk than the domestic banks, but their clients usually weren't Senegalese. To investors in the Arab and other African markets, Senegal is either an inexpensive or relatively transparent place to invest. Without evolving Senegal's banking system, it would only be a matter of time before the foreign banks completely eclipsed the Senegalese financial institutions' ability to finance small-scale entrepreneurial activity.

Mamadou's plans to become a real-estate mogul never materialized. After a few months of married life, he continued to look for work. He wanted a job with Sonatel—the national telephone company. He also was looking for a job in a bank but nothing was available. After struggling to find decent work for a few more months, his nest egg was nearly gone. It was at this point that he decided to go back to Italy with the hopes of earning more money before starting his family. A week before he left, Fanta announced that she was pregnant.

Arriving in Italy: Act Two

Mamadou's return to Italy was much more focused than before. He had an even greater reason to make money since he had a wife and child to support. On this second tour of duty, he decided to live in the medieval section in the port city of Genoa full of transnational merchants from Asia, the Middle East and Africa. The density of transnationals living and working in such a small section of the city was less alienating for Mamadou while offering him greater opportunities to work in the service sector. To him, this was preferable to selling fake Louis Vuitton bags. Mamadou rented an apartment with two other men—a man from Thiaroye, a Dakar suburb on the Cap Vert peninsula, and another man from Cambérène, near Pikine. Ousmane, who came from Thiaroye, was married the longest and had been working in Genoa for almost ten years. His eyes were always bleary and blood-shot. He had likely stayed in Italy for too long. Fluent in Italian and addicted to cash, a part of him was running away from the Senegalese lifestyle. Mustafa, the third roommate, was closer in age to Mamadou, but had no family except for a brother and a wife. He was very religious and very protective of both Mamadou and Ousmane.

For two years, Mamadou worked as a street vendor, then in the kitchens of a couple of restaurants, and even in an Internet café. He eventually got his official working papers and found a job in Mirafiori near Turin. He decided to leave Genoa because he thought that shift work at a factory would provide him with a more balanced life while still being able to save some money. His apartment in Mirafiori was in a working-class area where some neighbours were having trouble accepting West African immigrants, even though most of them had once been outsiders themselves, having migrated from Southern Italy in the 1960s to work for the automobile manufacturer Fiat.

The last year before moving back to Senegal, Mamadou managed to send enough money back to his wife so the two of them could buy a small piece of land on the edge of Keur Massar—a developed area farther away from Dakar than Pikine, but very close to his uncle. The property already had cement blocks delimiting its boundaries and Mamadou's uncle went out to the site every couple of weeks to check up on things. Plots were being slowly developed, gradually creating the beginnings of a neighbourhood.

Burned out from living away from his wife and newborn child Fatou, Mamadou decided once again to pack it in and move back to Senegal. Leaving wasn't going to be so easy this time as there was a lot of pressure for him to return with lots of cash in hand. But during his last three years in Italy—and the two years in Rome before that—Mamadou grew wiser, more mature, and certainly more skeptical of the various laws surrounding work permits, employment law, racism and the costs associated with transferring money back to his family. Italy was ready to receive another transnational. Mamadou was ready to go home.

Finally Going Home

Getting a cheap flight out of Italy on Air France, Mamadou flew to Paris and then on to Dakar. The stopover in Paris was stressful. The French had developed a natural mistrust for the Senegalese—a feeling that was thoroughly reciprocal. As a former colonial power, most Senegalese always preferred to avoid France if at all possible. Once in Dakar, Mamadou's cousin Coumba, along with Fanta and three-year-old Fatou, met them at the airport. Mamadou's heart was ecstatic, even though he was exhausted. They all piled into an old Citroën and drove off to Keur Massar, where his uncle was putting together a big dinner at his house to honour Mamadou's return. Driving out to Keur Massar, a thick, salty ocean breeze filled his lungs. Listening to the call-in radio shows in the car, everyone listened in silence to the latest stories about the life of a *modou-modou*, with young Senegalese telling their stories of loneliness and hope, of ambition and despair. Arriving at his uncle's home, goats huddled under a nearby tree, or slept beneath parked cars. The local Internet café was filled with kids surfing all kinds of websites on Islam, schools in the United States, or immigration law. And, of course, there were a lot of instant messaging and social networking sites flickering on the screens as the owner shuffled in and out of the café, wearing cheap plastic sandals purchased from one of the new Chinese discount-goods merchants that recently opened in the centre of Dakar. Next door, two Mauritanians operated a local convenience store while making sure their freezer filled with precious ice cream bars was locked at all times. They relied on the Senegalese for business, but rarely trusted them. The feeling was often mutual even though people rarely talked about it.

Mamadou would sometimes find himself along Route des Almadies around sunset, driving in his father's old Peugeot. Located near the airport, it was here where the most lavish homes in Dakar were being built—homes typically rented or owned by foreigners and transnationals. Some of the larger and more ostentatious houses belonged to Senegalese who had left the country years ago. A few houses would remain under a perpetual state of construction and were thus being rented out to Pulaars from the countryside for a small fee. It was a good idea to have somebody occupy these unfinished hulking homes while the more entrepreneurial Senegalese were off in Europe. The houses were usually built in an Italianate style, but the sight of goats eating garbage strewn across the houses' empty, sandy lots lent these structures a surreal quality—a barren landscape inhabited by speculative painted stucco houses complete with odd-shaped arched windows, columns and balustrades made of cement, with plaster applied anywhere and everywhere possible. The sparsely populated and slightly melancholic neighbourhood was a reminder to Mamadou that the once-tight social network found in communities across Senegal was beginning to erode, largely due to the phenomenon of transnationalism and its effects on increasing income disparity. Some of those who came back from abroad would opt to leave their family neighbourhoods behind, or live near those with whom they had worked with in Europe. This rebuilding of community was not always a good thing, and it was changing the delicate social balance of Senegalese society.

As a modern-day transnational, Mamadou learned a lot of lessons about life when he was in Italy. He also learned the value of a home and family. Even though he was able to live in two societies at once, he never experienced Italy as an Italian. Mamadou never abandoned his roots despite the fact he felt as though he was part of the new generation of global citizenry, one that can live and achieve success across nation-states; and where one can cross geographical and political boundaries almost as easily as a wire transfer or a call from a cell phone.

***

BRUSSELLES, BELGIUM, 2010

CALL SHOPS: A NEW ARCHITECTURAL TYPOLOGY FOR CALLING HOME

BY
RIITTA OITTINEN

This is a story about Brussels. But it's not about the Brussels of chocolates and lace and the landmark Manneken Pis statue. Nor, in fact, does it touch on the intricate and interminable constitutional and political wrangling between Belgium's Dutch and French speaking communities. No, this story is more mundane but, hopefully, will prove as delightful as the former, and as fascinating as the latter. This tale takes a close look at two forms of small and medium sized enterprises, call shops and laundromats, both of which I have come to know surprisingly well.

When I moved from Helsinki to Brussels over a decade ago, I started taking long aimless walks. To use the fancy term, I was engaging in *flânerie*. To be perfectly honest, owing to my poor sense of direction and the dearth of street signs, even some of my better-planned excursions devolved into clueless strolling. Yet according to the inventor of *flânerie*—none other than the illustrious 19th century French poet Charles Baudelaire—the Belgian capital was not a place in which one could enjoy his concept of wondrous wandering. *Flânerie* in Brussels was simply impossible: Baudelaire complained about the awful, irregular pavements, the narrow streets, the general clumsiness of pedestrians, and the lack or interruption of sidewalk space. The poet's complaints about the condition of the streets, or chance encounters with pushy pedestrians, may still remain valid. It is his view of Brussels as a *boring* place, however, that I simply cannot fathom. Brussels has certainly changed since Baudelaire's day into an increasingly vibrant and exciting place to explore.

In Brussels, the high degree of variety and visual quirks are, in fact, further obstacles to finding my way around. Taking in the city landscape and breathing in urban microclimates offer endless experiences, which often come at the expense of efficiency. This is not a complaint: I am always struck by the ways in which small businesses interact with their clients, but also with their environment and the world at large. Their signs, displays, decorations, and goods take you to Asia, Africa, the Americas, the Near East, and Eastern and Western Europe. By January 2000, almost a third of the population of a city of one million inhabitants had foreign citizenship, though these figures do not account for undocumented immigrants. Further, perhaps up to half a million people commute into Brussels daily to work or study from neighbouring provinces in Flanders and Wallonia, while about a million tourists visit Brussels each year. This "away from home" population, broadly considered, would seem to constitute the majority in Brussels during daytime.

On the whole, the city is home to more than a hundred nationalities, and likely an even greater number of languages. Almost half of Brussels' households are culturally mixed and multilingual. International organizations such as the European Union (EU) and NATO are polyglot in the extreme, and while other workplaces are less so, English is gaining ground. Employees in businesses serving the city's many ethnic communities quickly change languages to suit the needs of the client. I have wandered into both areas and enterprises whose language combinations are quite stunning after all, the commingling of tongues like Arabic and Lingala, or of Modern Aramaic and Swedish, are evidence of remarkable mobility resulting from historical and geopolitical causes. In Brussels, however, they may be among the languages available at your corner bakery.

Brussels has a very diverse mix of immigrants. Several large communities are the result of official immigration from Mediterranean countries. The first workers to arrive were from Italy and subsequently from Portugal and Spain. The Turkish and Moroccan communities in Brussels are also the result of an extensive call for foreign labour launched in the 1960s by the Belgian authorities as part of the official immigration policy. The African, and especially Congolese, presence reflects Belgium's colonial past. One neighbourhood marked by the Congolese diaspora in Brussels is more or less officially called Matonge, after a district of the same name in Kinshasa. More recent waves of immigration include asylum seekers since the second half of the 1980s. The lack of a capital gains tax has attracted very rich inhabitants from neighbouring countries, such as France and the Netherlands. Successive waves of enlargement of the EU have enabled people from the new member states—such as Poland and Romania—to seek employment, especially in the construction and service sectors. The recent increase in shops catering to people from Latin America confirms another current immigration trend.

Back to our protagonists. This story of Brussels will be told jointly by the city's call shops and laundromats to anyone who wishes to walk its streets. While call shops and laundromats differ greatly in physical and functional terms, they are poles of attraction to many of those who are not entirely at home in Brussels, either as recent immigrants or as temporary visitors. I will first describe how these institutions serve those who are "away" in Brussels.

Call Shops – Not Just for Phone Calls
Call shops are a modern example of a phenomenon where entrepreneurs, whose position need not differ greatly from the working class, meet the needs and preferences of a global, often very poor, labour force. They are holdouts against the megamarts, and reflect the background, personal style and wealth of their owners. Brussels has hundreds of call shops, also known as phone shops, *téléboutiques*, global communication centres, public phones, publique phones, phoneboxes, cyber cafés, cybernetphones, Internet clubs, international telephone centres, *cabines téléphone (Belgique, Europe, Étranger)* or, as they are officially known, private telecommunication offices (*Bureaux privés pour les télécommunications*).

Call shops are the result of Belgium's general telecommunications market. Both landlines and Internet telephony at home remain expensive due to limited domestic price competition. Call shops pop up where communities of users emerge. They also offer good rates on calls to mobile phones, which are dominant in developing countries. The network of call shops is dense in the less well-off parts of town.

Two opposing factors influence the prevalence of call shops. On an international level, the EU has had success in deregulating the European telephone market, which has made it much easier for call shops to meet the technical requirements of the business, allowing many to register with the Belgian Institute for Postal Services and Telecommunications. Simultaneously, however, local authorities in Brussels regulate zoning (*implantation spatiale*) for call shops and businesses that operate at night. In practice, the Brussels Region—which I call Brussels here—is made up of nineteen autonomous municipalities, of which the City of Brussels is, in essence, only one constituent. To add to the confusion, local authorities have shown themselves quite zealous in decreeing all kinds of regulations on call shops, many inconsistent with the rules in other parts of the city. For example, in Koekelberg, the minimum distance between call shops must be 400 metres, and no call shops are allowed to operate within 100 metres of a school, senior centre or housing, hotel, cultural centre, or place of worship. Local authorities can also prohibit the operation of call shops on certain streets. It has been suggested that businesses catering to the tastes of more affluent citizens do not face such fundamentally arbitrary restrictions or *de facto* quotas.

Unlike chain stores and other easily recognized urban service formats, there is no universal colour scheme that designates call shops. Many inhabit relatively nondescript storefronts, but their façades, window displays, or large advertising panels often deploy the brightest colours setting them apart from the rest of the building. Yet, there are also extremely low-key operations. It was the colourful ones that initially caught my eye, and fuelled my inspiration. Increasingly, my peregrinations through Brussels would become photo expeditions, and I would document the excesses, as well as the restraint, of shop façades. Shown side-by-side, a "call shop city" emerges from the light-table, a mix of the unobtrusive and the garish, the functional and the flamboyant aspects of a business that might go unobserved by the uninitiated.

Call shop city may be a colourful place, but it also overwhelms. The displays tend to induce information angst. First there are the eye catching slogans such as *Ring-Ring, Hello!* or *Toujours moins cher*. Other forms of advertising, whether painted or taped on to the shop window, or hanging from the external wall, occupy the rest of the available message space. The current trend is to list per-minute prices and indicate destination countries with flags in the window. For example, the elegantly painted panel that surrounds the window of the *Téléphone par satellite* call shop on Chaussée de Mons—Bergensesteenweg provides interesting demographics on the origins and reach of their clientele: Pakistan, Rwanda, Lebanon, Brazil, Tunisia, Europe, Syria, Ghana, India, Togo,

Algeria, Ecuador, Morocco, The Democratic Republic of Congo, Cameroon, and Nigeria. Sometimes little or no light enters the shop through the thicket of ads, which probably protects the computers from glare too.

It is easier for phone shop operators to express their social preferences and political views than it is for, say, supermarket staff. Available surfaces, while mainly reserved for ads of mobile operators, international money transfer companies and snacks sold at the shop, are usually able to devote a limited amount of space for posters related to social and religious concerns, cultural and sports events, "for rent" ads, and even missing persons flyers. Passers by can admire Bollywood stars or reproductions of artworks from around the world. During elections you can try to deduce the call shop owner's ethnic, community, or political sympathies from election posters. A typically Belgian feature are stickers expressing 'sympathy' for the police, the fire services, or waste disposal services, usually sold door-to-door by persons identifying themselves as representatives of these professions to allegedly support their socio-professional activities.

The range of advertising media is broad. Some advertise with hand-written sheets of paper only, others have illuminated signs, plaques and panels, often hand-painted in vernacular, multilingual typography. By far the most common iconic theme is images of telephones, the blinking neon hand-set sign is especially popular. Pictures of computers, satellite dishes and the globe, as well as the @ symbol, are commonplace. Many signs are a result of a variety of influences and aesthetic tastes, while typography includes both historic and modern typefaces. Some sign-boards are truly charming pieces of skilled workmanship, whereas others are intentionally bland.

As many of call shop city's business owners are of West or North African, Turkish or Middle Eastern origin, establishment names often evoke the old country: *Köprülü, Ben's Phone, El-Maarif, Ali Baba, Al Noor Hot Line* and *Tam Tam Phone* bring variety to an urban landscape once dominated by French and Dutch. I have also noticed a smattering of Globish names, such as *Belgium Internet, Euro E-café Phone*, and *World Communication*. Images of camels, palms, mosques, or national flags in the window are another way of indicating something about the owner's identity.

Investment in the shop and facilities is often so low that no renovations are made after changes of ownership. There are some aesthetic and ecological advantages to such conservatism: call shop floors or external walls are sometimes decorated with durable old ceramic tiles typical to Brussels. That the windows of call shops have to be repaired with tape, plastic bags, or cardboard tell more about tight profit margins than a trendy preference for recycling.

The interior decoration of call shops is often design-and-do-it-yourself. The no-frills shops only have a few chipboard booths and a couple of tables with PCs. It appears that some call shops get their phone booths as part of a turnkey installation. The biggest shops have over ten booths, numbered in a manner somehow reminiscent of the burn-me booths at tanning salons. More up-market call shops have a number of computers, a scanner and a fax, although the latter seem to be on the way out, judging by the increasing difficulty I've had finding one when I need it.

The design scheme always includes a cash desk with a computer, which the clerk uses to monitor call prices. Behind the desk there are often personal effects, such as images of saints, amulets, family photographs, or postcards. The better-equipped stores may include both a deep freeze advertising Mecca Foods' *halal* meat products, which may in fact contain ice cream, as well as a cooler space sponsored by Coca Cola or Lipton.

Although the regulations limit call shops to selling goods only for consumption on the premises, the rules appear to be interpreted flexibly. At least some of them have other business lines as well. Apart from snacks and soft drinks, I have also seen cigarettes, stationery, stamps, small gifts or sale-priced, Dutch, wax-print textiles bought mainly by African clients. You may also have your television, radio, mobile phone, fridge, computer or camera repaired, rent a video, or get your hair done—or even buy braids and cosmetics at *My Afro Style*. I have also seen international money transfers, currency exchange, air freight services, photographic printing, and Internet gaming being advertised. There are food shops and night shops advertising "phones" and Internet access, sometimes even using the term "call shop," although this would seem to be against the law.

Some call shops provide services that clients without a permanent job would otherwise find difficult to obtain, such as translations or help with filling in official forms and using the Internet. A copy machine in the corner caters to the insatiable demand of the Belgian administration for paperwork. "*Service bureautique*" was offered by the late *Multimedia center-Internet Teleboutique*, which also made "*carte de marriage et visite*" and laminated identity cards. A call shop downtown even offers video conferencing as *Vision conférence*.

Local politicians and councils often take a dim view of call shops and night shops. Some politicians seem to demonize them as alleged centres for illegal activities. They have their supporters as well, such as our local night shop and laundromat entrepreneur, who tried to get my vote in the last elections, when I visited his shop to buy samosas. He was disappointed to learn that I live on the other side of the street, and thus in a different district. Proponents of free enterprise and opponents of ethnic or social discrimination, sometimes in the same person, have criticized communal restrictions on the right of free establishment. Some politicians have also argued that call shops and night shops, far from posing a general security risk, are often the only lighted spaces that provide a safe haven and free entry to the vulnerable on dark and potentially dangerous streets at night.

At their best, call shops offer the same kind of support and social networks as local cafeterias and bistros. Popular call shops have a steady stream of clients until late in the night, partly because of time differences. Some clients know each other, or at least the staff or the owner: discussions at the counter can be so intense that a stray customer, such as myself, may have difficulties in getting any attention. In distinction to laundromats, groups—usually of men from the neighbourhood—meet in front of call shops.

The shop creates a space for business and domestic affairs and social interaction, an ersatz home and office, as well as a connection to one's country of origin. I would not say that many of them are comfort zones, and few of them are as homey as small cafeterias can be, but there is something comfortable in their DIY spirit. It has been said of American neighbourhood corner stores that they are the purveyors of its public life. The same could be said of the corner, night, and call shops of Brussels. It is noteworthy that both men and women use phone shops, whereas other seemingly public spaces such as certain types of "male bonding" cafés accept women only as staff or cleaners, if at all.

It is impossible to estimate the economic impact of call shops and modern communications. I remember once walking by a group of three Congolese men having a beer in front of a call shop located next to a company offering cheap freight rates and money transfers to the Democratic Republic of Congo. Despite the ordinary circumstances, they were engaged in a heated debate on whether chartering a light aircraft or a helicopter would be better for their business venture, presumably in the D.R. Congo, and quite possibly involving the export of minerals used in mobile phones. Although I am not sure how this particular deal was concluded with the Congolese counterparty, it is safe to say that the humble looks of phone shops are not a reliable indication of their economic and social value for their users at either end.

Automated Consumerism: Laundromats
Those who do not need a laundromat may not even notice them, unless they are struck by the odour of detergent or the grey puffs of water vapour emanating from the cooling vents. The visual contrast between laundromats, on the one hand, and corner shops, call shops, or small cafeterias, on the other, is immense. Unlike customers of the latter, laundromat customers do not usually spill out onto the street, with the exception of the occasional customer smoking and talking on the mobile phone outside.

There are more than a hundred laundromats in Brussels, with the market divided roughly in two between four large chains and scores of independent operators. The non-staffed approach definitely rules. Laundromats are a good indicator of metropolitan lifestyles within an urban area. In Brussels they tell about a very dense urban structure with rental accommodation, where the inhabitants might not have a single laundry washer in the building, let alone a communal laundry room. Another sign of the lack of laundry rooms are carpets that are laid on chairs and put on streets to dry in the summer. It is no wonder then that some clients come to the laundromat to use the dryer only. Conversely, you also see customers take damp clothes home to dry in order to save on costs.

Laundromats are interesting in their minimalism. They are fully automated and coin or token operated. From a legal perspective they are private spaces, but they feel like public spaces such as waiting rooms at bus or railway stations. They are all designed to prevent vandalism. For security reasons, visibility inside the laundromat is always kept unfettered. (Some communities require that only 20% of the window area of call shops is covered, but this principle seems to be respected more in the breach than in the observance.) I have not seen laundromats integrate other services such a cafeteria, perhaps because there is almost always a café nearby in Brussels anyway.

Laundromats have an almost uniform concept of decoration and equipment. One reason is that there are companies selling turnkey operations. A Brussels company operating *Ipsomat* laundromats and franchizing *Airwash* laundromat systems says that installation costs range from 120,000 Euros to more than a million Euros. In franchize operations, the owner is asked to pay at least a quarter of the costs and will retain a share of the profits. *Airwash* stresses that the owner's contribution to the running of the business is minimal, no commercial credit is required for the operations, and there are no inventories. *Airwash* takes care of analyzing the geographical location including five key demographic variables, part of a larger feasibility study offered to the prospective laundromat entrepreneur.

Siranet, another large Belgian turnkey operator, offers very clear criteria for choosing the location: a sufficient number of passers-by; an "engine" pulling in crowds, such as very well frequented shops within 100 metres of the laundromat; no uninhabited zones or "natural frontiers," such as a canal within 500 metres; a large façade with proper lighting; ideally a bus or tram stop, or a metro station nearby; preferably in the old city centre, not in an area exposed to vandalism, with parking possibly difficult but not impossible; and sufficiently far from the closest competitor. In other words: location, location, location.

The key operating principle is that there is as little to steal as possible. The equipment includes washing machines, at least one tumble dryer, a detergent dispenser, a banknote changer and, optionally, a token dispenser. There is usually a large table for sorting laundry. A wall clock is indispensable for keeping track of cycle times. There is a waste basket, perhaps even a recycling bin. The odd plant may stand in the corner. The inevitable wringer and telephone are also coin operated. Cheap plastic chairs may be available, but mostly the seating is sturdy and fixed to the floor. The fixed models look similar to the chairs at Brussels metro stations. The better equipped laundromats also have coin-operated vending machines for coffee, soft drinks, and snacks. You can consider the laundromat especially well equipped if there is an umbrella stand and a coat rack. These places suggest that self-regulation only works when there is very little to regulate.

Laundromats typically have few posters or ads adorning their windows, doors, and walls, but space is sometimes provided to ad agencies for extra revenue. The occasional poster affixed by a customer or the operator gives the customers a glimpse of the world at large. *Salon Lavoir Wassalon* had a huge poster with a large soap bubble with the text: "*Grippe Mexicaine! Desinfecte automatiquement. Votre ligne pendant chaque cycle de lavage!*" (Mexican flu! Disinfect your laundry automatically with each cycle!) The walls are generally left undecorated, with the exception of printed instructions, price lists, no-smoking signs, and the inevitable sponsored calendar. Handwritten instructions may add a little personal touch to mono-colour painted or tiled walls. Metal, plastic, and ceramics are popular materials because they are the easiest to clean.

While eerily intimate, the atmosphere of a laundromat is simultaneously impersonal, hospital-like and threatening. There is almost never anyone to give a helping hand or keep clients in check. Staff only visits to maintain the machinery or to clean the place up. The only security is provided by a CCTV camera, the existence of which is indicated with an image and the text "*souriez, vous êtes filmés*" (Smile, you're being filmed). Laundromats are open-all day all-week, so there are no dynamic LED "open" signs to attract clients.

Time and space almost disappear in the more clinical laundromats. In contrast to other types of small business, they seldom reveal anything about the life history of the entrepreneur. An exception to this rule is *Salon Lavoir Kapoor & Sons* in my neighbourhood. The neon sign includes an elephant and the flag of India in addition to a washing drum. With the exception of laundry chains, it is the advertising signs that usually contain the sole element of a personal touch. The aesthetics stress a rather uniform clarity and cleanliness with white and blue as the dominant colours. Bubbles are the favourite theme, but clouds, water droplets, and waves abound too. Washing machines, clothespins, and white laundry hanging on a line are also popular motifs. *The Blue Wash* even has a large mural painting with a blue sky, the sea, and a swimming pool surrounded with deck chairs.

It is the clientele that creates the greatest variation in laundromats. Newcomers to the city, civil servants living in temporary quarters, *au-pairs* living on their own, freelance and contract workers, immigrant families, football teams, and long-term tourists all join the cause. Some sit and stare at the washer drum, others read or escape to their own soundscape, while others leave the premises for the wash cycle. Children, in-laws or friends provide company.

The obvious demand for alternate uses is severely restricted. I came across this note on the window of a laundromat near a school: "Students who arrive at or leave the Lycée are requested to refrain from loitering around the school. The Place Bremer laundromat is not a meeting place. It is reserved exclusively for clients. Equally, at noon, the doorways of neighbouring houses are not places to have a meal or to leave detritus of varying sorts. Pupils caught violating these rules will be systematically and seriously sanctioned."

Random meetings and discussions among clients are typical. They may be limited to the practicalities of using and sharing washing machines. These were the topics of my discussions, too, when I used the laundromat up the street, having just arrived in Brussels. The fact is that many formerly easy routines become difficult in a new environment. It was somehow a relief to read the English-language travel blog *The Random Walk* on the use of self-service laundries (*laverie libre-service*) in Paris. Their first hint is that "if the door doesn't open if you pull, try pushing." It might say "poussez-push" and "You can fill multiple machines, just like in the U.S., if no one else is using them. The dryer works the same way—put the clothes in the machine, select the number of the machine from the central board, put in the money and press the button."

Laundromats are, in their own peculiar way, havens of peace. Excepting the humming of machines—which can lead to protests from neighbours— there is little by way of distraction, such as bubbling discussions or visual clutter. The steady spinning of the wash drums may induce you into a kind of relaxed hypnosis. It is also comforting to know that if you follow the instructions, the outcome of the process should not create any surprises.

On the whole, though, I find laundromats depressing. The force of circumstances is the only reason for frequenting them, and you wish to leave as fast as possible. Here the inhabitants of the global village are alone together. In the independent short film *Launderette*, a female customer crystallizes her wish to get away for good: "I want my own washing machine so that people cannot look at my knickers."

A Sense of Place and Belonging

Small and medium sized enterprises also have another, subtler function of creating space for the identity of those who have arrived in the city, and started to make it their own. In addition to call shops and laundromats there are, of course, a wide variety of other businesses run by owners and staff originating from or expressing an affinity towards some other part of the world. Some of these businesses cater mostly to the culinary or cultural tastes of a particular community or a geographically defined clientele but they serve, with the exception of a few religious shops, anyone—after all, they are entrepreneurial.

What is interesting about many of the businesses is how they reflect a singular presence that relates to multiple locations. One approach is to fashion such connections out of physical locations that exist or may have existed, geographically speaking. Another approach is to link historical, geopolitical, or mythical concepts that have at least some basis in geographic reality. Both approaches make way to understanding what it means to belong to different places.

These messages fall into a number of categories. A typical example of business communication that indicates such multiple belonging are the scores of businesses that associate Europe or Europeanness to a non-Belgian, even non-European, location. National flags are the most common form of expressing such an association. For instance, the flags of Poland, Pakistan, Portugal, India, or Turkey are often displayed with the EU flag. *Euro-Bangla*, *Euro-Punjab*, *Euro-India*, or *Euro-Afro* represent a fairly common type of business name in Brussels. This belonging seems to have a further social message. It would seem that linking the attribute "Euro" to the name of a location outside Europe expresses, among other things, some kind of an aspiration or achievement. It seems, for example, that this Euro attribute is used more often in association with Europe's old colonies. The linkage of formerly colonized countries with Europe could signify, then, that the formerly subservient region should now be treated on an equal footing. Conversely, I have not observed any *Euro-Australian*, *Euro-Canadian*, *Euro-American* or *Euro-Chinese* business names or signs. There is reason to think that these regions are seldom, if ever, linked to Europe in business signs because there is no great aspiration in these areas to being considered part-European, or that being on par with Europe would not be considered an achievement by the local population.

As a counterweight to the enthusiasm about Europe, there are business names that refer to the owners' and/or clients' home village, region, or personal past involving real or imaginary communities. In my neighbourhood, shops and cafeterias owned by Christians from the border region of Turkey, Iraq, and Syria are typically named according to this pattern. Business names such as *Medyat*, *Tur Abdin*, *Le Bon Samaritain*, *Les Jardins de Babylon*, *Mesopotamia*, *Michelangelo Time*, or *Chez Gabriel* all signify aspects of a Syriac-Aramaic-Assyrian culture with allusions to Mesopotamia as a geographical region defined by the Euphrates-Tigris river system, home of the Tur Abdin/Midyat region. A cradle of ancient culture, it is an area of Biblical reference and is home to modern-day Aramaic speaking settlements, as well as Christian communities. It is also a place where angels have had a strong role in many belief systems.

In addition to naming, the visual world of SMEs promotes historical buildings, regions, and images, along with historical and mythical characters. For example, the Polish food shop *Polski Sklep* has a large business sign juxtaposing two images that perfectly capture the divided Europe of the 1950s: the cultural palace of Warsaw, commissioned by Stalin, and the Atomium, a building modelled after the iron molecule in celebration of the peaceful use of atomic energy and built for the World Exhibition of Brussels. It is difficult to say if this sign is post-modern irony or a sincere attempt to finally make two (or three, if you include Stalin's Russia) countries on either side of the Iron Curtain shake hands, or both. What should we think of the deli that's sign sported the flag of Yugoslavia, together with a bunch of sausages, years after the country has fallen apart?

Brussels teems with areas where the past and present of social, ethnic, and cultural groups live parallel lives that sometimes intertwine, sometimes compete for cultural hegemony, and occasionally clash violently. A journey through Brussels with a focus on its SMEs helps us to understand the complex ways in which individuals from different backgrounds, when confronted with competing historical narratives, reflect upon and re-vision their identities and sense of belonging. It also gives us clues of the varying ways of cosmopolitan sociability.

On the whole, corner shops, cafeterias, call shops and other semi-public meeting spaces—with their signs, ads, displays, and decorations—bring back memories from various corners of the world. They also bring alive whole epochs: the time of Belgian colonialism, the collapse of the British and Ottoman Empires, the age of emancipation and independence struggles, the birth of nations and the disappearance of almost whole peoples, the legacy of regional conflicts, the organized immigration of workers and the unexpected arrival of their families, the Cold War era and, more markedly, the arrival of post-communist entrepreneurship. Even many of the older periods are still surprisingly present in Brussels, if you care to notice them. What could be tucked "away" in time or space, or retained only in the private memories of its inhabitants, is surprisingly "here" in Brussels.

***

LEARNING IDEOGRAMS: A STORY OF HOW CONGO'S BRAZZAVILLE IS BEING BUILT ANEW BY CHINESE COMPANIES

BY
SERGE MICHEL

As he awaits his limousine on the steps in front of his office, Claude Alphonse N'Silou scans André, his private secretary, indifferently. Everything about their appearance reveals the second man's hierarchical subordination to the first. The minister is grandiose: dark bespoke suit, white shirt, cufflinks, and a tie with black, blue, and grey stripes. The secretary slouches slightly, standing duck-like in oversized shoes. He has forgotten to remove the label (bearing the name of an anonymous brand) from his jacket's sleeve.

The minister responsible for construction, urban planning, housing, and land reform is an intimate of the President. He owns a number of well-situated villas in residential districts of Brazzaville, some of them rented to Western diplomats. He sent his children to school in France. We instantly recognize him as someone who has done very well for himself. The secretary, on the other hand, doesn't always take home enough money to properly feed his family. He got his job through a mentor to whom he remains in debt, and his fate hinges on the results of an election—a dangerously close race.

"Have the tiles arrived?" Claude Alphonse N'Silou asks.

"Only half of them, sir," André answers.

"Not broken?"

"Not too broken, sir."

The secretary hangs his head. The minister pushes out an angry sigh. He glances meaningfully toward a journalist who has just spent the last hour sitting in a leather armchair in the minister's air-conditioned office. That brief glance seems to say, "You are European, I was educated in Europe—we understand each other, we both love Africa, and we can't let it get screwed over!"

It can be frustrating to be a cabinet minister in the Congo, where roadblocks seem to shadow your every move, making any successful action even more improbable. The Roman tiles for the villas in the Bacongo district were ordered from Italy a year ago. Paid for in cold hard cash, then unloaded on the Pointe-Noire docks two months later. The shipment was badly stored, and part of it disappeared, no doubt sold on the black market by corrupt port or customs workers. Then there was no space to be found on the freight cars of the Congo-Océan railroad, whose crumbling line carries supplies to the capital in fits and starts. The rainy season came, mud jammed the tracks, the trains stopped running, then the trucks got stuck in the mud on the road parallel to the tracks. In Brazzaville, prices for food and construction materials soared—and still there were no tiles. At the Bacongo jobsite, the Chinese company has tried to protect the nearly finished roofs as best it can. "Why Italian tiles?" the minister was once asked by the Chinese foreman, a stocky, bowlegged man so short he barely reaches the knot in the minister's tie. Windows, doors, plumbing: all the Chinese materials for the 40 villas had arrived long ago. In the Republic of the Congo, the Chinese have means that cabinet ministers do not. Because they sell locomotives to the Congo-Océan railway and promise to repair the tracks, they can dictate which goods make it onto the freight cars.

Why Italian tiles? Because the minister studied architecture in Italy, where he wrote a thesis about modern airports. He even designed some Italian villas for Bacongo. He is very proud of them—two floors, Greco-Roman façade, garden and balcony, small garage. He believes his efforts to renew the neighbourhood are the perfect illustration of the mission the President has given him: to revitalize Brazzaville's urban landscape as part of the great national "New Hope" program. In the eyes of Claude Alphonse N'Silou, it's a simple business: he designs and the Chinese build. So what if the first manifestation of "New Hope" is housing for Congo's upper classes, most notably in Oyo, the President's home village, 400 kilometres north of Brazzaville, where every member of the Congo's ruling class has had a villa built by the Chinese to increase the odds of running into "the Prez" on weekends? And so what if the only truly driveable highway in the country is also a Chinese production that just happens to lead to Oyo, a route of little use to the average Congolese? What matters is that things are moving forward, and that the country is reawakening from the civil war that raged in the streets of the capital less than a decade ago.

The car, a black Peugeot limousine, finally appears. It is 11 o'clock in the morning and, with the sun high in the sky, the ministry buildings cast almost no shadow. Nor do the luxury autos parked in front, nor the trees bordering the grounds. The driver was probably ordered to wash the car—to impress the European reporter—but not having had enough time to wait for it to dry, the vehicle is now speckled with dust. Claude Alphonse N'Silou grimaces as he settles into the backseat. The convoy sets out, led by a silver jeep filled with armed guards. The jeep opens a channel through the capital's traffic jams. Another jeep, a blue one, brings up the rear. It is full of functionaries who have been summoned to the minister's tour of the Bacongo construction site.

Driving across Brazzaville in these conditions is an interesting experience. Ensconced in his seat, Claude Alphonse N'Silou points out, with a sweep of his arm, the buildings now being renovated by Chinese companies, repairing the damage caused by fighting a decade ago between the Ninja rebel movement and the government—the headquarters of the national electric company, those of the national oil company, a shopping centre.

"The Chinese are fantastic," he says. "They did the Alphonse-Massamba stadium for us, the department of external affairs, and the television station. Now they're working on the Imboulou and Ngiri dams, and the water system in Brazzaville. They're doing the airport. They're going to do the Pointe-Noire to Brazzaville highway. They're building housing for us. They're going to build an amusement park by the river. It's all decided, all done deals! It's all win-win! Tough luck for you French, but the Chinese are fantastic. As far as we Africans are concerned, the Chinese build things, but the Europeans never get around to building much."

A short detour via Camp-Clairon, where yet another Chinese company is busy tearing down Breton-style flats built in the late 19th century for French colonists. Under the minister's orders, they will be replaced by one thousand apartments in four buildings arranged around a tree-lined square and a shopping centre. The minister orders the convoy to stop on the shoulder of a dirt road where citizens of modest means are walking, carrying goods on their heads. A gaggle of wretched barefoot urchins stops playing football for a moment to check out the glittering limousines. The minister opens his tinted window to point out a giant billboard showing what Cité du Clairon will look like. The poster features five elegant people, including a couple with a baby stroller and another with a suitcase, positioned within a computer rendering of the complex. We can see façades punctuated with large windows and balconies rising above a patio shaded with yellow parasols. This might as well be Frankfurt.
"You know," says the minister after closing the power window, "we're rich now! With oil, wood, minerals, and everything else, we're growing at 6%. Better than Europe!"

A bit farther down the road stands the monument to the city's founder, the Franco-Italian explorer Pierre Savorgnan de Brazza, whose remains were returned to Brazzaville last year with much fanfare. The monument is a small pantheon, with a metal and glass cupola sitting atop 500 tonnes of marble imported from Carrara, Italy. Brazza is seen as a national hero, because he fought the brutal exploitation of the natives by the colonial companies of his time. Indeed, he is completely forgiven for having always travelled in a litter carried by black servants.

We pass the presidential district and the French cultural centre, the sight of which inspires the minister to take some jabs at the former colonial ruler.

"I'll be frank," he says. "The French can be so patronizing. The way they talk down to us—it must stop. It's a complete waste of time. And where are they now, anyway? They're getting the hell out of Africa! The French economy is going down, unemployment is going to go up in France. You know, I don't care if you're black, white, or yellow as long as you have something I'm interested in. It's win-win cooperation, as the Chinese say. You win, I win. We do business. Except with you French, all you care about is elections. Whether everyone got his ballot. Come on, enough already," he laughs. "Those kinds of relations are starting to annoy the people. The world is changing, the world moves very fast. Today our children want to go study in China, the United States, or Canada, rather than France. Attitudes change. And if France isn't careful, she'll have to go to the Chinese to buy things that could easily have been had here. France is incredibly blessed. France had a treasure, but at some point she forgot about it. She preferred to fight for something else, for democracy, governance, human rights. For *discourse*! It's a real shame. France's decline saddens me deeply. Good Lord, my children are French, you know! France allowed me to raise them under good conditions. I would very much like, if I ever had the chance, to be of service to France, but she refuses to give me the opportunity. I have a friend in the government who was visited by a Frenchman, who told him, 'I fought to have France resume cooperation with the Congo, and now I have something for you. I have a very nice project for you.' 'What is it?' my friend asked. 'A rainwater recovery project,' said the Frenchman. My friend looked at him in disbelief and just about tossed him out of his office on the spot. Rainwater recovery! That's a good project for Israel! We've got plenty of water here! There's water everywhere! The problem is getting it to people. Building water mains, like the Chinese are doing. Otherwise, just dig a ten-metre hole and voilà, you've got water."

The convoy passes the Pierre Savorgnan de Brazza School, once famous for its instruction in Russian. In 1965, five years after gaining independence from French colonialism, Brazzaville established relations with Moscow. A friendship pact followed in 1981. Many of today's Congolese architects and engineers were educated in the Soviet Union. They learned their Marx and Lenin by heart. They spoke the language fluently. When the USSR collapsed, the orphaned Congo descended into grinding poverty and a decade-long civil war. Help finally came from China, the other Communist power. But this was not about friendship between peoples, that pet topic of Soviet professors, but about raw materials. The growing Chinese economy, which some compare to unfettered capitalism, is so hungry for oil, iron, copper, and wood that it started to cause prices to soar. And that immediately translated into wealth for African producers. Deeming it too risky to simply be a buyer, China decided to set up shop in Africa, while insisting that the move was not at all a colonial venture. In recent years, a half million Chinese have moved to Africa. In every one of Africa's fifty countries, China buys its way in by funding the major infrastructure projects (bridges, roads, dams, railroads, housing) that the Western powers and their organizations, such as the International Monetary Fund and the World Bank, can no longer stomach. It has reached the point that the Pierre Savorgnan de Brazza School is now acclaimed for its Chinese courses. Every year the number of students studying Mandarin doubles.

The largest Chinese company in Congo is the International Economic & Technical Cooperative, from Weihai, a city of nearly three million (as many people as live in the entire Congo) on the shores of the Yellow Sea, in Shandong province. The city was recently twinned with Brazzaville. In the early 20th, Weihai was within a 700-square-kilometre territory that the British leased from China as a sanatorium and summer base for the British Eastern Fleet. In those days Weihai was known as Port Edward. Across the strait, Russia leased Port Arthur on the same terms. Today, Congolese cabinet ministers routinely visit Weihai, just as Chinese officials visit Congo. The Chinese never miss an opportunity to remind the Congolese that they too were once the victims of European colonialism, as a way of forging a fraternal bond with the Africans.

After passing the expansive grounds of the French ambassador's residence, we finally reach Bacongo. There are no lawns here, no fancy driveways. A single crumbling street, lined with humble shops, shacks, and eateries, runs parallel to the river. In the middle of the district, on the left, is a high wall broken by a gate. The gate's two pillars are decorated with silver Chinese characters on a blue background, proclaiming the efficiency of the Weihai International Economic & Technical Cooperative, while on the beam is a yellow banner with the words, "The ambition to do more for you—Vote N'Silou." It is the missing link explaining the minister's interest in this forty-villa construction site—his urgent desire to see the Italian tiles laid.

Claude Alphonse N'Silou was not only mandated by the President to revamp housing in the Congo, but also to be elected to represent Bacongo in the country's parliament. And that is no small thing, because most of the area's residents hail from the forest region of Pool, located along the river between Brazzaville and Pointe-Noire, where people took up arms against the President, to punish him for overthrowing his predecessor with the help of the Angolan army. In the Pool region, the rebellion was led by a dissident priest, and in Bacongo, by a former prime minister. Ten years ago, combat raged in the capital. That is why Bacongo's forty Chinese villas are not simply a cluster of Italian-inspired luxury homes, but a place of profound national importance: if they help elect Claude Alphonse N'Silou, they will symbolically snuff out the last remnants of the rebellion and complete the President's reconquest of the country.

The minister's convoy passes through the construction site gate, where it is greeted by the cheers of a hundred or so blue-uniformed Congolese workers who appear to have endured a lengthy wait in the sun. A dozen Chinese foremen stand beside them, most of them wearing green shirts, over which some wear a white T-shirt boasting a symbolic message in red letters: "Thank you, Mr. President." Without wasting any time, Claude Alphonse N'Silou enters a villa and reappears on the balcony, where he proudly expounds on the project. There he meets two Chinese workers who are painting the railing. He greets them.

"How's it going? Ah, you're here too? Hi, how's it going? Good? Ni hao! Doing well, guys? Ni hao! Ni hao! You see that roof over there? Congolese workers are laying the tiles, with just one Chinese foreman, and all at once we're solving the housing problem, the training problem, the knowledge transfer problem. Where's the Chinese who's running the site? Call the Chinese boss! Where is he? Get him up here! Where is he? Hello! Ni hao! See? I even speak Chinese! The company that's working here is involved in many industries, all over the country. They're also involved in mineral prospecting. Nobody speaks Chinese here, it's annoying. How's it going? Good? How are you doing? They work at night from six o'clock until what time? Eleven? You hear that? Not bad! They work until eleven at night! It isn't easy to rebuild a country. It takes lots of patience. For us, the most important thing is to lead the way, show that it can be done, that poverty isn't eternal, that we can modernize our cities. That's all I care about, showing that we can do things as well as others, that we can transform our urban fabric, transform the place where we live. What we want is to develop our country. If you're with us that's good—if not, then too bad! The most important thing for us is to develop the country. It doesn't matter who our partners are!"

The minister points out the houses, of which about ten seem nearly finished. The roofs are partially covered with Roman tiles that have been trickling in from Pointe-Noire. There are three models of villa, distinguished by the number of bedrooms. Named after fruits—safou, mango, and papaya—they are designed for the modern Congolese family: a husband and wife, each with a job and a car. The well-ventilated garage leads to a small sitting room, more intimate than the large dining room across the hall. The spacious kitchen opens onto the backyard in order to allow the servants to prepare some of the food outdoors. To ensure diligent homework, the two children each have a bright room with ample closet space. They share a double-sink bathroom, so they can brush their teeth together.

Does this Congolese family really exist? Or is it a dream, the fantasy of a cabinet minister educated in Europe? Bacongo families, whose traditional dwellings we see beyond the gates, have more than two children. Several women live with one man, along with numerous mothers-in-law and elders. Cooking is done in a hearth in the middle of a small courtyard, which does double duty as a henhouse. To make way for the first forty villas, the minister had the Chinese company raze a hundred or so earthen shacks with corrugated metal roofs. He generously compensated the residents, who are supposedly first in line for the new villas thanks to a sophisticated government loan program. In reality, the expropriated families have pocketed their cash and moved on to other neighbourhoods, such as the very popular Poto-Poto, while the eventual occupants of the villas will most likely be members of the Westernized government elite. The process seems to have been completely accepted: the expropriated families didn't ask for anything more, the remaining owners in the area have seen property values rise, and Bacongo's merchants are eager for more affluent people to move in.

From the balcony you can see the river, two or three hundred metres down the hill, wide as an ocean bay before it narrows into rapids a few kilometres downstream. On the other side of the river are the towers of Kinshasa. Eventually, every lot between the Bacongo road and the river will be expropriated to make way for a hundred more Italian-Chinese villas. To the right, there is a break in the metal barricade surrounding the construction site, to give the locals access to a drinking-water supply drilled by the Chinese. And indeed the locals are here to greet the minister, with considerable enthusiasm. Everyone seems to have a Chinese-made wheelbarrow inscribed with "Courtesy of N'Silou," in which they haul their water in jerry cans (another Chinese import), again inscribed with "Courtesy of N'Silou." Above the well a large placard proclaims: "A personal gift from N'Silou before the election, to help families and stop children from drowning in the river. Vote N'Silou."

It is noon and the Chinese crews are starting to leave the site in a pair of blue trucks for lunch at their compound, a kilometre away. On the balcony, the minister has finally been joined by the site boss, the short man who barely reaches his tie knot or, at times, even his knees, what with all the bowing and scraping he does. Embarrassed greetings: Claude Alphonse N'Silou knows only two words of Mandarin—hello and thank you—and the Chinese man cannot speak a word of French. The minister plucks a cellphone from the inside pocket of his jacket and calls Mireille, an interpreter. He tells her he would like to go meet the Chinese workers in their canteen, then passes the phone to the Chinese man. More bowing and scraping. Before getting back in his limo, the minister speaks to the Congolese workers, who remain gathered near the gate. He expresses his confidence in the progress he sees at the site and in the success of the President's "New Hope" program. He closes by saying how optimistic he is about his election prospects: if he doesn't win outright, he'll surely take it in the runoff. He receives a long ovation.

"This is the most difficult neighbourhood for this election," he says after settling into the Peugeot's backseat. "It was the neighbourhood of Bernard Kolélas, the rebel leader. But I think I can win. I'm the one who wrote the expropriation law, I'm the one behind the very generous compensation. One of the very encouraging things, which shows how much I'm appreciated, is that the people who received compensation wanted to demolish their houses themselves! And when you pass through there, the people wave and smile. Many of these families were destitute. The money we gave them for their piece of the shantytown was really unexpected. It allowed them to go into business, pay off debts, send their kids to school. Really, they're living better than before! Until now, the government never did much for the people. It was discredited and nobody took its promises seriously. Some time ago, people started to believe, because we're doing things differently. It's new, it's concrete. Slowly, slowly, we've started to lift a few of our fellow citizens out of poverty."

There is more applause for Claude Alphonse N'Silou when he walks into the Chinese canteen. A hundred-odd workers look up from their bowls, put down their chopsticks, and start clapping. "See, they're eating!" he says, beaming, to his secretary, and raises his arms in triumph. He shouts *"Bon appétit!"* and "Thank you for your work!" To get back to the limousine, the minister must walk a series of planks laid across the ground. The Weihai International Economic & Technical Cooperative compound is a vast mudflat punctuated with rusted-out machines and spare parts, rather Spartan dorms and showers, trucks, tires, stacked bags of cement, and great heaps of rebar. The only fastidiously kept corner is a large vegetable garden tended by the Chinese cooks, who grow

Chinese vegetables for the Chinese workers' meals. Congolese are not allowed within the compound, save the minister and his entourage. "I've got work to do, I've got to go now," he says as he drops off the European journalist in front of the Bacongo development. "Come see me at home tonight to continue our talk!"

The construction site is deserted. The Congolese workers have also gone to eat, in one of the modest eateries, which the security guard points out. To get there one must navigate earthen streets clogged with playing children. In a fly-ridden room, about fifty men stand and wait as the cook, a portly woman wielding a ladle, fills one bowl after another with manioc and a few vegetables. The workers are in a surly mood, and all are eager to express their frustration.

"We're paid at the bottom of the scale—1,800 francs (2.75 euros) a day—even though the minimum wage is 2,500 francs a day. Lunch costs 500 francs. To get to work in the morning and home at night is another 500 francs. So we're left with just 800 francs a day. We don't have a contract. No days off. No insurance. When we get injured on the job, we pay the costs. If it's a serious injury, we get fired. The Chinese are inhuman. They never stop working. They're aggressive. They treat us like slaves. If you make a mistake, they hit you with a board or a shovel. They hit you to hurt you. One day, I splashed a Chinese with a bit of wet cement. He got mad and hit me. Another time, I cut my thumb with a circular saw. No compensation, not even some medicine. The Chinese are bizarre. We have to deal with them because that's the way things are, but they're bizarre. They mistreat us. They call us monkeys."

Night falls over Claude Alphonse N'Silou's sprawling villa. One enters the finished part by crossing a construction site that seems to be the future site of endless colonnades and pillars topped with triangular gables. The future U.S. Embassy, next door, looks like a humble bunker by comparison. The Congolese workers lie down on the shoulder of the road, waiting for the minibus that will carry them home. The Chinese workers, on the other hand, have lit floodlights so they can keep working. The minister waits, lounging in a leather-trimmed sitting room, flipping through French television channels on a huge wall-mounted plasma TV set. The scuttlebutt in Brazzaville is that the Chinese gave a villa to every member of the government who does business with them. Claude Alphonse N'Silou claims he is paying the going rate for the work being done for him privately by the Weihai International Economic & Technical Cooperative, which he can afford thanks to the rent paid by the United States ambassador for another villa he owns.

"With the Chinese," says the minister, "nothing is free. They want money, and we also want to win. Once the two parties agree, we sign a contract. It's true that they do a little dumping, but as long as it works for us, it's OK. What we Africans want is to win. You say my fellow Congolese workers complain about being underpaid and mistreated by the Chinese? We have laws here, and I personally see to it that they obey the law. It's true that the Chinese have a slight tendency to cheat, but when we catch them we punish them. We monitor things. I've sent Chinese workers home because they behaved badly toward Congolese workers on jobsites. They don't always respect my countrymen. We aren't like them, our way of life is different. There are three million of us and more than a billion of them. So our attitude toward work isn't the same. In China, it's a matter of survival. Here too, but not in the same way. And when a person comes here and pushes another man to work beyond his physical limits, it becomes an act of aggression and I say 'stop.' There's something important to know about the Chinese. When they're in a hurry, they work in three shifts. And when that happens, the Congolese aren't on board, because we believe in living on a certain schedule. Only the Chinese work the night shift, and I don't like it. I'd like to see more Congolese workers on the Chinese sites. The problem is that our character is somewhat laid-back. Some of our young people still haven't grasped the importance of work, and often the Chinese get irritated by that. That can lead to harsh words, or sometimes even acts of violence."

A servant arrives with French sparkling water and leaves the sitting room, shuffling his feet across the marble floor. The minister is on a roll.

"I'm telling you, the Chinese are dangerous. I don't know how they do it, but they study every senior official, every cabinet minister. They ingratiate themselves, establish friendly relations. Once I had dinner with a group of important officials from both countries. One man from the Chinese commerce ministry talked to me about jazz, about Greco-Roman architecture. My God, those are precisely my interests! So I realized that it was a set-up. At the end, he told me we had things in common and we'd continue discussions. He called me at every stop on his tour of Africa—from Angola, from South Africa—and even after he got back to China, just to ask me how I was doing. Afterward, we realized that they did the same thing with every Congolese cabinet minister. Everyone had his own Chinese! Watch out—in ten years, they'll own the world!"

The minister is interrupted by a phone call. He takes a cellphone out of an inside pocket, and then a second one, and finally a furiously vibrating third one. André, his secretary, is calling. He says the tiles have all arrived, that the Chinese will work day and night to install them on the roofs of ten villas, and that the presidential visit to Bacongo can go ahead as planned in three days. The visit will take place the day before the first round of the parliamentary elections. There will also be a mass giveaway: more Chinese wheelbarrows, jerry cans, and T-shirts. The whole event will take place amidst a group of villas just completed by the Chinese—if Claude N'Silou is elected, it will be largely thanks to the Weihai cooperative. He puts down the phone with a smile and picks up the thread of his geopolitical musings.

"I'm under the impression that the Chinese who come here feel as though they're on a mission. For them, business is a vehicle of conquest. I think China's goal is to reclaim its status as the world's greatest power, as it was more than a thousand years ago. The Chinese have realized that Africa is a clean slate, a place forsaken by the West. And that it was ripe to be conquered. They've decided not to impose their values on people, but rather to come to us with respect for our way of life. It's a different approach. The Europeans preach development, democracy, and elections. The Chinese are interested in construction and trade. The Chinese know perfectly well that if they're too lax back home, it'll be chaos. And if China explodes, the whole world will pay. So a bit of strictness is needed. That's why they can approach somewhat authoritarian regimes with an understanding attitude. They don't try to change us, they don't want to teach us anything about governing. They believe peace depends on economic development. As far as they're concerned, when a country develops there's less social conflict. That's why Africans' point of view is much closer to that of the Chinese than that of the Westerners."

Postscript: Two weeks after this day spent with Claude Alphonse N'Silou in Brazzaville, N'Silou was elected, against all expectations and in the runoff, to the Congolese parliament for the district of Bacongo.

***

TORONTO, ONTARIO, CANADA, 2002

FEELING FOREIGN: WHAT HAPPENS WHEN A HOSPITAL LOOKS JUST LIKE A SHOPPING MALL

BY
DAVID THEODORE

Bloody hospitals. Sometimes English words are the best ones to use. *Damn.* Some words are round and solid in your mouth. Or in your head. Even when you don't say them out loud. English ones are good for that. But why can't they speak our language? Just talk to us. Ask us what we need. We are the most. We are patient. We need the help. We are the sick ones. Our children need attention, succor, care. Why should we adapt ourselves to them? Don't they have sick kids? Don't they understand what it means when Queenie is sick? Shouldn't they be adapting to us?

Sometimes they talk about changing. Changing things to suit us. Changing the way they talk. But that's not what happens. What happens is we change to suit them. Can they change the way they talk? The way they see? The way these bloody waiting rooms make you wait and wait and wait? All that glass and green steel. Big-big. Speedy elevators. We do what they want. Where they want. When they want. Meryam told me Muslims gave one million dollars to a hospital in Brampton. What for? Sickness is not just doctors. Health is not just doctors and waiting rooms and machines. Health is food and family and water and money.

We know sickness. We know doctors. But hospitals? Hospitals are a Toronto thing. Like Burger King and Disney and cancer. People here go to the hospital to have their babies. Then they go to the hospital not to have their babies. Then they go to the hospital to die. Here they are always going to the hospital.

Here they love hospitals! They always think just because they have something that it's special. I mean, a coloured man for president, what's so special about that? What was Ghandi? Chairman Mao? It's a difference that makes no difference.

What do they do with a million dollars? That would buy a lot of posters. And a lot of Halal dinners and biryani. I hate the posters. I do not have venereal disease. I do not want my children to have checkups. I do not want my children to be diverse. They need to be well. I would be grateful if they could be well. How does a poster make them well? How does a poster about good food give food to my children? That's not what I mean. I mean, my children have good food. But for the other children who don't. How does having a poster in this plastic place bring food to children? Or the Winnie the Pooh sticker? Just silly.

They put up travel stuff here, too. Mountains and trees. White people skiing and bumping little beach balls around. Like we are going to go on a little trip. A little vacation. Who thinks of these things? And all these magazines. Who wants to touch them? If we weren't sick before we got here, just touch some of those magazines! Then for sure you will have diarrhea. That's the problem. Everything here is something to look at. Posters, magazines, all the hospital people in their colourful uniforms, the plastic chairs, the yellow elevators, the artwork, and that dancing pig! Is it supposed to take your mind off the sickness? Doesn't it just make you sick?

Well, it's not too bad today. But Queenie is not so sick. This is just a checkup.

I don't want to checkup. Why when one child is sick does my whole family have to come here, to a place of sickness? How is that healthy? Do sick people here go shopping? Do they take sick kids to ride on the Ferris wheel? Why does this damn place look like the shopping mall?

Sometimes here is where you are, and there's no sense making it like you're somewhere else. Maybe they'll make a prayer room. A million dollars! Maybe a prayer room is as bad as a Disney movie about a talking fish or Aladdin. It's out of place. In the wrong place. Fake. Like a plastic tree. Or a nurse who smiles but isn't friendly. Why are Muslims giving money away? To put plastic chairs in waiting rooms? Is it to make here look like there? Or to make us part of the furniture here? A plastic chair. A vinyl cushion. A flat-screen television. A mother with her sick daughter. A help desk. Just so long as people fit in. *Damn.* Just as so long as we don't look out of place. Don't look foreign. Lost. What is she doing now? *What are you doing now Queenie?*

This is not our place. It's our turn soon. This waiting is easier than before, easier than when Queenie had to stay here. That was hard. That was harder than sitting waiting to get a checkup. They put her in a private room without any other kids! How was she supposed to like that? All by herself in a room. Just imagine. What kind of crazy idea is that! Just silly. I tried to stay with her. There is a bench that folds out into a bed. But then I couldn't sleep. And I couldn't look after Buzzie and Irfan. Queenie spent her time asleep.

I guess it was not different really. I waited there, too. She was sick. So pale. Waiting for the doctor. Waiting for the nurse. Waiting for morning. Waiting for something to stop. To start. What could I eat? There's no food here. They have Burger King. I guess that's for the bigger kids. The kids who play the Internet and eat burgers and pizza and French fries. But that's not food. Not here! And not at home. French fries? I sometimes went down to the food place and ordered some soup. All bright yellow and red and plastic. And green benches. Not a place you want to eat. Not when your child is sick. Bloody damn. It is just like when we go to the shopping mall. Is that what families do here? Go shopping? Even when their child is sick? It makes me want to scream, but I don't. I won't smile though. I won't. I wanted to turn that place upside-down.

Later I could take her down to the fountain. But going up the slope to get into the restaurants—to where the pizza is—that's hard for a wheelchair. Especially for me because I had to push both her and the IV. More tubes. More plastic tubes. *Bloody stupid.*

Queenie's room looked down into the atrium. Not even outside. No window to see the people outside and the buildings and lights. But like outside. Fake like so much here. Water fountains like it was a big outdoor park. When I am sick I don't want to go to the park. Queenie didn't notice the fountains. Or the pig... is it a pig? But Buzzie did. He liked to come with me, even though it was scary to see Queenie and all those tubes and machines. So pale. Buzzie liked the elevators. The transparent windows. I liked those because they make me safe. If the elevator stopped, then everyone could see we were in there and could climb a ladder and get us out. He liked watching people go up and down. He could see when Murzad arrived to take us home. He liked to ride the elevator all the way down. He says they are yellow because they are for kids. He likes the wheels and pulleys coming down. They're fast. They're really fast. All the way up and all the way down. So pale.

Queenie come sit down. No. Come now. At least they've taken that disgusting yellow tape off. How can you watch your kids in a place like that? Every second chair cover in yellow tape marked "danger." You don't want to bring your kids to a place like that. Not when they're sick. *Bloody damn.* Of course they blamed that on the Asians, too. SARS. The nurses told me that at Sunnybrook Hospital it was worse. Here they just closed down the atrium. They made everyone wash their hands when they came in. And you had to sign up, check your name off on a list.

So much for making it like a city street. The big entrance, that is. The big big big glass wall and the fountains and everything. It's supposed to be just like walking in a street. There are shops to buy clothes, and yogurt and Starbucks and Body Shop and a library and a gift shop. And a pharmacy. That makes sense. I liked the pharmacy here. I don't like asking Murzad to go to the shopping mall. I don't have to find some other place to get medicine. And someone from the hospital can translate and explain, make things clear. I'm sure some mothers come here even when their kids aren't sick. Just to shop. But with SARS, the shops stopped making sense. What kind of street do you need permission to walk down? At Sunnybrook, they had to close everything down. They had thirty-six entrances and had to close them down. Or something like that. They only left the main door open. They started the yellow tape thing, apparently. It was supposed to keep you from getting sick. I guess it worked. I never got SARS! And I had to come here a lot. But what were we so afraid of? Something invisible? Something that might happen? Queenie's doctor looked so tired. That bloody tape changed everything. Like it was Asia's fault. Like I was not supposed to be there. Like I should be ashamed she was sick because someone else was sicker.

Anyway, everyone knows doctors and hospitals don't do much. I mean, if you break your leg, they know how to fix it. If they want to take pictures of your brain or your baby, they can do that. But make you better? How? Their babies don't die here. Or their mothers. I've seen a lot of dead babies and dead mothers. But that was in the countryside. It's not so bad in the cities. Here it's not so bad everywhere. We are grateful, I guess. But that's because of food, not doctors. Life is hard in the countryside. Bad water. Dirty food. War. Those things will make you sick. And no doctor will make you better. No hospital, either. If you go to the hospital and you get better you'll get bad again as soon as you go home. Buildings aren't magic. The hospital is just there to make the doctors feel smart. Like they were actually helping you. The buildings just make it easier for the doctors to see a whole bunch of people at once. That's how they get paid so much. Hospitals. But they don't make you better. They're just big-big. They just make the doctors feel good. They make the nurses feel friendly even when they don't know they are insulting me. Without respect. They make that bloody information lady feel helpful. Well, I can smile too. Under the big glass dome. All that green steel. A big cow. Restaurants, food, shopping. *Bloody damn.* You can get used to it, but you can't adapt. We are not finches.

Meryam says I should be grateful. But I'm not. I'm grateful that Queenie is well. That all this plastic and Winnie the Pooh is some other place. This is not my life. This is not my place. That this is just a checkup. I am grateful. I'm grateful that Queenie is well. That Buzzie and Irfan are well. That they can grow up here at least for a little while with Murzad's parents. That's better than the countryside. Even though it's hard too. That's better than the little places outside the city I remember with bad water. But the hospital did none of that. The hospital just tries to make us more like them. More shopping. More smiles. They fix you up. But they can't make you well. I am grateful for the fix-up. I am not grateful for the big glass walls. The glass ceilings. The green steel. These plastic chairs.

I know I'm different. I know I'm different *here*. They got Queenie to be part of a study. They signed her up. A couple of young women. Students, they said. They want to know what kids have to say. They tried not to be disrespectful. They were friendly. They were trying to be helpful. They took her around the atrium and asked her questions. That was better than waiting here for the doctor. Better to be studied than just to be waiting. Maybe something good will happen? That's what I told Murzad. He was angry, I think. Was it disrespectful? What if it helps someone else? What if it helps Queenie?

She got a camera to take pictures. They wanted to know about the building. What does a child know about buildings? But she had lots to say. That's Queenie! She says it doesn't smell like old people. She says she doesn't like the stairs. She counted them. If you walk up to her floor, that would be one hundred steps. Twenty steps for each floor. And she doesn't like the cages. I don't know if that's what they are, but that's what they look like. Green metal cages on the balconies. You could sit in them and look through them and look down at the fountains and the people and the pig. The wires made her worried like someone has done something like jumped off them before. Are they protecting someone? Who needs protection in a hospital? Are we not safe here? Where is she? *Queenie! Come sit down here. Come.*

But it was fun. Queenie got one of her photos printed in the toaster. She told them what she thinks. She's not a goodie-goodie. She wouldn't want to just say something pleasant. To be nice. She may never get a husband. Unless it's a new one. I mean, not a new one really. One from here. A man who likes baseball and not cricket. Ha! One who was born in a hospital. How will he convince Murzad? Will Queenie fight? *Queenie? Be patient now. Yes, be patient now.*

We put it up at home. The photograph. She took a picture of a tree. Not inside, but outside. Across the street. I think it's sad. All of these kids, cooped up like chickens in a big coop. Getting fatter. The wires are like cages. I know they're benches, but why do they have to be wires? Queenie was funny. She said it was good for kids in wheelchairs. Maybe she just doesn't remember how it was before. How could she? She said that with the wheelchair, she didn't want to go out of the room with the gown. She didn't want to be seen wheeling around in the gown with dirty hair and all that jazz. So she liked her room. It's just me that felt trapped there. She thinks those windows are special because you get to see the people down there — when you're locked up — well not locked up — but when you are in a room — you kind of feel like you are with the other world. It's not a problem for her. Just for me. For the family. She likes people and talking with strangers and nurses a lot. She can charm Murzad now. But he's not going to like it. Once she starts talking back. Questioning. Will he blame the hospital? He already hates it. I think he's proud we know our way around here.

Bloody bloody damn! No. Here. Take this. Please Queenie. All right. There's no light in the waiting room. When will it be our turn? No sunlight that is. Everything that looks natural is fake. There are no windows. They have big wall-size photographs. Big-big. Trees almost as big as real trees. Bloody mountains. What a laugh. It's like having a picture of a tree is just as good as having a tree. I would have a tree. A real tree. And windows. Real windows. And I would take away the clinic. The nurses. The other patients. The fake walls. The nurse says sick people get better faster in rooms with a view outside. What about waiting rooms? Do sick people get better when they all wait together in one room? Shouldn't they have a window outside? But I don't want to look outside, really. Outside of here would still be the wrong place. It's like the big glass walls. And the glass ceiling. Glass doesn't make anything disappear. You can see through it, if the light shines just right, but that's all. Walls are walls. You're on one side or you're on the other side. Even fake walls. And here both sides of the wall are wrong. They're both the wrong place.

We are waiting for our doctor here, but not really our doctor. Not the doctors who have come over here like us. When our doctors get here, they are told they aren't doctors. They have trained. They have been to school. They have helped people. Healed them. Watched them get sicker and die. Consoled the crying mother. Told you the bad news. The bloody diagnosis. But once they get here, that's not good enough. They can't be doctors here. All they did is change places, change countries. Move from one building to another. In one they were doctors. In the next they were taxi drivers! Suddenly they don't know anything. They are stupid. They don't know how to practice. Instead they drive taxis. Doctors driving taxis!

No one respects you when you're not wearing blue jeans. And then no one respects you when you do. They think I am trapped here. Because I cannot leave home by myself. I have to wait for Murzad to bring me here. Because he's my husband. The nurses think I wait too long. That I get sicker waiting for him to help. Or that my kids do. That it's his fault Queenie got worse. Yellow elevators can't fix that. Pigs on tightropes and Disney posters can't fix that. Do they really help people here? Can they help anyone? Is it any better if I have to come here by myself? Why can't they come to me?

Meryam had the best idea. They don't know our language at the hospital. They don't know how to treat each other with respect. With respect for family. With respect for mothers. And they don't let our doctors work here. Our doctors are taxi drivers. So when she has a medical problem, she calls a taxi! Then she can speak to a doctor in our language. "Culturally sensitive help." That's what she says. "In an accessible and non-intimidating space." I like Meryam.

Doesn't anyone understand how stupid this is? It can make you feel very intimidated and kind of scared, like, especially if you're a young person and you're just walking into the building and you know that you're here for medical reasons. Because when you go to a hospital you're in a hospital because of a bad reason. You're in here because you're not feeling good, or something's wrong so you need something to cheer you up. Does the pink pig do it? Does it make the kids feel good? Maybe for Buzzie. But not for Queenie. And not for me.

Kids get diarrhea. Now Murzad has diabetes. All that glass. The steel. The yellow elevators. It's supposed to help you find your way. So we won't get lost here. But we are lost here. Or not me. I know where I'm coming from. I don't have to smile like this is a real park. Like this is a real place. Like being here makes me healthy. Makes us better.

Sometimes where you are is where you are. Where are you? *Queenie? Where are you?*

***

AMSTERDAM, THE NETHERLANDS, 1968-1995

INTERPRETING MODERNISM:
HOW AN AMSTERDAM HOUSING DEVELOPMENT
CHANGES WHEN SURINAM GAINS INDEPENDENCE

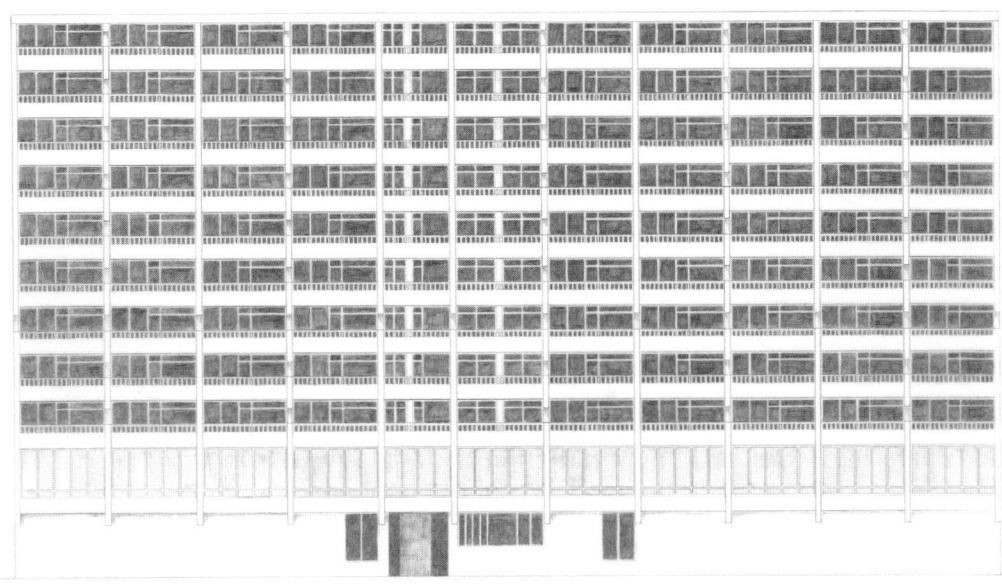

BY
WOUTER OOSTENDORP AND JOUKE SIESWERDA

This is the true story of a fictional flat. The events described in this story all happened in various places throughout the Bijlmermeer from 1968 to 1995. For the benefit of the narrative we have condensed these events and tell the story of one exemplary building.

Prologue
She was built at the end of the post-war reconstruction era in the capital of the Netherlands: Amsterdam. She was, however, not an ordinary building, nor located in an ordinary part of town, but part of the most beautiful and most modern town ever: the Bijlmermeer. The Bijlmer (as this part of Amsterdam is colloquially called) was the architectural embodiment of the Dutch welfare state and a shining example of Modern urban planning—better than the canals, better than Berlage, and better than the General Expansion Plan (Algemeen Uitbreidingsplan or AUP).

She was raised to be the ultimate solution for the polluted, dilapidated, and crowded cities. A modern city expansion in its purest form: large dwellings arranged in high-rise flats, placed in a lush and green environment. A strict segregation of program would guarantee a quiet and clean neighbourhood with an abundance of leisure possibilities. It would be the safest living environment in the country, as the motorized traffic—lifted high above the ground—was completely isolated from pedestrians and cyclists. She was taught the principles of light, air, and space; an emancipatory machine that would allow (middle class) people and communities to flourish, she was, in short, the "city of the future."

It is apparent that her parents had, as parents do, great expectations. And, as often is the case, her life story is much less straightforward. It was more like a winding road with a lot of unexpected turns. It is not a happy story, but it is not a tragedy either: between the lines interesting things can be found and important things can be learned.

Youth
Although she was built in the late 1960s, she had existed in the minds of her designers much longer than that. As it became clear that the Western Garden Cities, built under the AUP, would not be sufficient to deal with the increase in population (the post-war baby boom) and the higher living standards (fewer people in bigger dwellings) a new solution had to be found; a quick, cheap and, at the same time, prestigious solution.

The name of her father was Siegfried Nassuth; he led the design team of Amsterdam's Department of City Development. He was a man with a strict egalitarian vision of society who drew inspiration from the socialist housing schemes designed and built in the Soviet Union. These housing projects were designed with collective facilities, which were meant to relieve the worker's load, stimulate communal life, and emancipate the masses. For the Bijlmer, Nassuth envisioned equal opportunities for everyone and ample possibilities for the personal development of its inhabitants; the urban fabric would express and facilitate these values.

If Nassuth was her father then Cornelis van Eesteren was her grandfather. The ideas of the Department of City Development in Nassuth's time stemmed directly from principles formulated by CIAM (1928–1959) and Functional Modernism. These were introduced to the Netherlands by Van Eesteren, who had been chairman of CIAM and the head of the Department of City Development before Nassuth. He also had been one of the designers of the AUP, which formed the basis of the new radial structure of Amsterdam; satellite cities fanned out from the city core, separated from each other by vast green spaces. To the southeast lay the Bijlmermeerpolder, the last remaining possibility for expansion. Here the next step in the renowned urban planning tradition of Amsterdam would be made. The Bijlmer had to be an even more thorough and consequent execution of the Modernist planning principles than the Western Garden Cities built under the AUP.

She was built with the latest industrial techniques. These were times of serious housing shortages and the challenge was to build fast and in great numbers. She was therefore cast in concrete, with a façade of concrete bricks and long concrete galleries. She rose ten storeys high and bent twice at a 120 degree angle. When she was ready they named her Bloemenoord.

Because of the pressing demand for middle class (single family) housing she was the first of a big family. Her siblings, born soon after her, were given illustrious names like Frissenstein, Grubbehoeven, and Kruitberg. The whole family together formed hexagonal patterns that from above vaguely looked like a honeycomb. All the flats were connected by an indoor pedestrian street on the first floor, but more importantly these corridors connected the whole family with the parking garages and through this with the highways and rest of the city. The inhabitants would reach the garage by car and walk to their homes without getting wet and without touching the ground. Traditional (crowded and dangerous) streets were made obsolete. It was a kind of Jetson-like fantasy, with fly-overs, sky bridges, ultra modern docking stations, and a baggage service that would reach from your car to your apartment.

Inhabitants would enter the Bijlmer via one of the elevated roads looking down on the green fields and parks. Due to industrialization and mechanization people would have much more free time; the green courtyards would be ideal for all kinds of leisure activities. Driving on the high roads one could watch the spectacle below. But the monumental apartment buildings would tower above everything else. Coming closer to Bloemenoord the exit-ramp would lead directly to the parking garage. From here the indoor street would provide access to the elevators. The street would be sunny and lined with collective facilities like bars, daycares, play areas, and hobby rooms; it would generate liveliness and form the heart of social life in the building. These collective spaces were essential to the Bijlmer plan as they would compensate for the drawbacks of living in a high-rise and would be the ultimate expression of collective living. The elevators rose up to the galleries, leaving behind the bustling activity. The galleries offered spectacular views and gave access to the private domains.

The apartments, with an average size of 100 square metres, were quite big, certainly compared with those in the Western Garden Cities, which measured 70 square metres on average. They would be equipped with the most modern kitchens, bathrooms and fixtures; ideal for modern living.

In line with Nassuth's egalitarian and industrial principles, he raised all his kids the same. Ninety percent of all dwellings in the Bijlmermeer were located in high-rises like Bloemenoord. And of those apartments the biggest part were intended for typical Dutch families and had five rooms. The layout of the plans was sober but well designed. There was a kitchen near the entrance, a living room down the hall, and three bedrooms and a bathroom to the right. The hallway between the bedrooms could function as a play area for the kids. The whole building was designed as a machine for living, and a very specific way of living at that.

Bloemenoord's youth was relatively carefree and her first steps were promising. The plans were met with great enthusiasm by architects and politicians. The scarce notes of criticism were drowned by the high praise of the press. Most people seemed to agree that this was indeed the future of the city. The first people to take up residence in Bloemenoord in 1968 were pioneers who believed a new way of living was possible here. These people, however, were not all large families with three or four children and a dog. They were intellectuals, artists, gays, and socialists. A different crowd than foreseen, but a crowd determined to make the most of their new home. They all came to the Bijlmer with a shared belief in a new society; a society where people lived *together* and had the opportunity to fully develop themselves.

The planners, however, had not really thought about the management of the collective facilities. Bloemenoord was furnished with a couple of undetermined spaces, but who was to pay for their use? When the housing corporation figured that the inhabitants had to rent these collective spaces if they wanted to use them, they remained empty... but only for a while. These pioneers had come to live here for a reason, after all. After a lot of meetings and much protesting to no avail, they simply broke open the door and squatted a couple of the spaces in the belly of Bloemenoord. They christened the space "Binnenpret" (inside joke) and started a bar, a cafeteria, and... a TV station. This was quite easy: all the TV cables were already built in; it was just a matter of tapping into the system. At first the transmissions were of a practical nature (cooking, do-it-yourself tips, etc.) but later on politicians also came over for an interview.

Soon all kinds of informal activity sprung up. Since a lot of journalists happened to live in the Bijlmer, a newspaper was easily started and would stay around for quite some time. Other establishments emerged, like the Café de Nachtegaal and the Bonte Kraai bar. After a few years, the corporations and the municipality finally caught up with the inhabitants and subsidized the building of a pavilion right between Bloemenoord and one of her brothers (of course connected with the corridors on the first floor). The TV station moved there, and the bar as well. There were places for meetings, tables for card games, and a snooker table. The famous musician/doctor Boy Edgar gave performances there and started something of a jazz tradition that carried on long after his death.

There was no lack of drive and initiative. The new inhabitants stuck together, especially when there were issues with the housing corporation or the municipality. When the architect of Bloemenoord decided it was time to install the plating on the (up till now) semi-transparent fence, the residents picked up their wrenches and screwdrivers and removed the plating in one evening. They were reattached more firmly the next time, but with crowbars they were just as easily taken down again. In the end the housing corporation let the people decide for themselves. The people from the Bijlmer knew very well what they wanted, and what they did not want.

The people in the Bijlmer were resourceful, but it is clear that the situation was far from ideal and more issues kept requiring their attention. Bloemenoord and her family found herself quite isolated from the rest of the city. The planned (and promised) subway connection to the centre had still not been built, neither had the big shopping centre (with all the facilities that a city needs). The few collective spaces that were actually built proved to be bare and expensive, and nobody had really thought about who was to maintain them and pay for them. It all came down to the enthusiasm and professionalism of the inhabitants.

Meanwhile, the rents kept going up. The ambitious plan had turned out to be much more expensive than expected: overall building costs had increased drastically and labour wages had exploded before construction began. Moreover, the contractors drove a hard bargain and the subsidies from the national government were cut. The apartments became so expensive to build that they could not be rented out as social housing any more and they were placed in the "free sector." Social housing was subsidized and regulated by the government while the free sector was open to anyone who could afford it. This shift was meant to keep the plan affordable, but more drastic actions were necessary. Under the influence of the contractors and the government the plan was stripped to its core. More and more siblings were born, but with fewer and fewer facilities: distant cousins without collective spaces, with smaller apartments, with longer galleries and fewer elevators. And, as there was no money left for the proper maintenance of gardens and parks, more and more of these identical apartments stood alone in an empty, windy expanse.

People started to protest against the high prices and the promises that were not kept. Where was the bustling liveliness? Where was the Garden of Eden? Where was the city of the future?

After numerous strenuous (but ultimately useless) protests, people started to abandon Bloemenoord. There were other places they could go, after all. Just as construction of the Bijlmer started, the national government enacted a new memorandum on spatial planning. Instead of dealing with the housing shortage within the city limits, the new strategy was to build on the outskirts of smallish towns and villages. Suburbia, the government had decided, was the new city of the future.

All of this led to an increasing vacancy rate and apartments were left empty. But when our heroine looked around her she could still see new nephews and nieces arriving. The municipality—in their haste to build as fast as possible—had already given out the contracts to the builders. Flats were still being built at a fast and steady pace, even though there was no one to live in them.

Adolescence
At this point another story becomes important. Forty-seven hundred miles southwest of the Netherlands lay one of the last remnants of the Dutch colonial empire: Surinam. It had been part of the kingdom since 1667, and since the 1950s Surinamese had been coming to the Netherlands in search of better prospects. The early 1970s saw increasing unrest in the colony as it was working towards independence. A lot of Surinamese were already living in the Netherlands by then, but a great deal more moved here while they were still sure they had Dutch passports. When Surinam gained its independence in 1975 the Dutch government offered the Surinamese people the choice over their nationality, which caused a drastic increase in Amsterdam-bound emigrants on the flights toward Europe. In the end there were almost as many Surinamese living in Holland as in Surinam.

The government had to deal with this increased influx of newcomers. Their initial strategy was one of dispersal. Spreading out these "new" Dutch citizens in small groups across the country was believed to stimulate the integration process. As the Surinamese arrived at Schiphol airport, their first stop was Amsterdam. Here they were temporarily housed, in decrepit but expensive pensions, awaiting their relocation to smaller towns all over the country. For a lot of them, however, Amsterdam was the final stop. No one really wanted to take care of these newcomers and the smaller municipalities simply did not have the means. The pensions proved to be very expensive for the city and, like a good deal of the housing stock, in very bad shape. Quickly, an alternative had to be found.

These newcomers, though, presented Dutch legislation with a problem. The strict rules and guidelines regarding the social housing sector were not designed for this situation. It was impossible for immigrants to apply for social housing. The only option that remained was the free sector.

This is where Bloemenoord re-enters the story. The complaints of the inhabitants had not gone unnoticed and the now overwhelmingly negative publicity in the press had caused her image to come to an all-time low, and as a result the vacancy rate was going up. At the same time, there were some 3,500 Surinamese stuck in pensions in Amsterdam urgently looking for a place to live. It did not take long before the municipality started to direct them to the Bijlmer, where there were enough empty apartments. The high prices, though, led to overcrowding as numerous families had to share an apartment in order to pay the rent. In one known case there were twenty-four people living in one apartment: twelve adults and twelve children.

For a large part this migration also happened in a more natural manner. The Bijlmer was close to the airport and a lot of Surinamese already had (distant) relatives living there. Moving to the Bijlmer was a logical step. Together they created a little piece of Surinam in the Netherlands. By now the airline from Paramaribo to Amsterdam had been nicknamed "the Bijlmer Express".

What these new Dutch citizens found there was not something they were used to. The newcomers imported a totally different living culture and they had a certain carefree way of adapting to their new surroundings. The tight modern machines, so specifically designed for the modern Dutch family, were reinvented in ways nobody had foreseen.

The generous apartments (by Dutch standards) in Bloemenoord were not big enough to accommodate the extended Surinamese families. As a result, some people simply connected multiple apartments themselves by breaking away either walls or floors. A bedroom turned out to be just as well suited for use as a dog kennel. Chickens could be kept in the kitchen sink. And why could a campfire not be lit in the living room?

Walking along the galleries you could now smell exotic food coming from the kitchens. Some of the apartments were even turned into makeshift restaurants. The smells and tastes from Surinam were never far away. A couple of floors down, the indoor street could be mistaken for a market. All kinds of exotic fruits and vegetables could be found here.

Bloemenoord was not designed for the specific needs of this totally different group of people. The Surinamese were used to spending a good part of their day outdoors. The Dutch climate made this impossible most of the year. Transferring all their activities inside caused some nuisance, to say the least. The poorly insulated apartments were not designed for extensive cooking, music making, animated conversation or parties.

They also imported their religious beliefs. Although for a good part Catholic, a lot of Surinamese also still adhered to traditional ideas about their ancestors' spirits: the winds or Winti. Some apartments doubled as informal Winti temples. People could come here to get medical or spiritual assistance from a Winti priest. Public life was not attuned to these newcomers. Where could they house their churches? Where could they celebrate weddings? Space was soon found in the disused parking garages. All over the Bijlmer churches nestled in the most tucked away places. Only the gospel music gave outsiders any clue as to what went on there.

What did catch the eye were the brightly coloured birds that would be brought out on warm summer days. In the parks of the Bijlmer the Surinamese continued their tradition of bird-singing contests. Two caged male birds would be placed next to each other and the one that sang most frequently within a five-minute time frame was the winner. Especially popular was the betting that took place during the contests. Illegal bird importation flourished: they were transported rolled up in a newspaper or strapped to a leg. The pet stores offered an enormous variety of tropical birds and other animals.

The way the Surinamese settled in the Bijlmermeer illustrates the self-organizing capacity of the neighbourhood and its inhabitants. This slightly anarchistic tradition was started by the idealistic pioneers and was carried on by the newcomers in the 1970s and '80s. Whatever lacked in their neighbourhood, whether it was a bar, a daycare or a church, the people from the Bijlmer just started themselves, informally.

Another great example is the petting zoo that sprang up at the feet of Bloemenoord; it is still there today. It started with two chickens and a couple of rabbits that needed to be looked after. They found a home in the storage facilities on the ground floor. Soon a rooster followed, and a couple of sheep. The farm had to move outdoors where, without any permits, a pigsty, a hay barn, a pony shed, and an information centre for school children were built. Everything was constructed by locals with materials that were lying around or could be obtained cheaply. The petting zoo was a big success. For a while the people from the Bijlmer even produced their own cheese.

Adulthood/Midlife Crisis

As said, all this curious and foreign behaviour caused quite some nuisance for the average Dutch population. It was not, however, just a cultural issue. Socioeconomics were also a factor, as a large part the Surinamese came from small villages; they were poor and still struggling to find their place in

Dutch society. They were busy adapting, and not too fussed about throwing the garbage in the garbage chute. It could just as easily be thrown over the balcony.

The green spaces around Bloemenoord were now filled with litter and the strangest things were hanging from the trees. The staircases were used as a public toilet. The collective spaces were closed due to bad management. Instead of a lively and social meeting point, the corridors were now generally a place best avoided.

Meanwhile, reports were published on the "criminal behaviour of the coloured people." Though it was true that the crime rate in the Bijlmer was relatively high, the population was also relatively young. Compared with native Dutch youths of the same age group the difference was actually not that big. But the problems were directly being associated with the high ratio of immigrants. This led in a lot of cases to a political and media focus on the ethnic factor, rather than a healthy debate about the social and economic issues that needed to be addressed. There was no doubt though that crime was an issue, and people did feel unsafe.

The housing corporation was very much aware of these problems and was afraid that they would accumulate in Bloemenoord. It enacted a dispersal policy: no more than 30% of the flats could be occupied by immigrants. This was, of course, racial discrimination but the alternative, they said, was the first ghetto known to Holland.

The corporation, however, was not able to cope with the high vacancy rate indefinitely and with the statement, "We do not discriminate," it abandoned the dispersal policy. This resulted in a further concentration of people who, because of their socioeconomic position, where not able to maintain their living environment. At the time, intensive socioeconomic assistance from the government did not yet exist so these people were left to their own devices. The disinterest in the living environment and its collective spaces was caused by the pure focus on survival, which was more important to its inhabitants than the maintenance of their neighbourhood.

The people that were already settled started complaining about the situation in Bloemenoord, first about the physical condition of the flats, but after a while more and more about the social problems. The municipality was not really interested in the socioeconomic situation of the people in Bloemenoord and the Bijlmer in general; the flats were, after all, free sector and therefore not their problem. The housing corporation, however, reacted to the situation by once again putting a stop to the Surinamese influx into Bloemenoord.

In the media and on the street nasty words like "Negro-ghetto" and "monkey-mountain" were heard with increasing frequency. Finally the Surinamese population had enough of the one-sided negative publicity. They broke into an empty school building and started a Caribbean Centre. They wanted to show the rest of the country what their culture had to offer. What is more, they finally wanted a decent place for their music, festivities, and social activities. They were not alone and got help from Antilleans, Hindus, and native Dutchmen. Future mayor of Amsterdam Ed van Thijn was one of the people supporting them; he called it a just cause, important for the whole country.

In the coming years, however, nothing really changed and the situation became untenable. As more people left the Bijlmer, more apartments remained vacant. As for Bloemenoord, more than 100 of her 800 apartments were vacant; apartments which were not appointed to the large number of Surinamese looking for a roof over their heads.

At this point, Surinamese people started to organize themselves into an action group called "the Beheersraad." They did not accept that Surinamese were kept out of the Bijlmer while the municipality spent lots of money on pensions in other parts of the city. Complaints about this situation led to the development of a subdivision called Housing for Surinamese and Antilleans in the Bijlmermeer. They planned protest actions to gain publicity in the media about the discriminating policies and the huge need for proper housing for this group of people. They warned the corporations and municipality of action if they did not improve the situation. It led to nothing so they took matters into their own hands and started squatting eighty apartments for eighty families.

Now that the newcomers had organized themselves they were able to communicate directly with governmental organizations and discuss matters on a political level. They formed Committee 80, an umbrella group of municipal institutes, corporations, and the squatters. Its purpose was to find solutions for the situation in Bloemenoord. After a lot of meetings, discussions, and failed alternatives, the municipality finally gave the Surinamese access to the social housing program. The squatters were in large part tolerated and the families could stay.

With their actions and negotiations the Surinamese managed to free themselves from the "social lock down"—being stuck between social housing and the free sector—and finally found solidarity in Dutch society. The squatting arose from both a political motivation and a spatial need; it was an expression of a socio-economic tragedy. The Surinamese took Bloemenoord and used her notoriety to get publicity for their dreadful situation vis-à-vis the Dutch housing authorities.

Numerous other problems still lingered. Overcrowding, the poor condition of the flats, the filthiness, the bad transit connections with the city, the area's bad image, and a severe lack of facilities and urban planning were issues that remained unresolved. As a result stable households left and people with a poor socioeconomic position took their place. During the 1980s and

'90s the problems kept piling up in the Bijlmer without any adequate response from the housing corporations, the municipality, or the government. Drug addicts and dealers started to find their way to Bloemenoord and the crime rates went up.

A lot of these shady activities were concentrated in the darker recesses of the Bijlmer: under the elevated roads, in abandoned parking garages, on the ground floor of the apartment buildings, that had been reserved for storage spaces. These storage rooms would become infamous throughout the country. Since the primary means of access to the flats were the corridors, people in their daily comings and goings had no reason to go to the ground floor. The plinths consisted of mostly blind façades hiding the storage units. There was no social control of the public space. The so-called "eyes on the street" were absent.

Bloemenoord's ground floor became the ideal place for shady activities. Her storage rooms were converted into makeshift apartments, semi-professional brothels or hideouts for junkies. It became a place where you would not want to linger at night.

The Bijlmer had gotten stuck in a downward spiral. The original inhabitants' criticism of the execution of the plan led to bad publicity early on, which made people stay away from the Bijlmer, resulting in vacancy. The vacancy attracted more problems and started a process of gradual slumming, which produced more negative attention.

Responsibility for the management of the flats lay with the housing corporations. Almost all of the corporations, however, were nearly bankrupt, and they were incapable of doing anything about the terrible conditions in the Bijlmer. Over the years there were numerous rescue plans for the Bijlmer, but they proved too little, too late. There was not the political will to save the Bijlmermeer. Not even a visionary plan from Rem Koolhaas in 1986 could change that. More and more people started considering demolition. In the mid 1990s the decision was finally made and a radical redevelopment plan for the Bijlmermeer was accepted. The renewal plan consisted of the demolition of about 50% of the high-rises, which were replaced by standard terraced housing units of two or three storeys: the same houses as everywhere else in the Netherlands. The future had finally caught up with the Bijlmer.

Old Age
Despite the numerous problems that arose, it is notable that serious *racial* tensions never occurred. The local soccer club was mixed from the beginning, there were bars where everybody walked in and out, and the youth also stuck together. And, where the people could not live with each other, they learned to live alongside each other. The Bijlmermeer functioned as the multicultural blueprint for the Netherlands. It was (and maybe still is) in

many ways twenty years ahead of the rest of the country.

It has become the cultural epicentre of many nationalities. Besides Surinamese, over the years a lot of Ghanaians, Hindus, and many other ethnic groups also came to live in the Bijlmermeer. The Bijlmer is now known as the home of over a hundred nationalities. And even people who eventually move out of the area come back every Saturday for the lively and exotic market, which cannot be found anywhere else in the Netherlands.

People from the Bijlmer have always tried to show this more positive side of the Bijlmer. Numerous events were organized that—besides being fun for the inhabitants—had the clear aim of breaking the stigma of the neighbourhood. Blij-met-de-Bijlmer (Happy-with-the-Bijlmer), for instance, was organized right outside Bloemenoord in the large park between her and one of the sisters. It was a festival with music, theatre, film, and activities for children. It was organized solely by volunteers and was a modest success every year it was organized (it lasted for more than sixteen years).

But one of the things that people associate most with the Bijlmer nowadays is Kwakoe: a festival that started as a series of informal, self-organized soccer matches. Like so many things in the Bijlmer, it just started. But, as people began to bring in food and music, this makeshift football tournament gradually evolved into a yearly festival in the Bijlmer park. The Kwakoe festival is still one of the multicultural highlights in the Netherlands. It is visited by people from every ethnicity imaginable. They play sports, listen to music, dance, stroll around the market stalls, and eat exotic food. Almost 400,000 people, spread out over several weekends, visit the festival.

Though the Bijlmer has unrecognizably changed over the years, the spirit it has generated is still there. The Bijlmer is still the Bijlmer, it is (re)created every day by its inhabitants. And Kwakoe might just be its new icon.

Epilogue
In 1995 Bloemenoord was demolished. The housing corporation and the municipality decided it was time for drastic action; a clear signal to all that things were finally going to change. Interestingly enough, she was in nowhere near the terrible shape that some of her siblings were in. She was, however, quite conveniently situated: next to the Bijlmerdreef and very close to the new shopping centre.

She was the first to go, torn down piece by piece. Gradually revealing the lives that had been lived within. As a half demolished skeleton she regained some of her former grandeur. For a short time it felt like she was under construction again. And all dreams and expectations could still be projected on the concrete structure. She revealed her potential for all to see.

In her life Bloemenoord played different roles for different groups of people. For some people she was a refuge; a place where you could live in perfect anonymity. The towering apartments offered seclusion and a magnificent view. The first pioneers used her as a way of creating a new social structure. For them she was a utopian machine, a way of changing society. For the newcomers she played an important role in an emancipatory process. She functioned as a tool for a minority that was fighting for a position, recognition, and solidarity in Dutch society.

For most people, though, she formed the backdrop for daily life. A place where, despite all the problems, a lot of people felt at home.

***

MAZARA DEL VALLO, ITALY, 2008

COMPROMISE IN THE CASBAH: HOW THE RESIDENTS OF A SICILIAN TOWN NAVIGATE SEVERAL LANGUAGES AND MANY DIFFERENT IDEAS ABOUT HOW TO USE SPACE

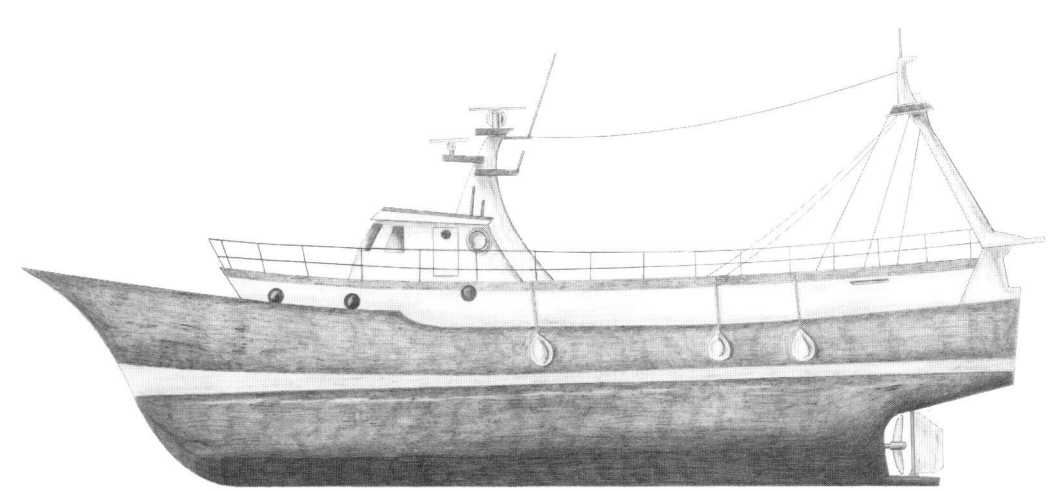

BY
GIOVANNA BORASI

"We came here because my father wants me to work on a fishing boat," I said. Eddie was looking at me. He had come for the same reason fifteen years ago. Eddie travelled back and forth to work on the fishing boats and left his family in Monastir.

"Pretty soon, I hope to sign on myself," I added enthusiastically. I had met Eddie five minutes before. With a few words and quick glances, we had communicated the main facts about our lives. There was probably a lot more to tell, especially about Eddie's life. We would be living nearby, a few metres farther on in the house next to his, facing the same courtyard.

"This is the bedroom," Vincenzo said, opening the flaking, blue, wooden door next to the kitchen sink. The room was large, with just one window, which looked out on another courtyard. It was late afternoon, and the late summer sun was less intense. Just the same, the room was hot. Maybe there were too many of us inside. Vincenzo went out and my father followed him. Together they passed through the glass door facing the courtyard, and we stayed in the room. My mother was looking all around, sizing up the walls and perhaps imagining how we could arrange our few belongings along them. I heard the men's footsteps moving away in the courtyard, until they reached the shadows at the far end. They were probably talking about money.

"Are we all going to sleep in here?" I asked. My mother didn't answer. My question was pointless. The house only had two rooms—the kitchen and this one. She answered me by changing the subject. "Your father's boat sails tomorrow already. He will be gone more than three weeks. They are going after the big fish," she said with a faint smile. But in her eyes I sensed a sadness.

We had arrived by boat from Tunis a few days before. Mazara was new to us. My father had been here many times to work on the fishing boats—a different boat every time, but I knew he liked the *Cesare Rustico* a lot. I liked it too. I remember the picture he showed me once. It was all white, with a big blue stripe on the side. He liked it because the captain, Paolo, was a *brav'uomo*, a good man. The rest of the crew changed constantly, but they were usually all Tunisian, like us. "It's good to be part of a ship's crew, Hosni," he told me one evening a few years ago, back home in Tunisia. "There are twenty of us, almost all from Mahdia, La Chebba, Monastir. We get along. In the long weeks at sea, when we're cleaning fish, we while away the time talking about home. It does you good to hear stories when you are far away and the dampness of the sea gets into your bones."

"Well then, Mahel," Vincenzo said returning to the kitchen with my father, "we agree on 130 euros a month. It's not that much and you're near the port. Pay me on the first of the month. I'll come and pick it up. We don't live in the Casbah, and since you're not from here, it would be too complicated for you to come to our house. We live on the Transmazaro, on the west bank of the Mazaro River. Instead of accepting government aid to repair this house, we agreed to go and live there." Vincenzo stopped talking all of a sudden, as if at that instant he was no longer sure about a decision he had made long ago. None of us really understood what he was talking about.

"That's fine. I understand, Signor Vincenzo," my father answered, eager to fill in the awkward silence. "I will make sure you get your money every month." I knew it was difficult for my father to commit himself to this, because pay on the boats changes depending on the catch.

Vincenzo looked around in silence. We had nothing else to say to each other, but he seemed not to have any reason to leave, or perhaps he had a reason to stay. He seemed to be thinking about something else. Then, as if nothing had happened, he started talking again. "I hope you will be comfortable here. We were for many years, until that accursed day when God decided to make the earth tremble! I remember it as if it were yesterday. How long has it been? Nearly thirty years! It was the summer of 1981. I remember I was here in the kitchen, and my wife was over there. When the ground shook, Holy Mother of God! 'Giuseppina, Giuseppina!' I shouted. I found her sitting on the floor near the bed with one of the children, the oldest, in her arms. Little Nino was in a corner. I picked him up, lifted my wife, and we ran out into the courtyard. All around, the Calcaras, the Morabitos, the Zagamis, the Di Dias had done the same thing, and then we ran into the street. Many houses had collapsed. The alleyways were even narrower because they were full of rubble, and everyone was crowding around, screaming. We ran until we had passed where the city walls used to stand. We never came back here to live. Now we live outside, in a new apartment building. Almost everyone did the same thing, except the Di Dias."

Vincenzo took a deep breath. He had just relived the drama of that time. Then he went on: "By the way, Mahel, have you met the Di Dia family? And the others?" My father shook his head. "Well, there's time, but if you want, once you are settled down I could introduce you," he commented. The word "hurry" was probably not in his vocabulary. "The Di Dias are the only Italians on this courtyard who stayed. Antonio Scimeni, who lives at 13 Via Goti, is another of the few who hung on. He renovated his house, but all around it everything is broken down. It's a dump. He says he would like to plant a garden, but I know him—he's always been a dreamer. The others never wanted to come back because their houses were in ruins, or because they're superstitious. And some were happy for an excuse to begin a new life. Since then, everything has stayed as it was. That's why there are so many abandoned houses. Experts came from Rome and said that 1300 unsafe buildings had to be torn down. Just think. I am happy to rent the house out, others do it too if their houses are in decent shape. But most Italians don't want to live here. The few residents are almost all foreigners like you, or Slavs or Romanians or Moroccans. You know, we call this part of the city the Casbah. In fact, it has always been called that because the city's layout is obviously Arab. But we call it that now because it's inhabited by more of you than of us. Some Italians are even afraid to walk through here. They say it doesn't even seem to be in Italy. In the street you hear people say, 'The Casbah has been overrun, they are destroying it. It's in Arab hands, it's a dangerous place, particularly at night.' But I tell them, 'What do you expect? You don't want to live here because the houses aren't in good condition any more.'" The fact that most Italians felt that the area was becoming too *foreign* was a detail Vincenzo kept to himself, adding, "All these people have to live somewhere, don't they?"

My parents nodded their heads as Vincenzo spoke. I wasn't sure if my mother understood everything. I picked up the meaning of what he was saying, and I liked listening to the sound of his hoarse voice.

There are still some Italians in Mahdia—very few any more, though. As a little child I had heard their language, listening to songs on the radio. Our two countries are only 137 kilometres apart. Mazara is closer to Mahdia than to Rome. So Sicily and Tunisia have "exchanged men" for centuries. My grandfather worked for an Italian boat owner who had settled in Mahdia to do business. Then, when my country became independent in 1956, Italian immigrants in the colony began a slow-motion exodus, most eventually trickling back to Mazara or Trapani. That's why my grandfather came here at first, then he convinced my father to do the same. I think that for him it was a way of continuing the same life, this time on the other side of the Mediterranean. In any case, my mother told me not to worry about the language because there are so many other Tunisian children here. I can even study at the home of Professor Hannachi Adbel Karim, who teaches in both Arabic and Italian. Everyone knows Hannachi, even back home. He was one of the first to arrive, a pioneer. He taught Arabic and married a Sicilian.

"You'll make friends easily. You'll see, there's plenty of Tunisian kids," Eddie told me the first day I was here. "Lots of Tunisian kids your age were even born here, and Mazara is home to them. They go to Tunisia in the summer, but only to visit their relatives."

"The fact is," Vincenzo began again after his question was left hanging, "at this point there are more than 400 fishing boats in the magnificent Mazara fleet, and more than half the workers are foreigners. They do all the work we Italians don't want to do any more. How awful we are! You know, Mahel, if you work on a boat, they'll never make you captain or chief officer! Those jobs are only for Italians. At first, people came to work for a few months and then went home, but now, like you, everyone wants to bring their family if they can."

My father looked at Vincenzo with a pensive, questioning look. Sometime later, I understood that at that moment he was wondering whether he had done the right thing to bring us here, where we didn't know anyone and would always be foreigners.

Vincenzo abruptly interrupted my father's thoughts with a slap on the back. "Well, Mahel, I really must be going." When he was at the door, he turned and added, "Oh, I forgot. I suggest that you not go onto the terrace. It's been shaky since the earthquake. Keep an eye on your kids, because there's an abandoned house in the courtyard. It's unsafe. And then, there are many who come to work here and don't have enough money, so they end up sleeping in the ruins. They always find an abandoned house. That way, at least they have shelter."

"Thank you Signor Vincenzo," my father said, accompanying him for a few steps in the courtyard, "see you soon." Vincenzo extended his hand toward my father and motioned goodbye with his chin to my mother and us, who had stayed behind in the doorway. He made his way through the courtyard, along the narrow passageway that led to the street. The sun was low in the sky. I followed his broad form with my eyes, until he disappeared around a corner.

***

When my mother woke me, the sun was still not very high. "Let's go. Get up. On your feet," she said under her breath. "Up! We're going to accompany your father to the port." It was early, too early for me. But I really wanted to see it with my own eyes, the fleet Vincenzo had spoken of. I got up quickly and, still half asleep, followed her into the bathroom. The cool water on my face made me see things differently, and suddenly the world around me acquired a sharp outline. I got dressed rapidly; my father had been ready for a little while, and my brother was sleeping in my mother's arms.

We went down along the alleys. It wasn't warm: The stone of the houses was giving off the cold that had descended on the city during the night. The air smelled like something—dirt, or perhaps cement or crushed stone. I especially noticed the smell whenever we passed an abandoned or ruined house. I thought of Vincenzo and what he had told us about what had happened to him and all of Mazara. From that moment on, I always associated this smell with the earthquake overturning the earth's deepest layers, and I imagined the smell still emanated from these abandoned houses.

We soon reached the port, where the bay opened up in front of us. There were so many, many fishing boats. Vincenzo had said 400. The number had seemed large to me, but I couldn't really imagine how many boats that was. Now, even if I couldn't count them, I saw how much space they took up in the water. Some were still moored, others were on their way out to sea. Gulls were flying around: maybe they could still smell fish in the air. The dock was a hubbub of activity. We had left behind the silence of the still-sleeping city.

My father went up to a man with a moustache who was wearing a crumpled undershirt and asked, "Do you know where Paolo is docked?"

"Over there, down at the end of the wharf," he answered. "This is a fine day to set out to sea. The sea is calm—it's a good omen." With a wordless smile, we took our leave and went over to the *Cesare Rustico*.

There it was, where the man had said. It was bigger than I had imagined. Now, I know why it was so big: it's a deep-sea trawler. About 40 metres long, the boats go so far out they lose sight of the coast. They're big boats because once the fish are caught they are processed on board.

On the dock opposite the *Cesare Rustico*, my father shook hands with a man, whom I took to be Paolo, now a legend in my mind. Looking at him, I tried to understand what made him a *brav'uomo*. My father gave us all a quick hug and jumped into the boat. Once on board, he disappeared into the ropes, barrels and plastic crates, instantly blending in with the other fishermen.

We stayed on the dock a while. Beside us, a lady was watching the same boat. "Let's hope they don't catch any people," she said, breaking the silence. My mother didn't answer or take her eyes off the *Cesare Rustico* for an instant. I looked at the woman to see whether she was joking or wanted to scare us.

This I now understand after being here a few weeks. The fishing boats often catch people, and not in a manner of speaking but in reality. Not everyone leaves the shores of Africa or Yugoslavia the way we did: some risk their lives aboard barges just to reach Italy, Spain or Portugal. That way they don't have to get permission, they don't need a passport. But the passage is very expensive. The barges are overcrowded, and many never make it to their destination. They sink, and the people end up in the sea, living with the fish. So the fishing boats pull them out of the water, sometimes alive, sometimes entangled in the nets.

I thought this was only a recent matter that concerned us Africans, until Tonino told me about his grandfather leaving for America in 1910 but never making it there. In those days, too, strange things occurred. He had boarded a ship with all his hopes. The ship sailed around Sicily for three weeks before letting all the passengers off on the same island, but in a different place. Tonino's grandfather had never left Mazara before and was so ignorant that he actually thought he had arrived in America, a land where he had been told he would find many Sicilians. It was not long before he happened to realize he had been duped.

***

Now that we have been living in Mazara for nearly a month, I am starting to know my way around the Casbah pretty well. This intricate group of laneways, extending from the Piazza della Repubblica to the Piazza Regina, reminds me so much of the medina where we lived in Tunisia. Buildings line every street, and a building's archway leads not into the building itself but into a courtyard lined with many buildings.

Our Tunisian neighbour, Eddie, explained why the city has this typical Arab layout: the Arabs invaded Sicily in 827, starting in fact with Mazara, and soon after gave the centre of town this system, which is why everything seems familiar to me.

We live at 8 Via Pilazza. In the courtyard at the back, there's us, and then a Slavic family, two Italian families and Eddie, who, since he didn't bring his family with him, lives alone. Then there is an abandoned house.

You enter the courtyard from Via Pilazza by passing under a stone arch, then you go through a long uncovered passageway created by the houses' tall stone walls. This opens into the courtyard, which has an irregular shape. In the courtyard there are also some old sheds, that have been completely boarded up, no longer in use. When I look at them, I wonder what they are doing there. I like spending my days in this open space. Sometimes I play with my brother, Fayel. My mother doesn't want us playing near the abandoned house because she knows it could collapse at any instant.

Almost everyone uses that space only as a corridor to get to their house. We all speak different languages, and not very good Italian, so we never gather together and all have a conversation. What would we talk about?

The Semzadeta family uses the courtyard for things like hanging out the laundry. I like seeing all their colourful clothes dangling. I also like to pass through them when they are drying and feel the damp on my face and arms.

On the other hand, my mother put a sofa in the courtyard so you can sit there in the evening. Sometimes when Ali comes to visit, he doesn't even go into the house. He sits on the sofa for a mint tea and some small talk.

I haven't quite figured out how it works yet, but I think there are invisible lines dividing our part of the courtyard from other people's parts. I only know that if we stray too far, it's not good, because we're in the Di Dias' section, or else the Semzadetas' or Eddie's, or in danger near the abandoned house.

***

I had never thought of this courtyard as a special place until today. I was sitting on my mother's sofa when some young Italians arrived, five or six of them. They were a strange sight in the Casbah. "Hi. Can we talk to you for a minute?" the tall one asked. I didn't say anything, which must have made him assume the answer was yes.

"We're students from the architecture school in Siracusa. We're doing a research project on Mazara, specifically on the Casbah. It is called *Abitare Straniero*." The fellow looked at me, and I'm sure that I looked perplexed. I certainly didn't put him at ease. He must have understood that the best thing would just be to come out with it and state plainly what he wanted. "I would like to propose a little game to you and your family, and all the families that live here. It uses a model of this courtyard," he said, pointing to a strangely-shaped piece of cardboard. "You can all move these elements around, the gate, the seats, tables, clothes lines, walls, awnings, wash tubs, and so on, to organize the space however you want, or you can think up other elements and arrange them according to whatever logic you think is most suitable."

I stared at him. The only word of his explanation that stuck with me was *straniero*. It meant "foreigner" and it was a word I had learned almost immediately, because when you go around Mazara you hear people saying, "He's a foreigner." I caught on quickly that this term referred to anyone who wasn't Italian.

Now, I thought, this fellow and his friends were interested in understanding how we foreigners wanted to live in this space we kind of divided among ourselves. Maybe it was an interesting idea. I had never thought about it, certainly not in those terms.

Basically, we are all using the courtyard, without really thinking about what the space was, for our own needs and in ways related to how we lived in the countries we all came from. For example, my family uses the outside space the way we did with our house in Mahdia, and I imagine it's the same for the Semzadetas and Eddie. As for the Di Dias, I don't know. I don't know what the courtyard was like when only they and "their kind" lived here, and there were no foreigners.

In any case, the game intrigued me. I explained it briefly to my mother, who had come to stand in the doorway when she heard voices, and I persuaded her to join in. The students knocked on the other doors and, little by little, Eddie, some of the Di Dias, and Saiti—the Semizdetas' oldest daughter—came out. Everyone gathered around the cardboard and started moving the components here and there.

It was interesting to see how everyone imagined arranging the pieces in a different way. For example, Saiti wanted to set up walls in the courtyard to separate the various families' spaces, perhaps because she is never happy when Fayel and I play hide-and-seek in her laundry. I became aware of a big difference: for my family, the courtyard was the front of the house, but for the Di Dias, the Italians, it was the back.

Certainly no one saw the space the same way. And in the weeks that we'd been living there, everyone had probably hidden their different viewpoints in silence. "Peaceful cohabitation among strangers," is what Hannachi called it when he talked about Mazara's different communities.

The tall fellow offered me his hand and said, "My name is Roberto."

"Hosni," I answered. He sat down next to me, and I made room for him. I could tell he felt like talking.

"What we are studying is obvious to you," he continued, "you experience it every day; you take it for granted. The Casbah is inhabited by people who come from places in a different world with different cultures and who, for one reason or another, find themselves living as neighbours. Today we played this game, but what we are trying to understand is far more complex. The city is what it is. Its original structure is interesting, abounding with possibilities. The system of courtyards interconnected by an intricate network of lanes is unique. The walls can't be moved. The city has been built to a particular density. Maybe our research will provide a chance to invent and activate new ways of inhabiting it, dictated by the need for different cultures to live together. But don't get the idea we mean to come in here and tell you how you should live. That's not it at all! On one hand, we are trying to understand how to solve a real housing emergency, with requirements different from Italian requirements. On the other hand, we want to figure out how this can be done while respecting the place's character, redeveloping often abandoned spaces, urban wasteland, in the in-between spaces. It's especially interesting for us architecture students," Roberto explained enthusiastically, "to see how—in this area where hardly any Italians live now because they don't think it's possible—you and the other new residents are appropriating and reinventing this place for yourselves. What for you is spontaneous or an act of necessity can become the basis of a project for us. Something could come out of the friction between cultures and places, out of competing for these spaces."

What Robert said fascinated me, and I especially liked the fact that he thought the courtyard, and the entire Casbah, were full of ideas. What for us, and for all the other Tunisians, Slavs, Romanians and Moroccans, was the only way we had found of living in this place could become an experiment for him to invent a new life for the Casbah. A new life that came from us.

While Roberto was talking to me, I didn't notice that Signora Di Dia had come over and was standing beside us. She didn't say a word, but eyed Roberto mistrustfully. The Di Dias were, of course, a rarity in Mazara. Yet, they had always lived there, and she probably thought differently about the future of the courtyard and all the Casbah. Unlike Vincenzo, they had requested the Italian government grant and had renovated their house instead of going to live somewhere else. It was probably the stubbornness of Concetta Di Dia—a worthy sea captain's wife—that had led to the decision not to abandon her house, not even if it fell into an abyss. Roberto realized it would be difficult to convince Signora Di Dia that his theories were sound. After forty years of Tunisians in Mazara, intermarriages were still rare—only 23. "*Donne e buoi dei paesi tuoi*," as they say in Italian—"Women and oxen from your home town."

Roberto went on thinking out loud, ignoring Signora Di Dia's discontented look. "There are lots of us here in Mazara today. We've come here a few times. We've drawn a map of the Casbah that shows the courtyards, abandoned buildings, roofs, and all the places we think would be good for projects. They are case studies. Sometimes the changes are minimal, sometimes more ambitious—for example, the idea of a multicultural library. Most are meant not only to suggest different uses for the spaces but also to bring social and safety issues up for discussion, like the idea of creating meeting places and gardens in the city's historic centre." Roberto seemed tired. He had been talking for quite a while.

"Maybe we'll see each other again," he said, smiling as he stood. "Your name is Hosni, isn't it?"

"Yes," I answered. "I don't know when you are coming back, but you many not find me here. As soon as there's a fishing boat that will take me, I'll sign on."

"You're going to sea, too? I would have loved that myself, but my father insisted that I attend university. I'm off. So long."

"So long," I reply.

***

"Mamma, I'm going to the port," I shouted. I was already running. It's beautiful at sunset. These days, there aren't many fishing boats. Even the *Cesare Rustico* hasn't returned yet. I'm beginning to get used to the rhythm of our life, set by my father's absence or presence, which is in turn set by the rhythm of fishing on the *Cesare Rustico*. I also like to go and watch, because soon that will be my life too. When the boats are in port, there is still plenty for the fishermen to do. Cleaning and repairing the nets is a laborious chore that takes days. The Italians say you have to have the patience of a saint for such work. But saint or no saint, whatever God you believe in, all the fishermen, foreigners or not, sit together on the dock on those coloured plastic chairs and run metre after metre of net through their hands. Their leathery skin has become so dark that it seems both sunproof and waterproof. "Spread that *sciabbica* out," is a phrase you often hear shouted at the port. Like this city's structure, the word "*sciabbica*" is familiar to me: we use the same word for big fishing nets in my language.

Not all the men are on the dock: some are working on the boats, replacing and changing parts. The discarded parts are heaped up in a mountain of debris at the end of the dock: pieces of metal, ladders and keel ribbing, the scrap of the maritime industry. Rusted and eaten away by the salt air, they are no longer of use on the fishing boats. But I am beginning not only to recognize these shapes on the dock but also to detect them in the Casbah. I'm not making this up—I've seen them with my own eyes. When I went to Via Bagno, for example, I noticed that all the houses on the courtyard looked abandoned. The street-level entrances are filled with stones, dirt, and plaster rubble—to all appearances, uninhabitable. However, there are actually people living in there. As Vincenzo said, many who come to work temporarily seek shelter in abandoned houses at night. I sat for a while on a piece of rock that must have been a door jamb once but was now leaning against a wall. It was very quiet. Then I heard noises over my head. The sun was strong, and I had to shift my position to look up without being blinded. I saw a boy walking on the roof. I recognized him from his pink t-shirt with *Pane fresco*—"Fresh Bread"—written on it. I know that t-shirt because it's from the bakery where my mother buys bread with *ciciulena*. I like that bread because it reminds me of the bread in Mahdia. We call sesame *gulkulan*: the Mazarans' name for it comes from the Arabic word.

He was a boy I had seen at the port, getting off the *Alibut*. I watched him pass from one roof to the other, walking quickly. He disappeared over one of the roofs of the courtyard then, all of a sudden, he reappeared two floors below, in the ruined house at the east end of the courtyard. Peeking in the window, I thought I recognized one of the metal ladders I had seen at the port. When I told Tonino this, he said that many people use that system to inhabit the old houses of the Casbah, to connect floors via the inside or the outside that are no longer connected or perhaps never were. Junked boats are also used to create a safe shelter in houses with precarious ceilings. These abandoned carcasses are still sound, so why not think up other uses for them? At the dock, they're like the skeletons of huge beached animals, and it's better for everyone if they are moved somewhere else. Maybe it is situations like these that interest Roberto: people making what they need with what they have, using ideas from various cultures. Who knows if he and his friends noticed all this as they walked through the Casbah. If they had, I bet they'll use it for their work—one of Roberto's projects. As for me, I'm just going to keep watching the sea, hoping to grab whatever washes up on shore.

***

TURTLE MOUNTAINS, MANITOBA, CANADA, APRIL 17TH, 1982

THE PRAIRIE IS VAST AND ENDLESS, UNTIL IT ISN'T: A MICHIF STORY

BY
JEAN TEILLET

Old Sarah shrugged, smiled and snorted all at the same time. To herself she thinks, "What kind of question is that to ask of me? Where did we live? How do I answer that?" Sarah rocks in her chair and stares off into the sky. It's a beautiful day and she spends much of her time now on the porch rocking and looking at that sky. She is old now, almost 100 years old, and she is secretly pleased that her view is unobstructed by any trees. She is distracted from the question while she contemplates the addition of trees to the prairies. The settlers, she knows, consider trees to be a beautifier and she likes them too—where they belong—in the river valleys. But they don't belong on the prairies. To Sarah's mind trees spoil the view and Sarah very much likes the long view.

Brought back to the moment by a gentle cough, Sarah returns to the problem of answering the question. She has been asked this question before of course, but usually she can shrug it off with a brief line, something like "well... we lived lots of places." But this questioner is different, a persistent girl from the University. She has a little machine that is silently recording Sarah's words. Sniffing around, Sarah thinks, like a *moshkwa*, a bear after berries. How do I say, and make her understand, that we lived everywhere; that a house was not our home; that we were born, lived and died on the plains, on a constant journey; that we were travellers, voyageurs. This is not something *les Canadiens* understand. They live in houses, behind fences, on farms or in towns. They have an address. We didn't live our lives in houses. Houses were for people who had things like furniture and stayed in one place; not for us; not back then. We didn't live in towns. We didn't have couches or chairs or beds. Furniture, Sarah thinks, even the word is heavy. And we did not stay in one place. We were *otipayemsuak*, the independent ones. With a sigh, Sarah decides that the only way to really answer the question is to start at the beginning.

"My people have many names," she begins quietly, "the Americans called us the Red River half-breeds of the North. The French called us Métis. The Cree called us *opetoygosan,* the half person. The English Canadians called us half-breeds. We called ourselves *les Michif.*" Sarah takes a moment to let this bundle of information sink in. She watches this *moshkwa* girl to see if she is just listening or if she is hearing. *Moshkwa* girl has sympathetic eyes and Sarah finds them hard to read, but maybe, Sarah decides, *moshkwa* girl hears.

"We lived on what the English in those days called the 'great plains'. We called it *le prairie* in Michif, the language of my people. I was born in 1882 on the plains on one of the last big Métis buffalo hunts. I don't know exactly where I was born. My mother said they stopped for a few hours on the plains—somewhere between the Turtle Mountains and the Montana Territory. I don't know, maybe we were in Canada, maybe we were in the

United States. I was born somewhere along the border, though back then the line meant very little to us. Maybe it meant something to the Canadian government far away in the east. Lots of things seemed important to those easterners that we didn't pay any attention to. Anyway, we crossed and re-crossed that border all the time. Our cart trails wandered south of the line out of the Turtle Mountains; sometimes we travelled north on the Canadian side as we moved westward. Sometimes we travelled south along the Milk River to the Cypress Hills. Sometimes we went up to Edmonton or over towards the Rocky Mountains. It was all beautiful, big and wide open—*le prairie*."

"By the time I was born, all of the buffalo were gone in Canada. So each spring my parents travelled deep into Montana to get the buffalo. We travelled in our Red River cart." Sarah stops suddenly, realizing that this *moshkwa* girl has probably never seen a Red River cart. "Did you ever see a Red River cart?" *Moshkwa* girl shakes her head. Sarah thinks about how to describe this cart that was so much a part of her life. "Big wheels" Sarah says, "that would be the first thing anyone noticed, the two big wooden wheels. Actually the whole cart was made of wood and we lashed it together with *shaganapi* – strips of buffalo hide. My Dad would wet those *shaganapi* and tie them around the axle, then it would shrink and tighten as it dried. Those carts held lots of buffalo robes plus some of us kids." Sarah looks at *moshkwa* girl with a dry chuckle. "Oh my girl, those carts were noisy. We didn't use grease because it would just get clogged with dust, so the wood on wood screeched all the time. We used to say it was like an old deaf *moshôm* —or word for grandfather—playing a fiddle out of tune – eieeeeieeieieieee." Sarah tries to imitate that screechy sound and gets a laugh out of *moshkwa* girl. Sarah laughs herself and says, "that sound travelled with us everywhere we went and when we stopped, someone would pick up a fiddle and we would dance. *Les Michif* went everywhere with the fiddle music and we never stopped moving. If we weren't travelling we were dancing. Movement was everything to us."

As if to emphasize how much movement means to her, Sarah sinks back into her rocker and silently rocks back and forth, staring again off at the sky. Remembering. Remembering the sounds of her life. Remembering the prized possessions—the Red River cart and their horses. "That was what we cared about, what we took care of—our Red River cart and our horses. They were our means of travelling and our lifeline."

"In my parents' day, the Métis went wherever the buffalo were, and the buffalo in those last days were in Montana. So they went to Montana with their horses and carts. They went with lots of other Michif families too; hundreds of families. It made a big party travelling on the prairie with hundreds of carts, thousands of people and thousands of horses. With the screeching carts you could probably hear them coming for miles. They'd make camps and send out scouts to look for the buffalo. When they finally caught up to the buffalo it was lots of work, butchering the meat and scraping the hides. I guess they were like a meat and leather factory on the prairie. They made pemmican – that's pounded meat mixed with fat and berries." Sarah looks at *moshkwa* girl and asks, "did you ever taste pemmican?" *Moshkwa* girl shakes her head emphatically. Sarah is not surprised. She hasn't met anyone for years who has tasted pemmican. No one makes it anymore. "Settlers who came out and first tasted it didn't like it much. But it preserved well and that's what my people lived on mostly; at least until the buffalo were all gone. Even then we made pemmican out of other meats. We also sold it to the fur traders and I hear they took it up north to feed the people who travelled on the boats. When in my parents' day, on those big buffalo hunts, once they got their share of the buffalo, they loaded their carts with meat and robes and made the long journey back to Red River to sell the pemmican and robes or hides. I heard that the hides were used to make belts and boots and for machines in that big American civil war."

"For many years my parents returned each year to the Turtle Mountains for the winter. The last year my family hunted the buffalo into Montana was the year I was born. That was when the Americans started to chase us back over the border and they started to demand that we pay them money, like a tax, for the buffalo we took. That was too much for us. It meant we would not make enough money to make the trip worthwhile. When we refused to pay, their army officers chased us back into Canada. After that we didn't go to Montana anymore and there were no more buffalo in Canada. That was the end of those good days and that good life. While it lasted, *les Michif* were proud and happy."

"We lived a free life and oh how we loved it. We camped wherever we wanted. There was green grass and clear, clean water to drink. We hunted all kinds of wild game and we ate duck eggs and sometimes for a change from buffalo we ate bear meat or antelope. We picked wild turnip, Saskatoon berries and wild cherries and we crushed the berries between rocks and dried them out to add to our pemmican."

Sarah has stopped rocking, caught up in her stories of the past. "What a beautiful life that was! Nothing bothered the Métis and there was no law to tell them what to do or where to go. They travelled with lots of families and when they camped at night it was like a big village of buffalo leather tepees. Every night there was singing and dancing. In winter we moved off the prairie and lived *en nick-ah-wah*, a wintering site. These were our refuges from the winter weather. The French called those places *hivernant*. The Hudson's Bay Company men said our *nick-ah-wah* were like the oases in the desert because they had water, trees and shelter from the weather. They were islands of shelter on a sea of grass. We used to say that *un hivernant…est toujours chez soi*. We had *nick-ah-wah* in the Turtle Mountains, in Qu'Appelle Valley, at Wood Mountain and in the Cypress Hills. There were lots more but those were the ones I went to with my family."

Sarah looks at the *moshkwa* girl to see if she is still hearing. *Moshkwa* girl smiles and gestures gently with her hand as if to say 'go on'. She is unusually quiet for a *moonia*, a white girl, Sarah thinks. Usually the *moonias* don't like silences. But this one seems very content to let the silence encourage the stories. Sarah looks around at the porch they are sitting on and the house she now lives in. A real house this one. Not like the *nick-ah-wah* cabins we built back then. "We built cabins in the *nick-ah-wah*" she tells the *moshkwa* girl, "well actually they were just shacks that were thrown together of cut logs with mud slapped in between. My Dad and his brothers could make one, sometimes two cabins in a day and we'd live there in the winter and leave as soon as the ground was hard enough to travel in the spring. Next year we never tried to find those cabins again. Indians burned them sometimes. Sometimes they just seemed to dissolve back into the earth."

"It's funny, you know. I was born on the buffalo hunt but I don't remember seeing the big herds of buffalo. I saw a few, but by the time I was old enough to remember the big herds were gone. For me the buffalo were stories told at night under the stars by my parents, my uncles and my grandparents. My life really began after the buffalo." Much of Métis life, Sarah thinks, has been lived in these 'afters'—after the buffalo, after the 1885 rebellion, after Riel's hanging, after the residential school roundup. To Sarah's way of thinking she has lived her whole life in these 'afters', though she doesn't say that out loud to the *moshkwa* girl.

"What I remember are the bones. That's what we did when I was a child. We travelled all over the prairies and picked buffalo bones. What a sight that was! Mountains of bones, sometimes piled higher than one of those big buildings I saw in Brandon and Winnipeg. White bones and so many you couldn't count them all. We went from being buffalo hunters to picking buffalo bones off the prairies. They tell me the bones made fertilizer for those farmers we'd see when we were travelling. You know, I remember thinking back then that the farming way of life was not good for much. I thought it would be very strange to live behind a fence or in a house where the stars are cut off from you even in summer. And then they were planting things all the time. Even planting trees on the plains; trees that spoil the long view." *Moshkwa* girl laughs, clearly amused at the idea that anyone would think trees were in the way. But Sarah is used to the fact that no one alive agrees with her on this. The new generations have all grown up with trees. They don't know, they don't spend much time on the prairie so they don't understand the power of the long view.

Sarah returns to *moshkwa* girl. "You need to understand," she says, "we were a pretty simple people, *les Michif*, we loved hunting, singing and dancing. We were proud. That's what the plains do to you. That big open space doesn't make shy people. It made us and we were loud singers, dancers, fiddlers, hunters and free people. We were proud to be Michif; proud to say we were free. The Indians knew us and the land knew us. I always knew, when we were on the plains in the storehouse of *le bon dieu*, that I was someone."

Sarah looks at the recording machine and for a moment watches the little wheels turn round. She can see them through the plastic cover. The machine is recording Sarah's words but also the pauses. "Where did we live you asked?" Sarah shakes her head. It's taking her a long time to answer this question. "Those *nick-ah-wah*, they were scattered all over the plains – Turtle Mountain, Qu'Appelle Valley, Wood Mountain, Cypress Hills. We stayed in all of those places. But did we live there?" Sarah looks at *moshkwa* girl, trying to emphasize her point. "What does that mean? Where do you live? Is it where we built a building? Or is it where we spent most of our time? And when? Do you mean where we lived in the fall or where we lived in the winter or the summer? Because, you know, we lived in different places each season of the year. If it's where we built a building, then we lived in the *nick-ah-wahs*. If it's where we spent most of our time, then it's on the prairie. Me? I prefer to say that I lived on the prairie when I was a young girl."

"After the buffalo bones were all picked, we began to stay in the Turtle Mountains year round. I remember the first year we didn't go travelling. It was strange for all of us. We didn't know what to do with ourselves, or our house. We weren't used to being there all year round. Then my father and his brothers began to take up trading. They would go on long trading trips to Red River and St. Paul and Edmonton. My brothers and I became the family hunters and fishermen. We hunted mostly ducks, elk and moose."

"Our home in the Turtle Mountains was a log cabin with a dirt floor and flour sacking for curtains. I remember those flour sacks. They had a red rose on them and we worked very hard to make sure those roses were centered in the curtains. We wore them too. We made dresses out of them and were very proud of the pretty rose on the front of our dresses. We thought we looked very pretty in them.

It was after we started to live in Turtle Mountain all year round that I first met my husband. He came home with my Dad on a trading trip and he never left again. He was a Lagimodière and I was a Poitras. They told me that some long time back we were second or third cousins, but I never did figure out how that connection worked. It seemed to me that I was a second or third cousin to just about everyone I met back then. That's the way it is with *les Michif*."

Sarah rocks for a long time remembering her fun-loving, fiddle-playing, sometimes maddening husband, now passed on these twenty years. She misses seeing that black curl that used to hang down on his forehead. She misses...well, truthfully she misses lots of things and lots of people, all long gone now. That's what you get Sarah, she tells herself, for living so long and living past everyone else – you get a time where you feel how much you miss.

"We had six children," Sarah says to the *moshkwa* girl. "Four boys and two girls. We didn't have a lot of money, but we never thought about it too much. My husband made pretty good money playing the fiddle at dances and he was much in demand for that. When we were young I liked to dance too, but once we had so many kids...well you don't dance too much when you have kids."

"My father, my uncles and my husband were traders and freighters. They were away from home a lot. That was one of the things that changed after the buffalo and the bones were all gone. We used to all travel as a family when I was a girl, but after the buffalo, it was the men that travelled. The women and children and old people stayed home."

"It was pretty good mostly. There were lots of other Michif living in the Turtle Mountains. We lived on the American side in the Dakota Territory for a while. The Michif named that place originally after our patron saint, St. Joseph, but they call that place Walhalla now. We lived at St. Joe's until the American government kicked us out. They said we were Canadians and we had to go back to Canada. I remember then that there was lots of talk about whether we were Canadians or Americans. We weren't so sure about it. Like I said, I didn't know if I was born on the American or Canadian side. Same with my brothers and sisters and even my parents. In the end there wasn't much we could do about it. So my Dad and my uncles came north of the line to see if they could find us a good place to live. In the end we moved just over the line and stayed in the Turtle Mountains but on the Canadian side. For us it was just another move. We built another log cabin on the Canadian side this time."

"You know what I remember most about that trip? I remember we were all in the carts and just before we crossed the border my Dad stopped and told all of us not to say we were Michif or Métis or half-breeds. If anyone asked we were French. He told us not to speak Michif to anybody outside the family and to speak French only. We didn't care too much then. We all spoke French and Michif and English and Cree. But that day, it didn't matter what we said because there was no one at the border. We didn't even really know we had crossed. Anyway, that day, no one asked us what we were."

"Not too long after we came into Canada the priests and the government people came to see us. All the men were gone on a freighting trip to Red River. Anyway, they came to our cabin and told us that all the children had to go to school. I remember we nodded." Sarah pauses for a moment, remembering the horrible misunderstanding. "That nodding was a problem. You see, the Michif, we have a habit of nodding or saying 'uh-huh' or 'heh-heh' when someone says something. For us, it doesn't mean we agree. It means we hear what you are saying and we are thinking about it. But I've come to understand that the English don't think like that. They think that it means we agree with them. We didn't know that then. We thought they were just telling us something and we could think about it for a while. So we were shocked when they then got up and started to round up the kids. We didn't mind the kids going to school. We used to have priests travelling with us on the prairies and they taught us stuff. We thought that was what they meant at first; that they were going to bring in priests to teach the kids. But we didn't understand that they meant to take our kids away. It never occurred to us that anyone would do such a thing. At that time I had three kids and my brothers and sisters and cousins had lots more. That day they took away 30 kids in all from our places in Turtle Mountain. That was a bad day. We fought them, but there were too many of them. I remember just sinking down on the ground and feeling…I still have a hard time to say how it felt. Maybe just empty. I could not imagine how we were supposed to live without children. What was the point of life if there were no kids?"

Sarah's rocking is more agitated now as she relives that horrible day. Even now, decades later she feels that panic and wants to cry. She looks at *moshkwa* girl who is also looking sad. Most people know about the residential schools these days and it's clear that *moshkwa* girl knows too. Good, Sarah thinks to herself, I don't need to explain. Still she wants to say something, because most of the stories about residential schools don't ever talk about how we stood up to them sometimes. They should know that we fought, Sarah thinks. I need to leave it on this recording machine that the Michif were fighters; that we never went down without a fight.

"A few days later our men came home and found us all weeping with the loss of the children. That night we built a big fire and had a council. The next morning the men loaded up their hunting guns, saddled up the horses and carts and went to the school. It was a long way away. Some of the men surrounded the building and my Dad and his brothers quietly went into the school with their guns. They didn't hurt the priests, but they picked up all our kids and packed them in the carts and brought them home. I was never so happy in my life when our kids came home. While the men were rescuing our kids, we women packed up everything we had. It wasn't much and it didn't take too long. But when the men came back with the kids we headed north and after many weeks of travelling around, we finally settled on the west side of Riding Mountain Park. We didn't stop for days because we were so afraid the police would come after us and make the kids go back to that school."

Sarah pauses again. She needs to let the bad feelings about that time fade a bit and to think of something else. Her mind goes back to the land they settled on near Riding Mountain. "It's funny now I think of it. Most of the settlers picked their lands for good soil – for farming. But not my Dad; he picked our land because it had a slough for ducks and because it had good trapping, hunting and fishing nearby. It's a good thing he never really tried to farm it, because it was bad farming land. Too rocky. We stayed there for a few years. But then we lost the homestead. The government came and made us move. They burned our cabin as we left so we wouldn't come back. They said we had to leave because we didn't pay taxes and didn't do any improvements. They were right about us not paying the taxes. We never had any money to do that. But we never understood how you could improve land. We didn't think of farming as an improvement because it ruined what we wanted the land for – hunting and trapping. It seemed funny to us to think that you could improve on the work of *le bon dieu*."

"Anyway, after that we moved to a road allowance near the Assiniboine River not far from Portage la Prairie." Sarah looks again at the *moshkwa* girl and asks, "do you know what road allowances are?" The girl shakes her head again. "The government sets aside certain corridors for roads. But they don't always build on them at first. So the land sits vacant. That's the land we moved onto. So many Métis moved onto them that they started to call us 'the road allowance people'. Anyway, we didn't know at first that the land we moved onto was a road allowance. We just knew it was vacant and there were no homesteads nearby. We built another log cabin and stayed there as long as they let us. At first we kept a guard. We worried that they would come again to take our children. So we drilled it into the kids, just like my Dad did when we crossed the border. If anyone asks – say you are French. Don't speak our half-breed language in front of others. Don't say you are a half-breed, don't say you are Métis or Michif. Say you are French."

Sarah looks at *moshkwa* girl again, "that's why people think the Métis are all gone you know; because we had to hide who we were so many times. We pretended we were French after Riel in 1870, and then again after Batoche in 1885, and then later to keep our kids out of the residential schools. We went underground really. We hid on the road allowances and pretended we were French. We did that for years and it's only now that we are beginning to resurface and say again with pride that we are Métis. You know, we didn't call ourselves Métis in my day. That's pretty new language, but it's what everyone uses these days. That's what my grandchildren say. They say we're Métis. I think Michif is a better word for us, but that's okay. Michif, Métis, it's the same people."

Sarah stops for a longer time now. She is trying to remember what she was talking about before. Something about the road allowance and schools. *Ah oui*, … "on the road allowance, we slowly began to understand that the best way to keep our kids from being taken away to school was to send them to school ourselves. We figured out that if we sent our 'French' kids to the day school the government would not come and take 'Métis' kids away to residential school. So we did that. My kids got a bit of an education. Not so much as my grandkids, but some anyway."

"I have come full circle now. I am back in the Turtle Mountains. I spend my days on this porch, summer and winter... as much as I can. They make me go inside at night to sleep. But I like it here. I don't feel the cold or the heat too much. I like to sit here and watch the long view."

Sarah starts to nod for a moment. This has been a lot more talking than she has done for a long time. *Moshkwa* girl has been quietly effective in getting Sarah to talk, something others who pester her with questions have not been able to achieve. The machine continues to record Sarah's short nap. Suddenly Sarah wakes up fully again. Now she is finished answering the disturbing question about where she lived. She wants to talk about something else.

"This morning the nurses here told me that today is April 17, 1982 and that the Métis have been recognized in a new Constitution for Canada. I was surprised, but pleased. You know why?" *Moshkwa* girl shakes her head and smiles back. "Because the Métis have been on a long journey. We were proud people once. We were the masters of the plains. We were great hunters. We were the translators for the Indian treaties. We lived in between the Indians and the settlers and we helped both sides to understand each other. We were the bridge between two different peoples but no one cared about us. No one even saw us as a people. They just saw us as a bunch of individuals who would eventually disappear. They thought we would just blend in with either the white folks or the Indians. We suffered after the buffalo and the defeat of Riel and we sank so low that we became road allowance people. But today, when they put us in a document like that, when they say the Métis are an aboriginal people in Canada. Well maybe in the future that will mean something to my people. I think maybe it means they will eventually see us as who we are. It means we can stop hiding and pretending we are something other than Métis. So it's a big day for us. It will mean something to my grandchildren and my great grandchildren."

Sarah rocks. She is pleased with the news she heard that day. "Do you know what else someone told me? They told me that the Métis cart trails that we made on the prairies can still be seen from an airplane. I've never been on an airplane, but I'm glad that there is something left of our Michif way of life. I wonder if the people in those planes know what they are seeing. I wonder if anyone knows what it was like to live like that. But I guess that's what you are doing isn't it? Getting me to ramble on about where I lived so that little machine can keep a record and you can write it down." *Moshkwa* girl nods and smiles kindly.

"That's good, my girl. It's good if someone remembers *les Michif*. You know, my people, we didn't collect things. If you move as much as we did, you don't want things. You don't want to carry them around. We never left things behind either. If we had any metal, it was precious so we kept it. Our cabins were made to fade back into the earth. We didn't make paintings or write books or make statues. We didn't build big skyscrapers or big churches like I saw in Winnipeg. We walked lightly on the earth and we left it pretty much as we found it. But that means people think we weren't there. They think we disappeared when they hanged Riel or when the fur trade died or when the buffalo were hunted out. People today don't know what the Métis did or where we went or even that we're still here. I like it. It seems right somehow that we left our tracks on the prairie. That's our art, our statement. Our tracks say – remember the Métis, we were here and we are still here."

***

COLONIA JAPONESA SAN JUAN, BOLIVIA, FEBRUARY 6TH, 2009

HOW RICE, PERSIMMONS, SOY AND A WHOLE HOST OF OTHER CROPS FROM JAPAN RESHAPED THE BOLIVIAN COUNTRYSIDE

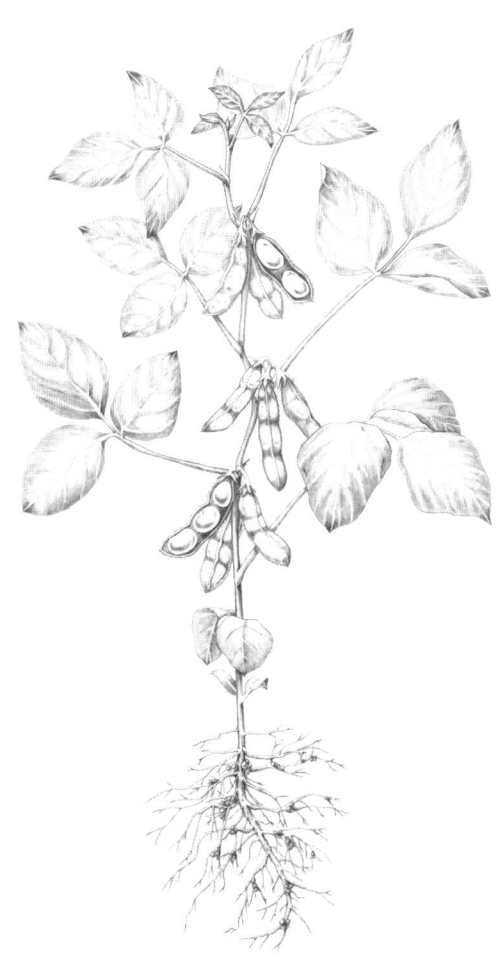

BY
KOZY AMEMIYA

Rice

A passionate debate breaks out among the group men having dinner at the end of an exciting day. They argue about which rice tastes best—and these men would know. They are not cooks; they are Japanese farmers in Colonia Japonesa San Juan and Colonia Okinawa. On this day of festivities, they were both hosts and guests, celebrating the National Day of Rice in the CAISY, the cooperative of Colonia Japonesa San Juan. Colonia San Juan is also designated by the Ministry of Agriculture, Livestock Farming and Rural Development as the "Rice Capital" of Bolivia.

"Blue Bonnet is not bad," says Seiji Yamamoto of Colonia San Juan.

"Yeah, but I think Carolina has a slightly better taste," says Tetuo Oshiro of Colonia Okinawa.

"None of those American varieties can match Japanese ones," insists Fumiyuki Sato of San Juan.

"True, but you should mix those American varieties with glutinous sweet rice. It tastes quite good. Try it," says Akira Chibana of Okinawa.

"How about *Grano de Oro*?" interjects Antonio Flores, a newspaper reporter from Santa Cruz covering the event, who is invited to join the farmers for dinner, and mentions the only brand name of rice he knows.

"*Grano de Oro* is no good," says Sadanobu Miyagi, a senior member of Colonia Okinawa. Everyone agrees.

"Why not?" asks Flores, "I thought it was very popular."

"Sure, it's popular among Bolivians," says Miyagi. "You know why? Because it increases its volume tenfold when it's cooked. With one kilo of *Grano de Oro*, you can feed twenty people. With Japanese rice, you can feed only seven. It's a matter of volume versus taste."

"Boy..." sighs Flores, "you guys take rice pretty seriously."

"Of course we do. Rice is very important to us," says Masao Kagawa, a senior member of San Juan. "We've been eating rice for centuries. Without good rice, we don't feel good about ourselves. Take sushi, for example. You might think sushi is all about fresh fish. Not so. Sometimes sushi is shellfish and rice. Sometimes it's pickled fish and rice. Sometimes it's cooked vegetables, eggs and rice, rolled and wrapped with a sheet of seaweed. You see, you can have sushi without fish, but you can't have sushi without rice. To make good sushi, you have to have good rice cooked perfectly, seasoned correctly, and kept at the right temperature. In other words, it's rice, not fish, which is essential to good sushi. Moreover, rice is the core of our culture."

"That's right," agrees Yamamoto, "Whenever I eat good rice, I feel so Japanese and happy."

"Indeed, I feel the same way," echoes Miyagi. "In fact, we came here to Bolivia to grow rice."

"We were not the first Japanese who came to Bolivia, though," says

Yamamoto. "The very first ones came through Peru and settled in the Amazon region at the time of the rubber boom. When the rubber boom collapsed, some of them went to the cities like La Paz. Most of them were sort of absorbed in the Amazon. They may have Japanese surnames but they are Bolivians. All of us here in San Juan and Okinawa came after World War II."

"Do you know what attracted us to Bolivia?" says Kagawa turning to Flores.

"It's the promise of 50 hectares of free land to each family. Fifty hectares may not sound all that big for farmland now, but in those days it was like a dream for us Japanese."

"It sure was," echoes Miyagi.

"This is before your time, Antonio," continues Kagawa, "but you probably learned at school about the 1952 social revolution of this country by the MNR. The new MNR government wanted to turn this lowland region into Bolivia's breadbasket and promised to give government-owned land to those who were willing to clear the jungle and cultivate it. So migrants came from the Altiplano and we came from all over Japan."

"And we came from Okinawa," adds Miyagi. "Okinawa was under US occupation in those days, and our lives were really miserable. We could escape from misery and get 50 hectares at the same time. It was more than a dream, we thought."

"But life was harder here in a way, wasn't it?" says Oshiro. "I was a small kid when my parents brought me here, so everything was play for me. But I knew grownups were having a really rough time."

"That's right," nods Miyagi. "The jungle was much thicker than we'd imagined. There were no roads so we were totally isolated. Besides, a mysterious disease hit us and practically everybody got sick. Fifteen people died one after another. So we had to move, and start clearing land again. Then we had to move yet again. Finally, we came to the current site of Colonia Okinawa and had to start all over again."

Silence falls on these men for a short while, whether they experienced this painful beginning or not.

"We were only lucky not to get hit by a disease in San Juan," Kagawa breaks the silence in a sympathetic tone. "Other than that, our conditions were no better. No roads, no machinery, no school as promised. But what could we do? We had to clear the jungle to grow rice. Did you see a metal water flask in our museum? Its top is missing, but the top had a small magnet that we used to make a basic compass for clearing lands and drawing boundaries. When we managed to clear enough land, we burned the dead trees. Finally, we began growing rice."

"Did you grow rice in the same way as it was done in Japan?" asks Flores.

"No, in Japan we grew rice in irrigated fields," says Kagawa. "We couldn't do that here right away. So we learned a lot from the local farmers. Do you know what a *punzón* is? It's a tool to make a hole in the ground and then drop in a few seeds. We got them from our Bolivian neighbours and sowed seeds. It worked very well. Slash and burn is effective for a few years, at least. We had a good crop in the first year. Some of us harvested rice with hand sickles that were brought from Japan and cut the stalks as Japanese would normally do. But others harvested in the Bolivian way and cut off each ear with knives or snipped it off with fingers. Then, we used threshing machines we'd brought from Japan. It's a simple machine and every farmer in Japan was using it. It really impressed Bolivians because they'd been threshing rice by beating it with long sticks. They admired it so much they asked us to thresh their rice with our machine. Someone made a small business by going around to nearby Bolivian villages, hauling his machine and its motor on a horse cart, to thresh their rice," chuckles Kagawa.

"Why didn't I think of that?" says Miyagi with a hearty laugh. His laughter has a ripple effect on everyone. He continues, "Our rice crop increased each year. You can even say we had a bumper crop around 1960. We took our rice to the market in Santa Cruz. It sold very well."

"Ah, I remember," says Flores, "my mom mentioning *Arroz Okinawa*."

"That's right," nods Miyagi, "we sold our rice by that name. But transportation was a huge task because the roads were so bad. It takes only a couple of hours now to Santa Cruz, but in those days it could take a whole week after the rain because the roads were just long strips of mud with deep mud holes." Miyagi grimaces as if it were still happening. "Getting our rice milled in the city was also a problem because the quality of their work was so inconsistent. But the biggest problem was the fluctuation of rice prices—we couldn't really rely on rice for stable income. You see, growing dry rice depends on rainfall. In Okinawa we often don't have enough rain."

"And sometimes we have too much rain in San Juan," adds Sato.

"That's right," continues Miyagi, "you need the right amount of rain at the right time to grow rice on dry land. But when the weather is perfect and everybody has a bumper crop, the market has a glut of rice, and the price goes crashing down. When we had bad weather, the market had a shortage of rice and the price went up, but we didn't have much to sell. We needed another cash crop."

"Indeed," echoes Kagawa. "We were growing vegetables from the very beginning, such as tomatoes, cucumbers, eggplants and green leafy vegetables, for ourselves. We wanted to sell the surplus in the local markets, but in those days Bolivians hardly ate vegetables."

"Did you grow anything else?" asks Flores.

"Oh, yes," responds Kagawa, "we grew cacao and coffee, but back then nothing really worked as cash crop."

"We also grew sweet potatoes, maize and *yuca*, but they were for us," adds Miyagi. "Throughout the 1960s, we were really at a loss. We felt as if we were in the deep dark hole and didn't know how to get out of it. On top of that, there were terrible floods, and all of us were so depressed…. Many farmers left for Santa Cruz de la Sierra or migrated to Brazil or Argentina or returned to Japan. Who could blame them? Life was unbearably hard here in those days."

Fruit

"But," says Yamamoto, "we never stopped searching for cash crops, did we? Watermelon was an early success. There were watermelons here before we came, though they weren't very sweet. The ones we grew with the seeds we'd brought from Japan were so sweet and juicy. Bolivians loved them. Then in the early 1970s we got a new variety of seeds from Japan. We knew by then our watermelons would sell well to Bolivians, so we planted them in a large quantity in San Juan. Sure enough, they were a big hit and became famous as *sandía japonesa*. The problem was that Bolivians loved our watermelons so much they saved the seeds and began planting them. Within five years, so many Bolivian farmers were growing *sandías japonesas* there was no point for us to grow them."

"You can say the same thing with pineapples," adds Sato. "We brought the pineapples from Hawaii. Who grows watermelons and pineapples now in San Juan? Nobody."

"*Ponkan* is facing the same fate," says Yamamoto.

"What is *ponkan*?" asks Flores.

"It's what you call *mandarina japonesa*. They were sent here from Kyushu in Japan, after initial success in Brazil, by the Japanese government's aid agency, the Japan International Cooperation Agency. We call it JICA for short. We imported young *ponkan* trees from Brazil. At first, the JICA research station here in San Juan tested its production, propagated it by grafting, and distributed the young trees to us farmers. We learned how to graft *ponkan* shoots ourselves quickly and the *ponkan* production spread like lightening. It was a huge success, as you know. Bolivia did have a few varieties of citrus before *ponkan* was introduced, but *ponkan* is far superior in flavour. It has made Colonia Japonesa San Juan famous with its production. But again, the Bolivian workers learned the technique of grafting and began growing *ponkan* themselves at far less cost. Look at the Santa Cruz-Cochabamba highway. Both sides are lined with *ponkan* orchards! And señoras and kids are selling *ponkan* at every highway toll station and at roadside stands all over Santa Cruz. Now Bolivians produce more *ponkan* than we do. *Ponkan* is still called *mandarina japonesa* among Bolivians, but it is now a Bolivian fruit, grown and consumed by Bolivians." Yamamoto pauses and looks at Flores, "It might as well be called *mandarina boliviana*."

Everyone laughs.

"But you still have *mandarina* orchards in San Juan," points out Flores.

"Yes, but very soon, we'll have to chop all our *ponkan* trees down," says Yamamoto with a touch of chagrin. "We take pride in producing the top-quality fruit. But our *ponkan*'s future is doomed. You know why? Because Bolivian farmers have neglected *ponkan*'s health maintenance, and their trees are infested with a serious disease. Our orchards are now surrounded by the diseased trees. So it's only a matter of time before the disease will attack our trees," sighs Yamamoto.

"What are you going to do then?" asks Flores, concerned but curious nonetheless.

"Oh, we've been mindful to diversified agriculture," says Sato, assuredly, "so we always have multiple things going at one time. The biggest thing that can take over *ponkan* is macadamia nuts. A long time ago, we brought macadamia seeds from Hawaii. It took the trees such a long time to bear fruit we found that it was not cost effective to grow macadamia nuts as a cash crop."

"I have such a tree in my garden," interjects Kagawa. "It's a giant tree now."

"Those early trees are now indeed giants," says Sato with a smile. "About thirty years after we brought macadamia seeds to San Juan, we got new varieties from Brazil and Paraguay. With those varieties, the commercial production of macadamia nuts is feasible."

"Ah, I've seen small bags of macadamia nuts at fruit stands in the Yapacaní market," says Flores, excitedly. "I had no idea they were locally grown!"

"They're in hard shell, aren't they?" Sato says matter-of-factly. "We have a processing plant at the CAISY to shell and process nuts."

"CAISY?" asks Flores.

"It's our co-op," explains Sato, "short for Cooperativa Agropecuaria Integral San Juan de Yapacaní. We export most of the shelled and dried nuts to the U.S. and Europe."

"I see," says Flores. "I also saw other things at the Yapacaní market that I'd never seen before. I believe they're Japanese. One is a big, long, white radish."

"That's a *daikon*. Yes, it's Japanese," confirms Kagawa.

"I thought so," Flores is pleased.

"I heard locals put *daikon* in soup," adds Kagawa.

"I saw another," continues Flores. "It's a squash but it's dark green and rather flat."

"That's *kabocha*, also Japanese," again confirms Kagawa.

"It was so interesting," says Flores beaming, "to see those Japanese things alongside traditional Bolivian varieties of potatoes, all in a local market run by Bolivians from the Altiplano."

"Yeah, but think about this. We include Bolivian food in our diet too, such as *yuca*," says Sato.

"When I was a kid, my mother used to make *kamaboko* with the snakes we caught," adds Oshiro.

"*Kamaboko*?" queries Flores.

"It's fish cake. Well, in this case, I should say snake cake," says Oshiro.

"If you're so blunt and honest, no guests from Japan will eat it," chuckles Chibana. Everyone grins knowingly.

"Getting back to macadamia," says Flores to Sato, "how many trees do you have?"

"None," answers Sato promptly. "A big fire burnt all my macadamia trees about fifteen years ago. All 3,000 of them."

"I'm sorry."

"Don't be sorry. For farmers, disasters are a permanent feature of life. Fires, floods, too much rain, too little rain, pests, you name it. That's why diversification is so important. I now grow persimmons."

"Persimmons? What are they?" Flores has never heard of them.

"They're fruit originally from East Asia, like China, Japan and Korea. I don't know how to describe them. They can be sweet, but their sweetness is very unique. And their texture is very unique too. Chinese and Koreans are crazy about them, and buy up all I can grow, regardless of price. I'd like to grow more of them."

"May I see the trees?" asks Flores.

"No, not here. It's too hot here for persimmons. I grow them in Samaipata."

"Samaipata?" Flores is surprised. "That's a resort area for the rich in Santa Cruz on the old Cochabamba highway."

"That's right," says Sato. "It's cool because it's in the foothills of the Andes, and yet it's close enough to Santa Cruz. I've also planted apple trees there. I want to grow peaches too. My wife's uncle grows organic vegetables there and can sell everything he grows."

"I know a Japanese farmer who grows flowers in Samaipata," adds Chibana.

"So the key to success for us," maintains Sato, "is to keep one step ahead of Bolivian farmers and to maintain the high quality of our produce."

Everyone nods.

Eggs

"It's not just fruit," says Kagawa, "we've also developed egg production in San Juan. Well, at first, we raised chickens for eggs for ourselves. Then some of us thought of starting egg production for a cash income, and started with 100 chickens. Soon there were eleven of us, with 1,050 chickens, and we formed a poultry farmers' association. I think that was in 1961. We sold eggs within the *colonia*, but soon we got more incubators, which meant more chickens, and then more eggs. In fact, we got more eggs than we could sell in the *colonia*. So the following year we began taking our eggs to sell in Santa Cruz. As we got more and more chickens, we needed experts' advice on how to house them, what and how to feed them, and so forth. So in the early 1970s, we asked the JICA for help and they sent us a Japanese poultry expert from Brazil each year. You know what? We came to produce 30% of the eggs in all of Bolivia."

Phew! Flores whistles.

"Unfortunately," continues Kagawa, "we were hit by fowl typhoid. It spread very fast and many of us had to stop egg ranching. During that time, wood was easily available, so some farmers experimented with battery cages. But it didn't work. The experts from the JICA used expensive vaccination from Japan and Brazil and tried other treatments, but they couldn't eradicate fowl typhoid. They came to the conclusion that we had to keep the chickens off the ground. So we decided on using wire cages and imported cages for 57,000 chickens from Brazil. That's when my family resumed egg ranching. Actually, it was my wife who was in charge of chickens, like most families here. Eventually, the CAISY bought a machine to manufacture cages, so it was much easier and less expensive to buy cages. I'm happy to say not a single case of fowl typhoid has occurred since."

"Eggs are not only good for us," says Yamamoto, "but also good for consumers. They're particularly beneficial for the poor, who can't buy meat, because they can buy a few eggs at a time."

"I know," Flores agrees, "you can buy just one egg at a local market. But where is your biggest market?"

"It's definitely La Paz," answers Kagawa. "We had a good network with Japanese in La Paz that helped us set up a sales office there in the 1970s. We trucked in our eggs over the Andes. In the early 1980s we were supplying about 90% of eggs consumed in La Paz."

"That's amazing," exclaims Flores, impressed.

"There's a photo of a cargo airplane at the tarmac hung on the wall at the CAISY's office. Did you see that?" Kagawa asks Flores. "Do you know what that is all about? That's a photo of stacks of crates being loaded onto the plane. In those crates were tens of thousands of fresh eggs all destined to La Paz. That was in 1982. In that year it rained so heavily that some parts of the road to La Paz were washed out. On top of that, hyperinflation was ravaging the nation, and transportation workers demanded wage hikes to keep up with the inflation and staged a strike that lasted a long time. Soon La Paz was running out of eggs. Some say that the mayor of La Paz telephoned the CAISY and begged for the shipment of eggs. But I think the sales reps in La Paz should get credit for this. Anyway, the CAISY chartered a cargo plane about five times and transported the total of 1.2 million eggs to La Paz. It was one of the proudest moments for the egg ranchers in San Juan. In that year we produced 50 million eggs."

"How about now? Do you still dominate Bolivia's egg market?" asks Flores.

"In La Paz, yes, though our share of its market is now about 60%," says Kagawa. "We produce and sell about 250 million eggs per year. And our share of the entire domestic egg market is now about 25%, down from 30% because some Bolivians with capital in Santa Cruz and Cochabamba began doing the same thing as we were doing. So, right now, the market has currently a surplus of eggs. Still, our eggs are very popular. Break one of our eggs and you see a really yellow yoke, and it's round, not flat like others'."

"So, again, quality is most important for you," says Flores.

"That's right," affirms Kagawa. "Our success in egg ranching ended up bringing about stiff competition, and we're going to survive the competition with quality."

"Two hundred and fifty million eggs are a lot," says Flores. "How many chickens are there in San Juan? And how many egg ranchers?"

"There are about 70 egg ranchers in San Juan," answers Sato, "and over 880,000 mature chickens in total. There are also semi-mature and juvenile chickens, as well as chicks, and every two months they replace the older birds. You must know one unique aspect of egg ranching in San Juan. That is, usually women are in charge. It's definitely so in my family. My wife has 16,000 mature chickens and 4,000 semi-mature and juvenile birds in her charge. But she says the señoras in San Juan are far better off than those in Japan because it's easy to hire farm workers in Bolivia. In Japan, they have to do everything themselves."

"It's true," says Kagawa. "My wife has recently retired and handed over her responsibility to our son. Taking charge of day-to-day operations for egg ranching is a lot of work. We have 18,000 chickens. I think having this enormous responsibility for keeping the chickens productive made her feel quite powerful." His eyes give off an impish sparkle.

"I agree," says Sato with a broad grin. "My wife says the only drawback of having chickens is you can't take a long vacation. After all, you're responsible for living things and you never know what might happen to them while you're away."

"Are there still any diseases for chickens?" asks Flores.

"No, it's not that," answers Kagano. "The main enemy of chickens right now is heat. Chickens are susceptible to heat stroke. When it's 40 degrees Celsius, chickens can die one after another."

"What do you do when it's really hot?" asks Flores.

"We spray water over the chickens," says Kagawa. "You know it's been getting warmer and warmer the last few years. That's worrisome."

"How about free-range eggs that are getting more and more popular in Europe and North America?" asks Flores.

"Ah, that'll be impossible here," says Sato, "because of the disease in the soil. My wife says she feels sorry for her chickens for being cooped up in a cage for life. But what can you do?"

Everyone nods in silence.

<u>Soybeans</u>
"How about Okinawa?" Flores asks Miyagi, Oshiro and Chibana. "Colonia Okinawa seems quite different from San Juan. Did you also try different crops?"

"Oh, yes, we did," replies Miyagi. "But we didn't get JICA assistance for a long time because we were under the jurisdiction of the United States through the Ryukyu government. We grew peanuts, *yuca*, maize and soybeans, and raised pigs and chickens. But nothing really worked to give us a steady income and we were really desperate for a primary cash crop. Finally in 1968 the Japanese government took charge of us. We had a terrible flood in that year, and many people left the *colonia*. So the prospect of getting the Japanese government's help gave us a sliver of hope. Around that time, a cotton boom began in Santa Cruz and we wanted to jump on the bandwagon. We were told that cotton was considered drought tolerant, and so it seemed a suitable crop for us. We experimented for a year, and growing cotton looked as if it was going to be really advantageous for the *colonia*. The JICA gave full support, and so with JICA loans we imported huge cotton harvesters from the U.S. and began all-out cotton production. Colonia Okinawa is twice as big as San Juan in terms of area, though we get less rain and are often subjected to major flooding from the Rio Grande. Cotton production seemed ideal." Miyagi pauses. Flores waits for him to continue. "But it turned out an utter disaster. We had bad weather, floods and pest infestation, and the market prices collapsed as a ripple effect of the oil shock. It was indeed an utter disaster." Miyagi falls into silence.

"In ten years," Oshiro takes over, "cotton production in Okinawa died completely. What we had left were immense debts. This caused another wave of exodus from Okinawa. As it turned out, this disaster opened the door to prosperity for those of us who remained. We could take over the lands that were left behind by those who had forsaken agriculture. We became quite land-rich though we remained very cash-poor. Then came the hyperinflation. It was so ferocious it devastated the country. But, ironically, it was beneficial for us with debts because, though we had borrowed U.S. dollars from the JICA, we were able to repay JICA in Bolivian pesos. When the hyperinflation ended, it practically wiped out our immense debts. I know one guy who had a debt of tens of thousands of dollars and paid back with only several heads of cattle. Another guy kept some U.S. dollars for several months until the Bolivian peso came down enough. He then exchanged the dollars he had to pesos and paid back his loan in full. Lucky, eh? But the most important thing is we mechanized for cotton farming and that gave us a great head start on large-scale mechanized farming. We had plenty of land, all we needed was the right crop."

"Was it soybeans?" asks Flores, already sure of the answer.

"That's right!" affirms Oshiro. "Around that time, soybeans were becoming an important crop for export in Santa Cruz, and we decided to try it."

"Actually," adds Yamamoto, "soybeans were first grown in San Juan at its JICA research station. In those days, Bolivians had never seen or heard of soybeans. I remember a CAISY representative took soybeans to Peru and Chile, but no one knew what they were. We were growing soybeans in order to make *miso* for our own consumption. We never dreamed that soybeans would be a key cash crop."

"*Miso*? What is that?" asks Flores.

"That's soybean paste we use for soup and other Japanese cooking," answers Yamamoto.

"When the soybean boom started in Santa Cruz," resumes Oshiro, "the JICA research station selected some American varieties of soybeans. Some of us tried them in Okinawa and hit the jackpot. In no time, soybean production spread all over Colonia Okinawa. Of course, there are good areas and not so good areas for soybean production, but overall soybean has been the top cash crop for Okinawa for the last twenty years. At one point Okinawa produced nearly 40% of the entire soybean production of Bolivia."

"The first-generation immigrants used to say," recalls Chibana, "we owe our lives to soybeans. They were so happy and so grateful. They went through such extreme hardships they were nearly broken. We grow soybeans in the summer. Some people also grow them in the winter for seeds. But the areas you can grow soybeans in the winter are limited."

"Some of us in San Juan grow soybeans in the winter for chicken feed," says Sato. "It works for us, too."

<u>Wheat</u>
"What do you grow in the winter in Okinawa?" asks Flores.

"Wheat," answers Chibana. "It's not easy to grow wheat in this warm climate. Our co-op, CAICO, and JICA did research on suitable varieties for tropical conditions, because wheat production is perfect for large-scale mechanized farming. Now there are good varieties from Brazil and Argentina, and we've succeeded in having the highest yield per hectare in Bolivia."

"Oh, yes, I remember," says Flores, "Okinawa is designated as the Wheat Capital of Bolivia."

"That's right," affirms Chibana. "Have you been to the National Day of Wheat that we host? No? It's just like the National Day of Rice in San Juan. Not only do the farmers come from different communities, but all sorts of agricultural associations, agrichemical companies, seed dealers, and government officials come, too. You should come."

"I'd be honoured," responds Flores.

"We even have our own flour mill," adds Chibana. "It's a medium-size mill. Now the CAICO is building a huge one, so that we can make pasta with our wheat."

"That's amazing," exclaims Flores. "So in Okinawa you grow soybeans in the summer and wheat in the winter?"

"In the summer we also grow maize, sunflowers and sorghum," says Oshiro.

"And on top of that," begins Miyagi with a grin, "I happen to grow something you're eating right now."

Flores, baffled, looks at the dishes on the table and points at each vegetable, looking at Miyagi each time. Miyagi shakes his head each time, amused.

"Can't you tell?" chuckles Miyagi. "It's the fish in front of you."

"But this is a *pacú*," says Flores, still confused. "Isn't it caught in the river?"

"You can catch a *pacú* in the river, yes," says Miyagi with a bigger grin. "But this one is from one of my ponds."

"Wow!" Flores is surprised. "How long have you been fish farming?"

"I started about four years ago. I dug ponds where the soil was clay and you couldn't grow anything else very well. Now I sell them to several restaurants in Santa Cruz. You can even order *pacú* at Okinawa's old restaurant, which is very popular among Bolivians. They didn't have fish in their menu before. It's my old-age pension. You don't have to go out every day and watch them grow." Miyagi lets out a hearty laugh.

"Do you think some Bolivians will copy your idea and start fish farming?" asks Flores, remembering what happened to fruit and egg production.

"Maybe. Or maybe not. It's too early to tell. When they see me making a lot of money, then they might start fish farming too. Just like everything else."

Back To Rice
"So," Flores changes the subject, "all these years you've worked on diversifying your farming, and you've succeeded. Now, however, rice seems very important again, seeing as we're celebrating the National Day of Rice here in San Juan. What's going on?"

"A very good question," says Kagawa, as if he were waiting for this subject to come up. "Remember we told you earlier that rice grew well on the dry land for a few years after slash and burn? But soon weeds overwhelmed the rice. Weeds are the biggest problem in growing rice. Wild "red rice" is another problem. Its seeds are mixed in with regular rice seeds, and it's so difficult to eliminate it at the seed stage. Once grown, it is even more difficult to eliminate it. But "red rice" doesn't grow in the water. So, wet rice production automatically solves the "red rice" problem."

"Another benefit of wet rice," interjects Yamamoto, "is that you can conserve the nutrients in the soil. If you keep growing rice in the same dry land it depletes nutrients in the soil, and you have to keep moving to new lands or apply heavy fertilizer. As you know, the remaining forests around Bolivia's Japanese colonies are now protected for environmental reasons. We have run out of land for such expansion. That's another reason for not growing dry rice so much any more. To start wet rice production, you do need a lot of capital to build canals and to level the elevation of the land, but eventually it's cost effective."

"How so?" asks Flores.

"Because," continues Yamamoto, "water itself keeps weeds from growing so you can reduce the use of herbicide. You can also reduce the use of fertilizer because the nutrients won't be leached from the land. Rice is a unique plant in that it can extract nutrients from water. You can keep growing rice in the same fields for years and years, decades and decades, and centuries and centuries, without depleting the nutrients in the soil. That's what we Japanese have done for two thousand years. Some Asian societies have been doing it even longer."

"Besides," adds Sato, "wet rice has a more stable yield than dry rice."

"To go back to the time when we switched from dry to wet rice," says Kagawa, "a few of us at first tried mixing wet and dry-land rice seeds and planted them when the rainfall was particularly heavy. We were delighted that we had a crop 50% to 60% higher than dry-land rice alone. Then we tried wet rice alone with rainwater we'd saved in the field. Everybody saw the success, so more farmers converted dry rice fields to wet rice fields each year."

"So you went back to the traditional Japanese method of growing rice?" Flores is curious.

"Well, not quite the same way as the farmers do in Japan," explains Sato. "Imagine. Japanese farmers' fields are very small. So they put a lot of labour, by transplanting young plants with machines, and produce high-quality, high-yield rice. Here, we have huge fields. I hire a transplanting contractor, and he brings a team of 60 workers. They do transplanting by hand, and it costs me $150 per hectare. But it's cost-effective to transplant. Still, I'm in the minority. Only 30% of the farmers in San Juan do transplanting. The

Japanese government donated a rice-transplanting machine to the San Juan rice farmers so that more of us could explore the possibility of adopting a transplanting process. A machine can transplant about four hectares a day. Another difference is we don't have an intricate irrigation control system yet, as they do in Japan. So, there's still a lot of room for improvement."

"Do you grow other crops in the same rice fields in the winter?" asks Flores.

"You could, but I don't. After I finish harvesting, I level my rice fields and prepare for the next year's crop. It's possible to have two crops a year, but I'd rather prepare my fields to be in good condition. I need to level my rice fields every two to three years. When I was growing dry-land rice, I worked on 400 hectares. Now I cultivate 250 hectares for wet rice, but I get a steady crop, much higher yields and more stable income with wet rice."

"Is dry rice still grown?"

"Oh, yes," answers Kagawa. "The total area of CAISY members' rice fields is about 10,000 hectares. Right now, 75% of that is wet rice. The proportion of wet rice is constantly increasing, though."

"How about your water system?"

"I draw water from nearby streams," says Sato. "I've also dammed one stream and created a pond. I'm pretty happy about my pond. It's not only useful but quite beautiful. You know another benefit of doing wet rice? More birds and animals of all sorts come to the fields than I've ever seen before. I see, quite often, alligators sunbathing near the stream."

"In my pond," joins Yamamoto with a smile, "there're a group of *capybaras* that have taken up residence. I had to tell my workers to stop shooting them—*capybaras* are considered quite a delicacy among the locals."

"Yeah, it's really wonderful to see animals in our fields, isn't it?" adds Sato.

"Do you have enough water?" asks Flores.

"Water is no issue in San Juan," says Sato. "I'm drilling a well right now and it's far from the stream. There's abundant ground water."

"How about in Okinawa?" Flores turns to the men from Okinawa. "Do you grow wet rice, too?"

"San Juan is a reservoir of knowledge when it comes to wet rice," says Chibana. "The National Day of Rice inspired me to come see what was happening in San Juan. I'd just had my seventh consecutive crop failure. Why? Oh, floods, winds, drought, you name it, I had it. So I decided to grow wet rice where the soil was clay and there was easy access to water."

"When was that?" asks Flores.

"Five years ago," answers Chibana. "It was around then that we began growing wet rice in Okinawa."

"Indeed, we're catching up with San Juan," answers Miyagi. "More and more farmers are growing wet rice in Okinawa."

"I think Okinawa is more suitable to grow wet rice than San Juan," says

Yamamoto, "because there's much more land in Okinawa so you can do it on a much bigger scale than we do. Also there are more sunny days in Okinawa. Sunshine is very important for the rice yield."

"That's very true," says Miyagi. "The biggest rice grower in Okinawa is probably the biggest in Bolivia. He has 1,600 hectares of land for his wet rice production."

"Our efforts are paying off," says Kagawa, contentedly. "We invest $7,000 a year in the CIAT in Colombia."

"What's CIAT?" asks Flores.

"It's short for the International Centre for Tropical Agriculture. It's a research institution for eco-efficient agriculture and has gene pools for rice, beans and other crops. We buy a lot of seeds from them. We're proud of the fact that 70% of Bolivia's revenue from rice is generated by the seeds we've brought in."

"You've been successful in wet rice production," summarizes Flores, "so I assume it's fair to say you're responsible for disseminating the knowledge of wet rice production here in Bolivia, right?"

"Yeah, I suppose," Kagawa is modest.

"That's why San Juan was designated as the Rice Capital of Bolivia," notes Flores. "So you host the biennial National Day of Rice and share the knowledge and technique of rice production with a lot of Bolivian farmers. Doesn't that create more competitors for you?"

"Of course the number of rice growers is increasing," admits Kagawa. "Ten years ago, San Juan was the centre of rice production in Bolivia. Not any more. Now, Bolivian farmers who have capital grow rice in a big way, any place where water is available in Santa Cruz and even Cochabamba because income per hectare from wet rice is greater than that from soybeans. But it's a good thing. The rice market is also expanding, too. Remember, Bolivia wanted us to come here to help make this country self-sufficient in food."

"That's right," echoes Sato. "Ask people from the Altiplano or Cochabamba. They never ate rice before we came here. Rice was mostly for the middle classes. Remember when *yuca* was the staple for Bolivians in the lowlands? Nowadays, they eat more rice than *yuca*."

"In fact," says Flores, "I eat rice quite often myself."

"You see?" says Sato, beaming. "My workers eat rice with every meal, every day. Their wives fry rice first before boiling it. That's the Bolivian way of cooking rice, right?"

Flores nods.

"Do you know *arroz con queso*, Antonio?" asks Yamamoto.

"Of course, I do. I eat it all the time at my favourite barbecue restaurant."

"Well, that's originally a Japanese dish."

"Really?" Flores opens his eyes big and wide.

"Yes. In Japan we feed a sick person a bowl of rice porridge with pickled plums or seaweed. You know the Hospital Japones in Santa Cruz was established with the aid of the Japanese government, don't you? When Bolivians were fed rice porridge there and got well, they came to equate their recovery with rice porridge. At least it has a good image, no? So some restaurants started making rice porridge, but with a Bolivian twist. That is, they put salted cheese instead of pickled plums or seaweed. That's how *arroz con queso* was born!"

"That's fascinating," Flores is amused, "I always thought *arroz con queso* was purely Bolivian."

"So did I" laughs Chibana.

"It's not just rice," continues Yamamoto. "Bolivians used to eat very few vegetables. Now they not only eat more vegetables, but grow Napa cabbages and *daikon* themselves. Of course, we've incorporated Bolivian food into our diet too."

"I think," says Flores, looking around the dinner table, "that's the main difference between you and Mennonite settlers. You mix with Bolivians, but the Mennonites don't. They're totally isolated and live among themselves without letting anyone in. I think they're quite nervous now with Evo and his land reforms."

"We were nervous, too, at first," admits Yamamoto. "Not any more. As long as we have clear land titles and work our land, no one will take it away from us."

"Besides," says Oshiro, with an impish smile on his face, "we hear Evo loves sushi. All the sushi rice in Bolivia is supplied by our biggest grower. We've got a good connection with our President." Oshiro laughs, and so does everyone at the dinner.

***

PERPLEXING PEREGRINATIONS:
ON THE TRAIL OF DRIFTING COCONUTS

BY
CURTIS C. EBBESMEYER

Apples by Land, Coconuts by Sea

I did not grow up in the Tropics. My ancestors date back centuries from northern European farming stock. After World War II, my father planted a small orchard in our backyard in the hot and dusty San Fernando Valley, Southern California. With water, everything seemed to grow there: peaches, almonds, plums, apricots, pomegranates, boysenberries, figs, pineapples, and apples.

In grammar school, my classes sang "Johnny Appleseed Grace." He became one of my boyhood heroes. While travelling large parts of the American frontier, John Chapman (a.k.a., Johnny Appleseed, 1774-1845) planted apple seeds, from which trees took root and pioneers prospered. Without apple trees, the Earth's temperate latitudes would be far different.

Later, I took up beachcombing, trying to understand the sea through the flotsam that stranded on the shore. With the passage of time, my files bulged with accounts of tropical drifters. Slowly, it dawned on me, amazing as the story of the apple seed is, the bountiful seed of another tree reached all around another huge band of the earth, to touch lives and shape tropical cultures, spread not only by human hand but by the whims of ocean currents. This grand world-traveller is the coconut.

In the grocery store, they are as different as apples and oranges, but beyond, on land and at sea, apples and coconuts bear many similarities. Commercial world production of both is about the same: 97 billion pounds for apples (2006-2007), versus 118 billion pounds for coconuts (2002). The coconut has become the most famous drift fruit and enduring symbol of the Tropics.

Tropical seeds have long been thought to be lucky charms, and many have medicinal value. My father loved the ox-eye sea bean (*Mucuna sloanei*; a.k.a. hamburger bean) because it contained high concentrations of the L-Dopamine drug he took to treat his Parkinson's disease. In Sanskrit, the coconut palm is known as *kalpa vriksha*, meaning: "tree which gives all that is necessary for living." It is an apt observation. I've observed nearly all the parts of the tree provide some benefit to those who live nearby. The coconut provides food, the leaves make fine roofs, and the trunks are suitable for construction.

To my beachcomber ways of thinking, Johnny Appleseed becomes the currents and apple seeds become coconuts. He, like the currents, went from farm to farm as the currents dropped coconuts beach to beach. He spread Christianity just as preachers dispatched tracts in bottles on the sea. He helped pioneers just as currents provided a plenitude of necessities for ancient mariners and settlers. Johnny wandered all his life; currents will wander as long as there is an ocean. Truly, the coconut is the apple of the tropics.

Many a time I have seen apples floating ashore from a cargo of fruit lost somewhere out at sea. Fresh apples float for days on sea water because air comprises a fourth of their volume. Coconuts can float for months and remain viable. They become seafaring apples—Johnny Appleseed dispersed the apple like the currents and ancient explorers spread the coconut.

Wandering Coconuts

Imagine Johnny Appleseed with handfuls of apple seeds stashed in his knapsack. Where did he plant them? How did they shape the lives of the pioneers who settled by the apple trees? Imagine the currents with a similar number of coconuts. How did the currents handle these hardy drifters? Let us follow the fates of approximately twenty coconuts. In the firmament of coconuts, what do these score represent?

We cannot imagine the travels and adventures of the trillions of unreported coconuts, though we know that each had individual genetic signatures (DNA codes). From a forensic point of view, the fates of these drifters are the ultimate cold cases. Coconut palms lead long, productive lives. They begin bearing nuts at the age of five to seven years, and continue doing so until they are seventy to eighty years old. In its lifetime, a single coconut tree may produce 1,200–3,500 seeds. Here's my speculation. The total number of coconut trees on earth may number in the hundreds of millions. I estimated 200 billion coconuts produced in three human generations by multiplying 100 million trees by 2,000 coconuts in the life of each tree.

I hoped to contrast fruits found in a supermarket with coconuts roaming the ocean. So, I purchased a coconut at my local supermarket, the Quality Food Center (Q.F.C.) in the University Village, Seattle, Washington State. Amongst other tropical fruit, beside pears and oranges, it had been de-husked and shrink-wrapped in orange plastic netting. The placard on the stick amongst the coconuts advertised "White Coconuts, $2.99 each, King of Tropical Fruit." The plastic tag affixed to the plastic netting announced that my "One Groovy Coconut" was the "product of Dominican Republic" under the brand name of "Brooks Tropicals" product #4262, and recipe hints for preparing the coconut. Elsewhere in the store, I found coconut meat in candy bars, cakes, ice cream, pies, and cookies.

Then I remembered the coconut I had received via priority mail from Captain Charles Moore a few days before my birthday in the year 2000. Charlie had mailed it from Holualoa, on the Big Island of Hawaii, as he was setting out on his epic studies of the Great Garbage Patch. It was a coco-gram, still with the husk measuring six by twelve inches, but coated in plastic and painted with a colourful tropical scene, *"Aloha from Kona,"* and a map of eight major Hawaiian Islands stretching from the Big Island northward to Niihau. It had been too large for the postman to stuff in my postal box. To this day, it resides on my shelves amongst other types of flotsam.

I pitied these poor coconuts, trapped as they were within the confines of human contrivance, far from the adventurous lives of their seafaring cousins. They'd been unnecessarily encased in plastic, symbolic of the age of oil. The one with the husk had been encased in plastic, the de-husked one in plastic netting. Nevertheless, they did have their travels, one via jet plane from Hawaii, the other via boat, truck or plane from the Dominican Republic.

Coconut Cachet

According to Wayne Armstrong, the noted botanist: "Of all the 250,000 species of seed plants on earth, only about 250 species are commonly collected as drift disseminules on tropical beaches, and only about half of these are known to produce seeds that can float in seawater for more than a month, and still be viable. This relatively small number of drift seed species does not include seed plants dispersed on vegetation rafts and drifting garbage from ships. Although the total number of drift seed species with long viability periods may be relatively small, nonetheless they form a floral flotilla comprising countless billions of individuals riding the ocean currents of the world."

The best known of all seafaring seed drifters is the coconut. The cachet of this drifty fame extends to seeds of three trees in the palm family (*Arecaceae*). There exist, from smallest to largest: the sea coconut the size of a golf ball (a.k.a. golf ball bean; *Manicaria saccifera*); King Coconut (*Cocos nucifera*) the size of a human head; and the CoCo-de-Mer, or double coconut (*Lodoicea maldivica*), which is, in fact, double the size of King Coconut.

Sea coconuts wash ashore in great numbers along beaches of the Caribbean and the southeastern United States. They drop from trees that are native to the Amazon River, and may be carried by the Gulf Stream and North Atlantic Current to beaches as far as those of Northern Europe. The sea coconut tree, or troolie palm, is unusual with leaves nearly eight metres long.

The Coco-de-Mer palm tree produces the largest seed in the world and grows on only two of the 115 Seychelles Islands in the Indian Ocean. Its fruit, the largest recorded weighing up to 20 kilograms (42 pounds) and measuring up to half a metre (1.6 feet) across, contains the double coconut, so called because it has two lobes, each resembling a coconut.

Sailors who first saw the double coconut floating in the sea imagined that it resembled a woman's disembodied buttocks. This fanciful association is reflected in one of the tree's archaic botanical names, *Lodoicea callipyge*, taken from Greek meaning "beautiful rump." The viable nut is too heavy to float, and only rotted nuts can be found on the sea surface, thus explaining why the trees are limited in geographical range to just two of the Seychelles Islands.

Wherever coconuts meet various cultures, they take on different values and significance. The origin of the generic name "Coco" for coconut may be traced to the three germination pores on the endocarp layer surrounding the seed. Iberian explorers found a resemblance to a monkey's face in the three round indented markings or "eyes" located at the base of the coconut. After the year 1500, Hispanic traders introduced the coconut into West Africa. Perhaps, too, they introduced a method for catching monkeys with coconuts, a story my father told to me when I was a boy.

The story goes that long ago, in Africa, India, and South East Asia, the natives employed a unique and interesting way to control pests. People relied heavily on their harvests, and monkeys were troublesome. To capture a monkey, a farmer would hollow out one end of a young, fresh coconut (an old, brown one would not attract monkeys), and emptied out the juice. He cut a hole just big enough to accept a monkey's hand (about one and a half to two inches in diameter). The larger the selected coconut, the better, so the monkey would have trouble lifting it. Then the native inserted a few peanuts. The monkey put his hand in the coconut and, when he made a fist around the peanuts, he trapped himself.

Because the monkey would not let go of the peanuts, its clenched fist could not be pulled through the hole, thereby preventing its escape. The natives pulled a string attached to the other end of the coconut and captured the monkey, with fist still clenched about the prize. This story comes down to us in part because of the enduring moral underlying the story, namely, that to survive it is sometimes necessary to let go of a treasured possession or situation.

No doubt the capturing of monkeys with coconuts predates the year 1555, when the word "coconut," first appeared in English print, taken from the Spanish and Portuguese word "Coco," meaning "monkey face." The Japanese culture retained the ancient mariner humour, for coconuts there are known today as "*Kokoyashi no mi*." Perhaps the humour came from the antics of capturing monkeys with coconuts.

The light, fibrous husk allowed King Coconut to drift on the ocean and propagate on other shores. We focus on the coconut king from here onward.

Travels with Coconuts

From my thirty years of beachcombing, what follows is a factual composite of the travels of a group of twenty-some coconuts. Perhaps the winds in a Pacific storm shook them from an unknown tree onto the beach below. I take, as a starting point, the Nesias (Micronesia, Melanesia, Indonesia), for this is thought to be their ancestral home. On this sandy shore, a giant coconut crab (*Birgus latro*) cracked one open; the tides carried the brethren to sea, probably with *Birgus larvae* within their husks. Birgus is the largest land-living arthropod in the world. It is known for its ability to crack coconuts with its strong pincers, and eat the copra.

This unique association of crab and coconut is an important one because the scientific community is divided as to how the coconut has spread around the world (e.g., prolific in South America, India, the Pacific Islands, Hawaii, and Florida). Whether viable coconuts floated to islands of the tropical Pacific has been much debated for more than a century. Some authorities have gone so far as to say that there is no shore where its presence is not due, directly or indirectly, to its having been planted by man. Other authorities cite localities where coconuts appear to have seeded themselves naturally, including cays in British Honduras (Belize), rocky islets in the Fiji Islands, the east coast of Trinidad, Cocos-Keeling Atoll in the Indian Ocean, and Krakatau and adjacent islets. Following the catastrophic eruption of Krakatau of 1883, coconut palms sprouted on Tetiaroa Atoll in French Polynesia.

But of all the arguments for a transoceanic dispersal of coconuts, perhaps the most interesting and persuasive comes from the widespread distribution of the coconut crab (*birgus latro*). With their strong claws, these giant crabs cut holes into coconuts and eat the contents, a behaviour unique in the animal kingdom. Careful study indicates that this large land crab could not have achieved its present widespread inter-island distribution with only a 30-day aquatic larval stage, unless they rafted to distant islands. It appears that the tiny post-larval (*glaucothoe*) stage may have been spent in the moist husk of floating coconuts. Ancestors of modern coconut crabs probably migrated concealed within floating coconuts.

A mature coconut eventually drops from the tree, unless it is picked. The embryo eventually sprouts out of the shell and becomes a young coconut seedling. At this point, the plant can survive for several more weeks or months on the food and water inside as roots gradually develop and extend out of the shell to anchor the plant in the ground.

As complete seed packages, coconuts have been known to travel to faraway lands to find new homesteads. Stories abound of coconuts floating their way across seas and oceans to be washed ashore on distant islands, rooting themselves in groves to greet visiting humans in search of paradise. Once the husk is removed, the seed dies. The de-husked coconuts at the supermarket are no longer productive seed packages.

My wife and I are avid watchers of *Forensic Files*, which is often broadcast on cable TV channels. There was one episode, for example, in which unburnt logs were found in a fire extinguished at a murder crime scene. Crime scene investigators needed to know if the logs in the fire pit came from the trees near the home of a suspect. Turned out, each tree has a DNA pattern as unique as each human does. Thus, I suspect that each coconut has a DNA pattern that could be traced to its parent tree. Someday, when DNA databases have further evolved, botanists will be able to trace coconuts, like we trace people, by their genetic code. The group of coconuts we are following here, having fallen from the same mother tree, probably carry similar DNA.

By the thirtieth day after our group of coconuts first fell from their mother tree, one coconut had drifted ashore with a load of *Birgus glaucothoe* where the crab eventually became established. By the hundredth day—the time a coconut may float and still germinate—the relentless flow of the ocean had transported the group hundreds of miles. Currents circling an island brought another one to shore where it sprouted. The others in the group drifted ever onward.

In time, religion, poetry, celebrations, and romance claimed the remaining coconut brethren.

Spell Over India
Coconuts enchanted India and other regions near the Indian Ocean. On the Nicobar Islands, at the southern tip of India, for example, until the early part of the 20th century, the Nicobarese people used whole coconuts as currency. Elsewhere, Sikhs inserted coins into coconuts to honour the 400th anniversary of the founding of their religion. In yet a third example, during *Raksha Bandhan* festivals, Hindus offered coconuts to the sea god *Varuna*, believing that the three eyes of the coconut (*stoma*) represented those of the god *Shiva*. Wondering how flotsam influenced history, I delved into these religious aspects.

Beachcombing opens doors to diverse lines of knowledge. On Wednesday, October 26, 2005, along Gulf Road in Apponagansett Bay, Massachusetts, Mike O'Reilly, Environmental Affairs Coordinator for the Town of Dartmouth, beachcombed a hairy brown coconut. Embedded in its husk he discovered an aluminum, squarish, five-paise coin minted in 1974 in India.

The Sikh religion makes much of the coconut and the paise coin. Sikhism began in 16th century Northern India with the teachings of ten Gurus. The lineage of living Gurus continued for centuries, until the tenth told his followers that a book of Holy Scriptures, known as the *Guru Granth Sahib*, was to be their future guide. The Guru Gobind Singh opened the *Granth Sahib*, placed a five-paise coin and a coconut before it, and solemnly bowed to it as his successor. Today, a five-paise coin has the approximate monetary value of a penny, but four hundred years ago, five paise was a substantial sum.

Sikhism is the only religion in which scripture is worshiped like a living Guru. In these teachings, the word "Guru" is composed of two words meaning light (RU) dispelling darkness (GU). Bowing before the *Guru Granth Sahib* is akin to bowing before Divine Light. On September 1st, 2004, Sikhs the world over celebrated the 400th anniversary of the first reading of the *Granth*. Many Sikh dignitaries gathered in the U.S.A. to celebrate it at the White House (perhaps they had heard of the famous coconut which sat on the desk of the oval office while Jack Kennedy was president—we will talk of this coconut later). To this day, coconuts are often presented as offerings throughout India. It is likely that on the shore five-paise and coconuts were offered to mark the 400th anniversary.

The condition of a coconut holds clues as to its drift longevity. When freshly dropped from its mother tree, it has a smooth, green skin. As it drifts, the husk disintegrates. "*It is quite possible that the coconut did wash in from open sea,*" wrote Mike. "*Apponagansett Bay — where I found it — opens to Buzzards*

Bay. And Buzzards Bay is wide open to the Atlantic. It is not at all uncommon to have debris wash on shore. It is mostly derelict fishing gear, but all kinds of overboard debris can be found. You find some unusual things that are kind of curious, but never a coconut."

Mike's discovery gave me a new appreciation for the significance of stranded coconuts. If others were set adrift in honour of the 400th anniversary, similar coconuts might have stranded around the North Atlantic Ocean. "*On August 15, 2006, one was found at Melvaig, near Gairloch on the Scottish west coast,*" reported Fiona Russell, a freelance journalist in Scotland. "*A couple of weeks later on August 31, another coconut was found on Dunnet Beach between Thurso and John o' Groat's. Both had most of outer husk intact.*" So, I considered the drift rates across the North Atlantic Ocean to see if Scotland might be the source of the coconut that washed ashore in Massachusetts.

My reasoning implies that Mike's coconut might have floated forty months. Given that the long-term average drift speed in the North Atlantic Ocean is seven miles per day, the currents could have transported the coconut nearly 3,000 nautical miles, thus ruling out India as a possible origin. Objects from India can reach the Americas along a drift route of more than 15,000 miles: south along east Africa, turn right around South Africa, then another right turn into the Atlantic Ocean to Florida and Massachusetts. The coconut hosted few barnacles, suggesting an origin in the North Atlantic Ocean as far away as Europe. Thus, Scotland along with other sources in the U.K., might be the location where the Massachusetts coconut could have originated, as described below.

After reporting the Sikh festival, I learned of Hindu beach festivals from the newsletter *Drifting Seed*, edited by my friend Ed Perry IV, author with John V. Dennis of *Sea-Beans from the Tropics*. Many Indians have immigrated to the United Kingdom where they continue celebrating ancient festivals. The following, derived from the reports by Dr. Roger A. Hewitt in the September 2009 issue of the *Drifting Seed* newsletter, come from the vicinity of London.

At the mouth of the Thames River facing the North Sea, Hindu beach festivals took place at Shoebury on September 16, 2007. A year later, on September 13, this festival was repeated during the noon high tide. Both festivals involved the floatation of coconuts. Most of them remained on the beach as broken shells. Another was seen, with a black skin and partly pink endosperm, on the Shoebury strand line formed two days after the *Raksha-Bandhan* festival on August 16, 2008.

During *Raksha Bandhan*, on the fifteenth day of *Shravan* (July or August), to honour *Varuna*, god of the sky, water, celestial ocean, law and the underworld, in some parts of India coconuts are offered to the sea. "In the days when the gods warred with demons, the consort of *Indra* (Puranic King of the Heavens) tied a *rakhi* (a silken amulet) around his wrist, by virtue of which, it is said, the god won back his celestial abode from his enemies."

As a mark of auspiciousness, coconuts are also broken at shrines and temples. However, at most places, it celebrates the love of a brother for his sister. On this day, sisters tie *rakhi* on the wrists of their brothers to protect them against evil influences. In some places, before tying the *rakhi*, barley saplings are placed on the ears of the brother.

Raksha-Bandhan appears to be when numerous coconuts are also floated in the canals at Southall in London. Like the Sikh August or September festival, "Hindu festivals are, at least in theory, timed by their lunar calendar and therefore to oceanic tides. For example, *Ananta-Chaturdashi*, worship of *Vishnu*, is observed on the day before the full-moon day of the lunar month *Bhadrapad*, and the start of the public festival of *Ganesha* is on the fourth day of that month when the full-moon day is counted as the 15th."

It is unlikely that these and the other stranded coconuts from Chalkwell and Westcliff originated from the Shoebury festival. However, before the major festival started in September 2005, coconuts stranded from earlier smaller Hindu meetings. A London coconut had floated 34 kilometres along the Paddington and Regent's Canal from Bull's Bridge. It had to pass three more sets of locks to reach the River Thames at Limehouse. Flotation tests conducted by Hewitt indicated that coconuts could remain floating for 722-1,571 days, long enough to float across the North Atlantic Ocean. These reports by Dr. Roger A. Hewitt reinforced the possibility that the coconut found in Massachusetts might have originated in festivals held in the U.K.

That these festivals have survived for centuries begs the question as to how far back in time humans have utilized coconuts. To find out, I turned to the discipline of archaeology.

<u>Kokoyashi</u>
For as long as humans have eaten apples (earliest records date from circa 6,500 B.C.), coconuts have been found in archaeological digs. The oldest known transocean coconuts were found near Fukui along the Sea of Japan in a garbage dump on the Hasu River, where it drains into Lake Mikata. In a layer deposited 5,500 years ago, Japanese archaeologists discovered pieces of four coconuts, along with other seeds (walnuts and acorns), earthenware, and wooden artefacts, as well as the remains of log boats and tuna bones indicative of fishing deep, offshore waters.

About four thousand years ago, 50 miles east of present-day Tokyo, on the beach of Choshi City, an ancient beachcomber carried home a waterlogged coconut. Later, the villager fashioned it into a container and lacquered it. Perhaps a catastrophe such as a tsunami, earthquake or volcanic eruption, buried it in the muddy sediments.

In a two thousand year old stratum elsewhere along the Sea of Japan near Fukuoka, a coconut was discovered, along with earthenware jars. Ancient coconuts drifted from tropical climes to both the east and west coasts of Japan, as do coconuts in modern times. This dig is located not far from where high school teacher Tadashii Ishii has beachcombed for many years. How many coconuts might the people of an ancient village have found? In twenty five years, Ishii found 656 coconuts on a mile of beach, for an average rate of 26 coconuts per year. Judging by the thousands of miles of Japanese shoreline, the prehistoric seas must have been alive with drifters.

Japanese have maintained a long and intimate relationship with the sea, including the use of drifting objects. I learned of their modern day influence on culture through beachcombing. In 2002, over coffee in Seattle, Nancy Yaw Davis asked if I'd help convene a meeting in Sitka, Alaska, concerning the drift of ancient peoples from Asia to the Americas. One should never underestimate the power of beachcomber gatherings. Some Japanese attended the meeting. Over lunch at Sitka's Little Tokyo Restaurant, they told me of the importance of coconuts in Japanese society.

Japanese Poem
In Japanese society, coconuts have long been symbols of romance. Atop Japan's Atsumi Peninsula, from the Irago Promontory, sightseers overlook a beautiful beach where coconuts wash up. Yanagida Kunio visited this beach and found a coconut. Later, he recounted his beachcombing to his friend poet Shimazaki Toson. In the year 1901, Toson romanticized the coconut's journey:

Coconut by Toson Shimazaki
There is a far away island, which
    I don't know the name.
From this island came one coconut
    floating on the ocean.
How long have you, coconut, been
    drifting on the waves,
    so far from the coast of your home?
Your tree must be grown over with
    thick, leafy branches.
Casting its shade all around.
I am also a drifter, wandering without
    a home.
I have used the seaside as my pillow.
Picking up this coconut and placing it
    to my chest, I feel such a loneliness.
And the loneliness of my drifting life is
    renewed in full.
When I behold the sun setting into the

sea, tears flow down my face.
For I am in an unknown place.
And yet, when my thoughts drift to the
comings and goings of the waves, I
> *know*

that one day I will return to my
> *true home.*

Another of the group of coconuts ended up in a different kind of celebration. The Ise Wan Ferry runs between the Port of Toba, Mie Prefecture, and the Port of Irago in Tahara, Aichi Prefecture. Between April and June, 1979, the Ise Bay Ferryboat Company celebrated its 15th anniversary by giving one thousand couples that were honeymooning on Rota Island (Marianas), a coconut to throw into the sea.

In the following months, beachcombers reported the honeymooners' coconuts downstream, in the North Equatorial Current near Guam, Miyake Island, and Mindanao Island in the Philippines. In a later effort, using coconuts to foster international peace, the Ise Bay Ferryboat Company screwed an aluminum medallion onto each coconut as if two friends were to toast: *"May the tides tie us together."*

Cupid's Archery Range
The Atsumicho Tourist Association (A.T.A.) has continued Japan's romance with coconuts. The waters immediately up current from Japan form an oceanic archery range in which the arrows (coconuts, like cupid's arrows) are thrown onto the Kuroshio Current (transport) which flows 300 miles north to Japan's main islands (target). Individuals, schools and companies sponsor coconuts for 2,000 Yen each (approximately $15 US).

A.T.A. released coconuts in the vicinity of Okinawa from the Vessel Southern Coral. Affixed to each coconut was a medallion: *"Coconut Message of Love, Journey of Love No. (Number assigned to Irakozaki - Flowers & the Sound of Waves, sponsor of the coconut), Atsumicho Tourist Association. Set this coconut adrift on the waves and your thoughts will reach the faraway Beach of Love."*

During seventeen years (1988–2004), A.T.A. sponsored the release of 1,964 Cupid Coconuts. The medallion affixed to each indicated the year of launch in Part Numbers in which, for example, Part II meant 1989, and Part XIV meant 2001. Each year, during the months of May through July, they released, on average, 115 coconuts. As the coconuts drifted northward, Japan divided the Kuroshio into two branch currents, one carrying coconuts into the Sea of Japan, the other branch transporting coconuts into the vast Pacific Ocean. Cupid, it turned out, fired many more coconuts to the east compared to the west. Of the

Cupid Coconuts reported to A.T.A., a few (11%) veered west into the Sea of Japan, whereas the majority (89%) turned east into the Pacific.

On the Kuroshio Current, the coconuts drifted 300 miles. Overall, beachcombers reported only one out of 26 coconuts released, a 3.8% reporting rate typical of scientific messages in bottles. The Black Current, as the Kuroshio has long been known to Japanese fisherman, carried most coconuts past Japan into the Pacific. At this time of writing, no Cupid Coconuts have been reported from Hawaii and the Americas, probably because, en route, the medallions fell from the coconuts. The medallions did not carry contact information telling beachcombers where to report the coconuts, and affixing the medallions may have caused the coconuts to leak and prematurely sink.

As their rotted husks fell away, some will remain adrift as the newlyweds celebrate their fortieth wedding anniversaries. We can be certain of this endurance from the fates of other coconuts, as we will see in the next section.

Endurance
It was, I suppose, inevitable that the scientific culture, inspired by the seed flotation tests of Charles Darwin, would address the long-term drift potential of seeds, including coconuts.

August 1971 found John V. Dennis beachcombing the sandy shores along southeastern Florida, where I have spent many an October searching for flotsam. John had in mind flotation experiments of long duration, much longer than Darwin's. He knew that his test would have to run for years before his seeds sank. He had picked his location well. The drifts of 85,000 scientific messages in bottles, released in the Caribbean and Gulf of Mexico, had shown that this location was a major collection spot for flotsam. Amongst all this flotsam, beachcombers had over the years reported 125 species of tropical seeds. He was searching for seeds that had already been floating for some time, seeds he could take home for his experiments.

John gathered up dozens of seeds and placed them in gallon plastic containers open at the top and filled with seawater. He picked up a King Coconut and a sea coconut, which were both plentiful along eastern Florida. Given that the coconut was without a husk, it may have floated for a considerable time before he put it in the container. Every few months, John exchanged the water in the containers with water from the nearby ocean. When a seed sank, he removed it and noted its time afloat.

The interior hard shell of a coconut does not crack easily. On and on, the seeds floated, the epic experiment gaining fame and taking on a life of its own. Finally, near the end of his life, he had no choice but to ask his friend, Ed Perry IV, to take over the water-bearing duties. As I write in 2010, after thirty-nine years, the sea coconut and King Coconut, stripped of its husk, both remain afloat in the tank.

These float times apply, of course, to laboratory conditions, so we cannot be sure if the coconuts we are following across the open ocean would drift for two score or more years. There is, however, some confirmation of John and Ed's experiment from a message on a coconut that washed up thirty-one years after it was set adrift in World War II.

Wartime Cocos
The most famous coconut-borne message must be the one dispatched during World War II by John Fitzgerald Kennedy, 35th President of the United States. While Lieutenant Kennedy commanded the Motor Torpedo Boat PT-109, a Japanese destroyer sliced his boat in half. The ramming killed two men and badly injured two others. The surviving crew swam miles to a small island by the name of Nauro. Kennedy carved a rescue message on a coconut and gave it to local natives to deliver to the Torpedo Boat base at Rendova Island, one of the Solomon Islands.

At great personal risk, through 65 kilometres of hostile waters, the native scouts delivered the following message: "NAURO ISL . . . COMMANDER . . . NATIVE KNOWS POS'IT . . . HE CAN PILOT . . . 11 ALIVE . . . NEED SMALL BOAT . . . KENNEDY." Kennedy and his men survived on coconuts for six days before rescuers found them. Later, President Kennedy kept the coconut on his desk in the White House oval office. It now resides in the John F. Kennedy Library in Boston.

Beachcombers often ask me to recommend non-polluting containers for their seaborne messages. They are concerned about introducing plastic and other non-biodegradable materials into the ocean. Following President Kennedy's example, I usually recommend coconuts because they are natural and plentiful. I also recommend coconuts as "messages in bottles" to beachcombers because of their flotation endurance, as exemplified by another example from World War II. According to Bert Webber, a Japanese soldier carved his farewell on the shell of a coconut. In 1942, as Japan's forces drove Americans from the Philippines, General Douglas MacArthur famously declared: "*I shall return.*" Among the invading Japanese, Tatsushiro Yamanouchi, 34, laboured as a civilian war worker. Two years later, the Japanese retreated before MacArthur's advance, abandoning Yamanouchi in the jungle.

Shortly before the final battle, Yamanouchi sealed a farewell to his wife in an empty, husk-less coconut. On it, he carved a message, telling where the finder could reach his wife. Three months later, MacArthur landed at Leyte. Within months, Yamanouchi perished in the jungle.

Thirty-one years later, a contractor found the coconut floating a few miles from Yamanouchi's home near Taisha Beach on the Sea of Japan. "*The coconut floated over the waves and finally landed on our home beach,*" said his widow, 65, recognizing Yamanouchi's handwriting, "*because my husband's great desire had reached the heavens."*

Where had Yamanouchi's message drifted? The absence of barnacles on the coconut suggested a short time in the sea. It looked as though blowing sand had abraded one side of the coconut till typhoon waves refloated it. Then, like a salmon reaching home after years at sea ranging over thousands of miles, it drifted northward to Yamanouchi's wife.

Three decades is a long time, time enough to circle the earth along pathways known as Grand Tours.

Grand Tour
King Coconut has a split personality. With their husks intact, coconuts float at sea and remain viable for several months; with their husks removed, they may float on as one bony, grey stone has done for thirty-nine years in John and Ed's tank flotation experiment. From this experimental endurance, I speculated on the grand journeys our coconut group might make aboard the currents that entwine around our planet.

My favourite Grand Tour takes twenty-five years for a round trip along a track around earth starting and ending in the Indian Ocean. From the coastal waters off Western Australia, the Tour runs west across the Indian Ocean to East Africa, where it turns south to the Cape of Good Hope. From the southern tip of Africa, the Tour heads north and west to the great promontory of South America, and thence northward through the Caribbean Sea and the Gulf of Mexico, entering the North Atlantic Ocean at the southern tip of Florida, U.S.A. From there, the Gulf Stream takes King Coco across the Atlantic to Norway, and ever northward into the Arctic Ocean. For years, King Coco makes its way along the coast of Siberia, finally turning south through the Bering Strait to Japan. Then across the North Pacific to North America, then redoubles the North Pacific back to the Philippines. Finally, comes the last leg on which King Coco threads its way through the island archipelagos of its ancestral home in the Nesias, and back to Western Australia.

How far could a free ranging coconut drift during the thirty-nine years while their cousin was trapped in the flotation test tank? Assume that these far drifters do not wash up on a beach and the currents persisted in transporting the epic coconuts for all those fourteen thousand days afloat. On and on they drifted, beneath the stars and the moon, conveyed ever farther at typical ocean speed of five to eight miles per day. Our marathon coconuts could have covered a total distance of a hundred thousand miles. Small wonder that the hairless palm stones often wash up. How I wish they had carried devices to record their travels like human runners do with pedometers strapped to their waists.

I'd like to think that at least one coconut adventurer drifted on and on, having made its way 40,000 miles along a continuous band of currents, threading through the sea like film in a projector, spooling around the gyres of currents, and orbiting the oceans between the continents. This journey holds great insight into our changing environment.

The value of travel, they say, lays not the destination so much as the adventures had along the way. Then surely, these coconuts on Grand Tours must have had the most fabulous journeys. If only these epic wanderers could speak as in the story *Manuscript Found in a Bottle* by Edgar Allan Poe. Our coconut adventurer no doubt has had many untold stories flow past it, an endless, undiscovered passenger making its way around the gyres of currents that continuously orbit the oceans. These gyres affect not just the waters they carry but the very climate above. With this in mind, the journey of our last coconut—as wondrous as its travels might have been—may very well hold even greater insight into our changing environment. Indeed, the oceans may very well be playing Johnny Appleseed with our world's future...

***

Kozy Amemiya holds a PhD in sociology from the University of California, San Diego, and is a research associate at the Japan Policy Research Institute. She has been investigating Okinawan and Japanese immigration to Bolivia since 1996.

Anders Bell holds a master's degree in assyriology from the University of Cambridge. He worked as an archaeologist in Turkey and as a research assistant to the Keeper of Antiquities at the Fitzwilliam Museum in Cambridge. He is a Curatorial Coordinator at the Canadian Centre for Architecture.

Giovanna Borasi is an architect, curator and editor. Curator of Contemporary Architecture at the Canadian Centre for Architecture since 2005, Borasi has worked on several exhibitions and books, with a particular focus on how environmental and social issues are influencing today's urbanism and architecture. Borasi was editor and writer (1998–2004) for *Lotus International* and *Lotus Navigator*.

Ilaria Brancoli Busdraghi holds a history degree from the University of Rome Tor Vergata. Her thesis dealt with the Italian stoneworkers who moved from Tuscany, Piedmont, and Lombardy to Vermont at the end of the 19th and beginning of the 20th century, a topic on which she has since lectured and published internationally. She teaches in the Italian department at Middlebury College, Vermont.

Lev Bratishenko is a Montreal-based writer, curator, and opera critic. He is Senior Web Editor at the Canadian Centre for Architecture and has published articles in *Mark* and *Cabinet*.

Ian Chodikoff is an architect and the editor of *Canadian Architect* magazine. He holds graduate degrees in architecture and urban design from the University of British Columbia and Harvard University respectively. His work explores the effects of multiculturalism in contemporary North American society. In 2003, as a recipient of the Druker Traveling Fellowship at Harvard's Graduate School of Design, he investigated the relationship among urbanization, and migration between Italy and Senegal.

Curtis C. Ebbesmeyer holds a PhD in oceanography from the University of Washington. He is co-author of the book *Flotsametrics and the Floating World* (with journalist and author Eric Scigliano, 2009), and since 1996 has published the quarterly newsletter *Beachcombers' Alert*. Report flotsam to him at www.flotsametrics.com

Bernard L. Herman is the George B. Tindall Professor of American Studies at the University of North Carolina at Chapel Hill. He collaborated with the anthropologist Svend Holsoe and the photographer Max Belcher on *A Land and Life Remembered: Americo-Liberian Folk Architecture* (1988). Herman is currently completing a collection of essays, *Troublesome Things in the Borderlands of Contemporary Art*, as a 2010 recipient of a John Simon Guggenheim Fellowship.

David Howes is a professor of anthropology at Concordia University in Montreal, and the Director of the Concordia Sensoria Research Team (CONSERT). His research interests include cross-cultural jurisprudence, constitutional studies, indigenous psychologies, and aesthetics, and he has published several books on senses and cultures. He is presently researching *the sense lives of things* in the Pitt Rivers Museum, Oxford. For more information, see www.david-howes.com

Serge Michel is a journalist and currently Editor-in-Chief of the Swiss daily *Le Temps* in Geneva. He has covered Switzerland, Eastern Europe, Africa and Iran, where his reports for *Le Figaro* and *Le Point* won him the Albert Londres prize in 2001. Working with the photographer Paolo Woods, Serge is the author of several books using travel-writing as a way to engage with subjects such as the global lust for petroleum, the war in Afghanistan, the invasion of Iraq, or the arrival *en masse* of the Chinese in Africa.

Maureen Power is the Curator of History at The Rooms in St. John's, Newfoundland. She holds a PhD from Memorial University of Newfoundland, where she was focusing on material culture and public sector folklore. Her PhD took her to Fogo Island, the largest of the offshore islands of Newfoundland and Labrador, for three months collecting a variety of folklore for the Digital Archives at Memorial.

Riitta Oittinen is a Finnish social historian, science journalist and critic living in Brussels. Oittinen is particularly interested in history and visual culture, especially photography and urbanism. Her current project, *Histories, Images and Europeans*, involves volunteer photographers who document manifestations of "Europeanness" globally.

Wouter Oostendorp finished a bachelor's degree in building engineering at the HAN University of Applied Science in Arnhem and a master's degree in architecture at the Delft University of Technology. He has worked as an architect at MVRDV and Baumschlager-Eberle in Hong Kong and recently has joined LIAG architects in The Hague. Oostendorp continues to be active in the field of research and design under the name Shelter + Strategy (www.shelterandstrategy.com).

Peter Sealy is a PhD candidate at Harvard University, where he studies the relationship between photography and architectural practice in the 19th century. He holds architecture degrees from McGill University and the Harvard Graduate School of Design. Between 2007 and 2010 he has worked as a Research Assistant at the Canadian Centre for Architecture in Montreal.

Jouke Sieswerda holds a graduate degree in architecture from the Delft University of Technology. His master's thesis, developed together with Wouter Oostendorp, dealt with the physical aspects of the social degeneration of the Bijlmermeer and similar post-war housing estates. He has worked as an architect for NL Architects and VMX Architects and is currently working at ZUS (Zones Urbaines Sensibles) in Rotterdam.

Jean Teillet is a partner in the law firm of Pape Salter Teillet, Toronto and Vancouver, where she specializes in Aboriginal rights litigation and treaty negotiations. She was lead counsel at the Supreme Court of Canada in the first Métis rights trial *R. v. Powley*. Teillet has several published works including a chapter in the second edition of *Great Questions of Canada*. Teillet is the great-great-niece of Louis Riel.

David Theodore is a doctoral student at Harvard University in the departments of the History of Science and of Architecture, Landscape Architecture, and Urban Planning and Design, where he is researching the intersecting histories of architecture, medicine, and technology. He is a Trudeau Scholar and was awarded a fellowship from the Social Sciences and Humanities Research Council of Canada. He has co-published articles on the history of healthcare architecture in *Technology and Culture*, *Canadian Bulletin of Medical History*, and *Social Science & Medicine*.

REFERENCES

LEV BRATISHENKO
WHEN A CUCUMBER IS NOT A CUCUMBER: AN E.U. TALE OF CUSTOMS AND CLASSIFICATION

Commission Regulation laying down quality standards for cucumbers (EEC) No 1677/88, O.J. L 150, p. 21–25 (15 June 1988). http://eurlex.europa.eu/LexUriServ/LexUriServ.do?uri=CELEX:31988R1677:EN:HTML (accessed August 26, 2010).

MAUREEN POWER
RE-CONFIGURATIONS: A TOWN IN NEWFOUNDLAND GROWS WHEN HOUSES ARE FLOATED IN FROM FAR-FLUNG OUTPORTS

Ennis, Ernest. "The Way It Was in St. Kyran's." Christmas supplement, *Monitor* 51, no. 12 (December 1984): 28. Archives of the Roman Catholic Archdiocese of St. John's.

Heritage Foundation of Newfoundland and Labrador. *Fisheries Heritage*. Website. http://www.fisheriesheritage.ca (accessed August 26, 2010).

Maritime History Archives. *Resettlement: No Great Future*. Memorial University of Newfoundland. Website. http://www.mun.ca/mha/resettlement/index.html (accessed August 26, 2010).

Walden, Scott. *Places Lost: In Search of Newfoundland's Resettled Communities*. Toronto: Lynx Images Inc., 2003.

BERNARD L. HERMAN
RETURNING TO A NEW LAND: HOW THE ARCHITECTURE OF THE OLD SOUTH MADE ITS WAY TO ARTHINGTON, LIBERIA

Belcher, Max, Svend E. Holsoe, and Bernard L. Herman. *A Land and Life Remembered: Americo-Liberian Folk Architecture*. Athens: University of Georgia Press / Brockton Art Museum/Fuller Memorial, 1988.

Miller, Randall M., ed. *Dear Master: Letters of a Slave Family*. Ithaca: Cornell University Press, 1978.

Tyler-McGraw, Marie. *An African Republic: Black and White Virginians in the Making of Liberia*. Chapel Hill: University of North Carolina Press, 2007.

Wiley, Bell I., ed. *Slaves No More: Letters from Liberia, 1833–1869*. Lexington: University Press of Kentucky, 1980.

DAVID HOWES
OH BUNGALOW, BORN BY THE BAY OF BENGAL, YOU CONQUERED AN EMPIRE—AND THEN THE WORLD—REDEFINING SUCCESS EVERY STEP OF THE WAY!

Clark, Clifford Edward, Jr. *The American Family Home, 1800–1960*. Chapel Hill: University of North Carolina Press, 1986.

Harrison, Percival T. *Bungalow Residences: A Handbook for All Interested in Building*. London: Crosby Lockwood and Son, 1920.

Howes, David, ed. *Cross-Cultural Consumption: Global Markets, Local Realities*. London: Routledge, 1996.

King, Anthony D. *The Bungalow: The Production of a Global Culture*. London & Boston: Routledge & Kegan Paul, 1984.

Lancaster, Clay. *The American Bungalow, 1880–1930*. New York: Abbeville Press, 1985.

Wilson, Henry L. *The Bungalow Book: A Short Sketch of the Evolution of the Bungalow from Its Primitive Crudeness to Its Present State of Artistic Beauty and Cozy Convenience*. Chicago: H.L. Wilson, 1910.

PETER SEALY
ON THE MOVE OF IROQUOIS, ONTARIO: HOW CHOOSING A SITE TO THE EAST OFFERS AN OPPORTUNITY FOR FUTURISTIC LIVING

Cantacuzino, Sherban. *Wells Coates: A Monograph*. London: G. Fraser, 1978.

Coates, Wells. "To the people of Iroquois: A plan with a message." Script of speech delivered August 31, 1954, Wells Coates Archive, Box 10C, Canadian Centre for Architecture, Montreal.

Cohn, Laura. *The Door to a Secret Room: A Portrait of Wells Coates*. Aldershot: Scolar Press, 1999.

Cowell, Elspeth. "Wells Coates' Toronto Island Redevelopment Project." *SSAC-SEAC Journal* 20 (June 1995): 41–50.

Richards, James Maude. "Wells Coates. 1895–1958." *Architectural Review* 124 (December 1958): 357–360.

Special issue on St. Lawrence Seaway. *Royal Architectural Institute of Canada Journal* 36 (May 1959).

ANDERS BELL
DEADLY RE-EVALUATION: WHEN THE IBIS, ONCE SACRED IN EGYPT, BECAME AN ALIEN MENACE IN FRANCE

Commission des Sciences et Arts d'Égypte. *Description de l'Égypte : ou recueil des observations et des recherches qui ont été faites en Égypte.* Vols. I and II: *Antiquités, Descriptions.* Paris: L'Imprimerie Impériale, 1809–18. http://descegy.bibalex.org/ (accessed September 1, 2010).

Marion, Loïc. "Annexe 2 : La dangerosité de l'Ibis sacré, mythe ou réalité ?" Report from a meeting of the Conseil Scientifique Régional du Patrimoine Naturel, Université de Rennes, France, September 4, 2006. http://www.pays-de-loire.ecologie.gouv.fr/IMG/pdf/Annexe_2__expos_ibis_L._Marion.pdf (accessed August 26, 2010).

Savigny, Jules-César. *Histoire naturelle et myth ologique de l'ibis.* Paris: Allais, 1805. Reprint. France: Nabu, 2010.

Yésou, Pierre, and Phillipe Clergeau. "Sacred Ibis: A New Invasive Species in Europe." *Birding World* 18 (December 2005): 517–526.

Yésou, Pierre, Phillipe Clergeau, and Céline Chadenas. "Ibis sacré (*Threskiornis aethiopicus*) : Etat actuel et impacts potentiels des populations introduites en France métropolitaine." Report. Rennes, France: Institut National de la Recherche Agronomique / Office National de la Chasse et de la Faune sauvage, March 2005. http://www.oncfs.gouv.fr/IMG/pdf/ibis_INRA_ONCFS.pdf (accessed August 26, 2010).

ILARIA BRANCOLI BUSDRAGHI
EXPATRIATE EXPERTISE: WHEN THE ARRIVAL OF SKILLED ITALIAN WORKERS TRANSFORMED THE VERMONT GRANITE INDUSTRY

Audenino, Patrizia. "The Paths of the Trade: Italian Stonemasons in the United States." *International Migration Review* 20 (Winter 1986): 779–798.

Avolio, Marcello. "L'emigrazione degli scalpellini di Baveno a Barre, Vermont (U.S.A.) dal 1861 al 1915." Thesis, Università degli studi di Milano, 1991.

Burattini, Roberto. "Italians and Italo-Americans in Vermont." Manuscript, ca. 1937, Vermont Historical Society, Montpelier.

Hathaway, Richard. "Men Against Stone: Work, Technology, and Health in the Granite Industry." In *Celebrating a Century of Granite Art,* edited by Gene Sessions. Montpelier, VT: T.W. Wood Art Gallery, 1989. Published in conjunction with an exhibition shown at the T.W. Wood Art Gallery & Vermont College Arts Center in Montpelier and the Barre Museum at the Aldrich Public Library.

———. "The Granite Workers of Barre, 1880–1940." In *We Vermonters: Perspectives on the Past,* edited by Michael Sherman and Jennie Versteeg, 225–238. Montpelier, Vermont Historical Society, 1992.

Hooker, George Ellsworth. "Labor and Life at the Barre Granite Quarries." Manuscript, November 1895, Vermont Historical Society, Montpelier.

Lane, Karen. "Old Labor Hall, Barre, Vermont: Preserving a Working-Class Icon." *Labor's Heritage* 10 (Spring/Summer 1999): 48–61.

Tomasi, Mari. "The Italian Story in Vermont." *Vermont History* 28 (January 1960): 72–87.

IAN CHODIKOFF
THE BACK-AND-FORTH CYCLE: HOW TEMPORARY SENEGALESE WORKERS LIVE ON THE EDGES OF ITALIAN SOCIETY AND RAPIDLY TRANSFORM THE BUILT ENVIRONMENT BACK HOME

Abdoul, Mohamadou. "Urban Development and Urban Informalities: Pikine, Senegal." In *Urban Africa: Changing Contours of Survival in the City,* edited by AbdouMaliq Simone and Abdelghani Abouhani, 235–260. New York: Zed Books, 2005.

Barbagli, Marzio. *Immigrazione e reati in Italia.* Bologna: il Mulino, 1998.

Cruise O'Brien, Donal B. *Saints & Politicians: Essays in the Organization of a Senegalese Peasant Society.* Cambridge: Cambridge University Press, 1975.

Diop, Momar-Coumba. *Le Sénégal contemporain.* Paris: Éditions Karthala, 2002.

Diouf, Mamadou, and Mara Leichtman, eds. *New Perspectives on Islam in Senegal: Conversion, Migration, Wealth, Power, and Femininity.* London: Palgrave Macmillan, 2009.

Guèye, Cheikh. *Touba: La capitale des mourides.* Paris: Éditions Karthala, 2002.

REFERENCES

Mboup, Mortala. *Les sénégalais d'Italie: émigrés, agents du changement social*. Paris: L'Harmattan, 2000.

Riccio, Bruno. *Senegalese Migrants in Italy: The Potentials of Investing Human and Financial Capital for Urban Poverty Reduction in Senegal*. United Nations: UN-Habitat, 2004.

Simone, AbdouMaliq. *For the City Yet to Come: Changing African Life in Four Cities*. Durham: Duke University Press, 2004.

RIITTA OITTINEN
CALL SHOPS: A NEW ARCHITECTURAL TYPOLOGY FOR CALLING HOME

Clerckx, Geoffroy. Geoffroy Clerckx, Conseiller communal, to Ministre-Président Charles Picque, Région de Bruxelles-Capitale. "Saint-Josse-ten-Noode – Règlement communal relatif à l'implantation et à l'exploitation de magasins de nuit et de bureaux privés pour les télécommunications – Demande d'annulation." April 14, 2008. Saint-Josse-ten-Noode, Brussels. http://www.geoffroyclerckx.be/reglementphonenightshops.pdf (accessed May 31, 2010).

De Boer, Joop. "Typologies in Launderette Design." *The Pop-Up City*, April 12, 2010. http://popupcity.net/2010/04/typologies-in-launderette-design/ (accessed May 16, 2010).

De Corte, Stefan, Eric Corijn, and Walter de Lannou. "From a Multicultural and Fragmented City towards the 'Mediterranean' Capital of Europe." In *The Contested Metropolis: Six Cities at the Beginning of the 21st Century*, edited by Raffaele Paloscia, 79–89. Basel: Birkhäuser, 2004.

Guldentops, Fred, Pascale Mistiaen, and Christian Kesteloot. "The Spatial Dimensions of Urban Social Exclusion and Integration: The Case of Brussels, Belgium." URBEX Series, No. 13, Fourth RTD Framework Programme, Targeted Socio-Economic Research of the European Union, Amsterdam, 2001. http://www2.fmg.uva.nl/urbex/resrep/r13_brussels.pdf.

Oittinen, Riitta. "In Hoc Signo Vinces: Eurosigns in the City Scenery of Brussels." In *Media and Urban Space: Understanding, Investigating and Approaching Mediacity*, edited by Frank Eckardt, 201–231. Berlin: Frank & Timme, 2008.

———. "Call Shops in Brussels." In *Unplanned: Research and Experiments at the Urban Scale*, 108–113. Los Angeles: Superfront Gallery, 2010.

Rouyet, Yves. "Règlement relatif aux magasins de nuit et aux bureaux privés pour les telecommunications." *Ecolo XL*. 2007. http://www.ecoloxl.be/spip.php?article277 (accessed May 31, 2010).

Telezynski, Bertie, dir. *Launderette*, 2010. Short film.

SERGE MICHEL
LEARNING IDEOGRAMS: A STORY OF HOW CONGO'S BRAZZAVILLE IS BEING BUILT ANEW BY CHINESE COMPANIES

Alden, Chris. *China in Africa*. London: Zed Books, 2007.

Broadman, Harry G., *Africa's Silk Road: China and India's New Economic Frontier*. Washington, DC: World Bank Publications, 2007.

Michel, Serge, Michel Beuret, and Paolo Woods. *China Safari: On the Trail of Beijing's Expansion in Africa*. Translated by Raymond Valley. New York: Nation Books, 2009.

DAVID THEODORE
FEELING FOREIGN: WHAT HAPPENS WHEN A HOSPITAL LOOKS JUST LIKE A SHOPPING MALL

Abrams, Norm. "Place and 21st Century Health Care Research: Concepts, Methods, and Findings." Presentation at the Health Care Technology and Place Workshop, Toronto, June 12–13, 2003.

Adams, Ann-Marie. "Yellow." *Azure*, Nov–Dec 2003: 98.

Adams, Ann-Marie, and David Theodore. "Medicine by Design." *Canadian Architect* 47 (March 2002): 14–15.

———. "The Architecture of Children's Hospitals in Toronto and Montreal, 1875–2010." In *Children's Health Issues in Historical Perspective*, edited by Cheryl Krasnick Warsh and Veronica Strong-Boag, 439–478. Waterloo, ON: Wilfred Laurier University Press, 2005.

Adams, Ann-Marie, David Theodore, Ellie Goldenberg, Coralee McLaren, and Patricia McKeever. "Kids in the Atrium: Comparing Architectural Intentions and Children's Experiences in a Pediatric Hospital Lobby." *Social Science & Medicine* 70 (March 2010): 658–667.

Adams, Ann-Marie, David Theodore, and Patricia McKeever. "Pictures of Health: Sick Kids Exposed." In *Depicting Canada's Children*, edited by Loren Lerner, 252–278. Waterloo, ON: Wilfred Laurier University Press, 2009.

Shakir, Uzma. "Exercise Your Rights to the City." Presentation at Citizenship in the City: Exploring the Kind of Problem a City Is, Trudeau Foundation Public Interaction Program Workshop, Ottawa, November 18–19, 2009.

WOUTER OOSTENDORP AND JOUKE SIESWERDA
INTERPRETING MODERNISM: HOW AN AMSTERDAM HOUSING DEVELOPMENT CHANGES WHEN SURINAM GAINS INDEPENDENCE

Bolte, Wouter, and Johan Meijer. *Van Berlage tot Bijlmer*. Amsterdam: SUN, 1981.

Diepen, Maria van, and Ankie de Bruijn-Muller. *De Kraakakties in Gliphoeve*. Amsterdam: Gemeentelijke Dienst Volkshuisvesting, 1976.

Dijkhuis, J.H., I.M.C. van den Broeke, L.J.G. van der Maesen, R. Melger, and M. Klaren. *Collectieve ruimten Bijlmermeer: analyse van een verschijnsel*. Amsterdam: Beheersgroep Bijlmermeer, 1975.

Heijboer, Pierre. *Wachten op de nachtegaal*. Amsterdam: Van Gennep, 2006.

Horst, Jenneke ter, Han Meyer, and Arno de Vries. *Sleutelen aan de Bijlmer*. Delft: Publicatie Buro Faculteit der Bouwkunde, 1991.

Mentzel, Maarten. *Bijlmermeer als grensverleggend ideaal*. Delft: DUP, 1989.

Stadsontwikkeling Amsterdam. *Grondslagen voor de Zuidoostelijke stadsuitbreiding*. Amsterdam: Afdeling Stadsontwikkeling, 1965.

Verhagen, Evert. *Van Bijlmermeerpolder tot Amsterdam Zuidoost*. The Hague: Sdu uitgeverij, 1987.

GIOVANNA BORASI
COMPROMISE IN THE CASBAH: HOW THE RESIDENTS OF A SICILIAN TOWN NAVIGATE SEVERAL LANGUAGES AND MANY DIFFERENT IDEAS ABOUT HOW TO USE SPACE

Cusumano, Antonino. *Il ritorno infelice*. Palermo: Sellerio editore, 1976.

Gangale, Davide. "Immigrazione. Mazara del Vallo 2: 'L'unica comunità aperta siamo noi'." In *L'ospite ingrato*. Centro Studi Franco Fortini, 2008. http://www.ospiteingrato.org/Sezioni/Conflitto_Lavoro/Gangale_2_18-08-08.html (accessed September 1, 2010).

Hannachi, Karim. *Gli immigrati tunisini a Mazara del Vallo: Inserimento o integrazione*. Gibellina, Italy: Centro Ricerche Economiche e Sociali per il Meridione (CRESM Editore), 1998.

Navarra, Marco. *Workshop: Abitare Straniero*. Siracusa, Italy: Università degli studi di Catania, 2008.

———. "Foreign Living: How Can Urban Waste Be Reused?" Edited by Maria Giulia Zunino. *Abitare* 488 (December 2008–January 2009): 150–153.

Sciascia, Leonardo. "The Long Crossing." In *The Wine-Dark Sea*. Translated by Avril Bardoni. New York: New York Review Books, 2000. Translation of "Il lungo viaggio." In *Il mare color del vino*. Milano: Adelphi, 1973.

JEAN TEILLET
THE PRAIRIE IS VAST AND ENDLESS, UNTIL IT ISN'T: A MICHIF STORY

Baldwin, Stuart. "Wintering Villages of the Hivernants: Documentary and Archaeological Evidence." In *The Métis and the Land In Alberta: Land Claims Research Project, 1979–80*. Edmonton: Métis Association of Alberta, 1980.

Barnett, LeRoy. "How Buffalo Bones Became Big Business." *North Dakota History* 39 (1972): 23–42.

Ens, Gerhard J. *Homeland to Hinterland: The Changing Worlds of the Red River Métis in the Nineteenth Century*. Toronto: University of Toronto Press, 1996.

———. "After the Buffalo: The Reformation of the Turtle Mountain Métis Community." In *New Faces of the Fur Trade: Selected Papers of the Seventh North American Fur Trade Conference*. Edited by Jo-Anne Fiske, Susan Sleeper-Smith, and William Wicken, 139–151. East Lansing: Michigan State University Press, 1998.

Ray, Arthur. "Determining Effective European Control in Alberta." Report for the Office of the Federal Interlocutor for Métis and Non-Status Indians. March 2009.

Taché, Monsignor Alexandre A. *Sketch of the North-West of America*. Translated by Captain D.R. Cameron. Montreal: John Lovell, 1870.

REFERENCES

KOZY AMEMIYA
HOW RICE, PERSIMMONS, SOY AND A WHOLE HOST OF OTHER CROPS FROM JAPAN RESHAPED THE BOLIVIAN COUNTRYSIDE

Amemiya, Kozy. "The Bolivian Connection: U.S. Bases and Okinawan Emigration." Working Paper No. 25, Japan Policy Research Institute, October 1996. http://www.jpri.org/publications/workingpapers/wp25.html (accessed August 26, 2010). Reprinted in *Okinawa: Cold War Island*, edited by Chalmers Johnson, 53–69. Cardiff, CA: Japan Policy Research Institute, 1999.

———. "Land, Culture and Power of Money: Assimilation and Resistance of Okinawan Immigrants in Bolivia." In *Encounters: Peoples of Asian Descent in the Americas*, edited by Roshni Rustomji-Kerns, 121–130. Oxford: Rowman & Littlefield Publishers, 1999.

———. "The 'Labor Pains' in Forging a *Nikkei* Community: A Study of the Santa Cruz Region in Bolivia." In *New World/New Lives: Globalization and Peoples of Japanese Descent in the Americas and Latin Americans in Japan*, edited by Lane Hirabayashi et al., 90–107. Stanford: Stanford University Press, 2002.

———. "Colonia Okinawa y Colonia Japonesa San Juan." In *Cuando Oriente llegó a América: Contribuciones de inmigrantes chinos, japoneses y coreanos*, edited by Banco Interamericano de Desarrollo, 179–196. New York: Inter-American Development Bank, 2004.

———. "Four Governments and a New Land: Emigration to Bolivia." In *Japanese Diasporas: Unsung Pasts, Conflicting Presents, and Uncertain Futures*, edited by Nobuko Adachi, 175–190. London: Routledge, 2006.

Asociación Boliviano-Japonesa Colonia Colonia Japonesa San Juan. *Hirakeyuku Yuko no Kakehashi: Ase to Namida, Yorokobi to Kibo no Kiroku San Juan Nihonjinijuchi Nyushoku 50-nenshi* [The Expanding Bridge of Friendship: Records of Sweat and Tears, Joy and Hope. The 50-year History of San Juan Japanese Colonization]. Santa Cruz, Bolivia, 2008.

Asociación Boliviano-Japonesa Colonia Okinawa. *Boribia no Daichi ni Ikiru Okinawa-imin 1954-2004. Coronia Okinawa Nyushoku 50-shunen Kinenshi* [Okinawan Immigrants Living on Bolivian Soil 1954-2004. The 50th Anniversary of Colonia Okinawa]. Santa Cruz, Bolivia, 2005.

Federación Nacional de Asociaciones Boliviano-Japonesas. *Boribia ni Ikiru: Nihonjin Iju 100-shunenshi* [Living in Bolivia: The Centennial Commemoration of Japanese Immigration]. Santa Cruz, Bolivia, 2000.

CURTIS C. EBBESMEYER
PERPLEXING PEREGRINATIONS: ON THE TRAIL OF DRIFTING COCONUTS

Armstrong, Wayne P. "Drift Seeds and Drift Fruits: Seeds That Ride the Ocean Currents." *Wayne's Word*. December 3, 1998. http://waynesword.palomar.edu/pldec398.htm (accessed August 26, 2010).

Ebbesmeyer, Curtis C., and Eric Scigliano. *Flotsametrics and the Floating World: How One Man's Obsession with Runaway Sneakers and Rubber Ducks Revolutionized Ocean Science*. HarperCollins: New York City, 2009.

Gunn, Charles R., and John V. Dennis. *World Guide to Tropical Drift Seeds and Fruits*. Malabar, FL: Krieger Publishing Company, 1999.

Muir, John. "The Seed Drift of South Africa and Some Influences of Ocean Currents on the Strand Vegetation." *Botanical Survey Memoir* 16 (1937): 1–108. Reprinted as *The Seed-drift of South Africa*. Stellenbosch, South Africa: Still Bay Conservation Trust, 2003.

Nelson, Charles E. *Sea Beans and Nickar Nuts*. London: Botanical Society of the British Isles, 2000.

Perry, Ed, and John V. Dennis. *Sea-Beans from the Tropics: A Collector's Guide to Sea-Beans and Other Tropical Drift on Atlantic Shores*. Malabar, FL: Krieger Publishing Company, 2003.

Seabean (private educational website). http://www.seabean.com (accessed August 26, 2010).

Smith, Jeremy. *Australian Driftseeds*. Armidale, Australia: University of New England, 1999.

LENDERS

In addition to materials from CCA Collection, this exhibition could not have been possible without the contribution of many individuals and institutions.

We would like to express our thank to the following contributors to the exhibition:

A7 Media, Fabrice Monod, Paris, France
A.G. Stacey Papers, Archives and Special Collections, Queen Elizabeth II Library, Memorial University of Newfoundland, St. John's, Canada
Aldrich Public Library, Barre, Vermont, USA
The American Geographical Society, New York, USA
Asociación Boliviano-Japonesa de Okinawa, Santa Cruz, Bolivia
Asociación Boliviano-Japonesa de San Juan, Santa Cruz, Bolivia
Egyptian, Classical, Ancient Near Eastern Art, Brooklyn Museum, Brooklyn, New York, USA
Claudio Aporta, Ottawa, Canada
Cooperativa Agropecuaria Integral San Juan de Yapacaní Ltda. (CAISY), Santa Cruz, Bolivia
Edward Burtynsky Studio, Toronto, Canada
Nicholas Metivier Gallery, Toronto, Canada
The European Union (EU), European Commission, European Economic Community
Ian Chodikoff, Toronto, Canada
Jouke Sieswerda, Amsterdam, The Netherlands
Resettlement Collection, Maritime History Archive, Memorial University of Newfoundland, St. John's, Canada
McGill Rare Books and Special Collections, McGill University, Montréal, Québec, Canada
Rare Books Collection, Missouri Botanical Garden, St. Louis, Missouri
Stadsarchief, Amsterdam, The Netherlands
National Film Board of Canada, Canada
Navarra Office Walking Architecture, Marco Navarra, Caltagirone, Italy
Nederlands Instituut voor Beeld en Geluid, Hilversum, The Netherlands
Netherlands Architecture Institute (NAI), Amsterdam, The Netherlands
The Office for Metropolitan Architecture (OMA), Rotterdam, The Netherlands
Peter F. Picco, Freshwater, Newfoundland, Canada
Resettlers Museum, Centreville, Bonavista Bay, Newfoundland, Canada
Natural History Department, Royal Ontario Museum, Toronto, Canada
Trow & Holden, Barre, Vermont, USA
Vermont Historical Society, Barre, Vermont, USA
Paolo Woods, Paris, France
Pierre Yésou, Nantes, France

COPYRIGHTS

Cover, p. 87 © American Geographical Society
p. 13 © European Union, http://eur-lex.europa.eu/
p. 21, 22, 23, 24, 25, 27 © Max Belcher
p. 32 © Homefinders Ltd (bottom)
p. 33 © Home Book Plan Company (bottom left), © Jack Fitzsimons (bottom right)
p. 35 © Martin Parr/Magnum Photos
p. 36-37 © Imperial Life Assurance Company of Canada / Group Desjardins
p. 39, 40-41 © Laura Cohn
p. 43 © Pierre Yésou
p. 45 Courtesy Nicholas Metivier Gallery, Toronto © Edward Burtynsky
p. 51, 53, 54-55 © Ian Chodikoff
p. 56-57, 58-59, 85 © CCA/Matthew Fellows
p. 60, 61 © Paolo Woods
p. 64-65 ©Amsterdams Stadsblad
p. 69 © Het Parool
p. 70, 71 © Jouke Sieswerda
p. 73 © Fortunato Pappalardo
p. 75 © NOWA
p. 76 © Department of Natural Resources Canada. All rights reserved.

Unless otherwise indicated, photographs were taken by Michel Boulet and Michel Legendre, CCA
© CCA

Illustrations by Erika Beyer
© CCA

Material from the CCA Wells Coates fonds is used by permission of copyright holder Laura Cohn.

Every reasonable attempt has been made to identify owners of copyright. Errors and omissions will be corrected in subsequent reprints.

NOTE FROM THE EDITOR

Journeys: How travelling fruit, ideas and buildings rearrange our environment is a research project by the Canadian Centre for Architecture. It analyzes how the movement of goods, ideas, architectural types, tools and various forms of expertise transform specific locations and their built environment.

What compelled me to initiate this project were the physical consequences triggered by these flows, migrations and encounters between different places and cultures. The challenge of such a project has been to find the right way to convey this multifaceted research and its surprising results in a comprehensive manner. As it progressed, the project took on a distinct narrative character, revealing itself in stories. Somewhat paradoxically, it seems that the very specificity of each topic—each "story"—begs an exploration of the larger implications at play. Even the tightly focused terms assigned to each situation studied—keywords such as "classification," "wayfinding," "negotiation," and "configuration,"—while perfectly aligned with the specific story they define, offer an interpretation of contemporary strategies and conditions in a much broader sense.

In the book, the stories are presented within a fictional framework, even though they are all based on real facts and archival research. Our approach was doctrinaire: very precise editorial requirements known as "the dogma" were adopted to fit these stories—involving different places, different eras and different cultures—into a cohesive compilation. In the exhibition, the project's narrative traits are funnelled into a focused selection of objects and the manner in which they are displayed. The reader and the visitor will notice one important detail: we made a special effort to not include any portraits in our selection of visual material. This, we decided, was the best way to emphasize that our focus here was not on the social or anthropological dimensions of migrations and movement, but only on the physical transformations involved.

GIOVANNA BORASI
Curator for Contemporary Architecture
Canadian Centre for Architecture

ACKNOWLEDGMENTS

Research for *Journeys* yielded findings so unexpected that we were forced to experiment with a different way to narrate, demonstrate and interpret its results. I would like to express my sincere thanks to everyone who contributed to this fascinating project.

First and foremost, I would like to acknowledge the role of Phyllis Lambert, CCA Founding Director, who supported this project from the outset. Journeys offered us an entirely new way to approach and present the extraordinary potential of the CCA Collection. In particular, I would like to thank Phyllis for being the person who introduced us to the Collection's amazing photographs of Liberian settler architecture by Max Belcher. I would like to thank Ralph Bernstein, CCA Trustee, for having introduced us to Ilaria Brancoli Busdraghi and her research on Italian immigrants in Vermont. Thanks also to Bruce Kuwabara, CCA Trustee, who from the start was interested in the broader issues this project would raise, and their particular relevance to a country like Canada. I would like to express my deepest gratitude to Mirko Zardini, CCA Director, for all his input on the direction of the project, and for the trust and freedom he afforded me in this experimental curatorial and editorial endeavour.

Extensive conversations during the research phase provided us with the insight and ideas that came to shape the content of this project. Many people took part, and we are grateful for their generous participation. In particular, I would like to offer our sincere thanks to Vered Amit, Patrizia Audenino, Sina Najafi, John Raulston Saul, Rhona Richman Kenneally and Rémy Tremblay. I am especially indebted to Gilles Clément, whose brilliant book *Éloge des vagabondes: Herbes, arbres et fleurs à la conquête du monde* gave me a conceptual starting point for this project, and who generously led me to the story of the Sacred Ibis.

The book and the exhibition would not have been possible without tremendous teamwork and engagement of the many individuals and institutions involved in the research phase, as well as those who helped us select and organize the various elements of this unusual project. A list of Lenders and Collaborators is in the back, but in particular I would like to thank those who were personally involved in the process: Claudio Aporta, Norman Akley, Pat Byrne, Edward Bleiberg, Paul Carnahan, Laura Cohn, Martha Davidson, Talitha van Dijk, Matthew Fellows, Heidi Frampton, Karen Lane, Suzanne Mulder, Mark Peck, Edna Penny, Vera Penny, Pascale Pere, Peter Picco, Bert Riggs, Joan Ritcey, Thomas Royden, Marjorie Strong, Scott Walden and Heather Wareham.

For their brilliant contributions, I am equally indebted to all the book's authors. Thanks especially for having accepted to be a part of our editorial experiment, respecting our strict editorial "dogma." You have helped us create a cohesive, unusual and witty book. I would also like to thank the many authors who provided us with content for the exhibition, or directed us to the sources of their material.

My deepest thanks go to Actar Publishers for their collaboration on this volume. In particular, I thank Albert Ferré who played a fundamental role in its editorial frame. I am grateful for all our conversations, for his enthusiasm, and for his understanding of the book's scope and content. Many thanks are also due to Ulises Chamorro, for his brilliant graphics, and to everybody else at Actar, for their perseverance. Special thanks go to Erika Beyer, whose ethereal and highly detailed illustrations give each of these stories a unique character.

I would also like to express my greatest appreciation for the work of Nargisse Rafik and Brendan Brogan, for their help with the editorial alignment of the stories in this volume, and for their contributions to the editorial process. My sincere thanks to Jennifer Harvey for her thorough fact-checking on all the stories. Special thanks also go to the eagle-eyed Katya Epstein, as well as to translators Albert Beaudry, Hélène Floch de Gallaix, Donald Pistolesi, Julie-Anne Ricard and Matt Sendbuehler, whose work shows respect for and faithfulness to the many different voices in these tales. We are equally grateful to Isabelle Canarelli and Lucinda Catchlove, whose proofreading skills impressed us all.

ACKNOWLEDGMENTS

I would like to thank Martin Beck for his invaluable contribution in developing the exhibition's conceptual framework. Martin played a fundamental role in clarifying the narrative and in establishing some pivotal notions about the connection between the content and the exhibition space. My deepest thanks also to Alex DeArmond, for his sophisticated graphic design and successful interpretation of so many curatorial ideas in another medium.

Journeys is the outcome of intense research and conceptual work conducted by a skilled and dedicated curatorial team at the CCA. In particular, I would like to recognize the role of: Anders Bell, Lev Bratishenko, Meredith Carruthers, Daria Der Kaloustian, Laura Killam, and Peter Sealy. I would like to thank all of them for having accompanied me with enthusiasm in this long process, and for doing so without hesitation when faced with the inherent risks posed by any experimental venture. The many discussions we had on the project's content and its curatorial and editorial processes strengthened our structure and our approach. I also would like to thank Shannon Harvey who contributed to the initial research phase.

I would like to thank Theodora Doulamis for her excellent skills in managing the project's many administrative requirements, as well as Sébastien Larivière and his team for always ensuring that the content of our show is presented with a wonderful sense of spatial clarity. My personal thanks goes to Natasha Leeman for her indispensable assistance.

Finally I would like to thank the many other CCA teams who worked tirelessly to bring this project to fruition. Our gratitude goes to the Collection for their invaluable assistance during the research phase; and to Collection and Program Services: special thanks to the Conservators and Registrar for processing and handling items from all over the world; to the photographers and the copyright officers for helping us prepare and secure the best visual material for our publication; as well as the CCA Communication Department and Theresa Simon for taking on the challenge of distilling such an unwieldy subject into a clear and compelling message. Thanks also to Lev Bratishenko for his ideas on how to transfer the content of this show to the project's website (www.cca.qc.ca/journeys), and to everyone who generously contributed to its online archive.
—— GIOVANNA BORASI

***

I'm deeply indebted to the people of Colonia Okinawa and Colonia Japonesa San Juan, Bolivia. I am especially grateful to Yumifumi Nakamura, Toru Higa, and Masahide Ikehara in Colonia Okinawa, as well as Masayuki Hibino, Jun Ikeda, Noriko Ikeda, and Toshio Ishizawa in Colonia Japonesa San Juan. —— KOZY AMEMIYA

I would like to thank Natalie Mayerhofer for being the ideal reader and Helen Strudwick for her Egyptian anecdotes. —— ANDERS BELL

I would like to thank the European Commission, Directorate-General Agriculture and Rural Development, Brussels; and the Community Plant Variety Office, Angers. —— Lev Bratishenko

I would like to dedicate my story to Fanta Diamanka-Sene and Ousmane Sene, without whom this story—and my journey—would not have been possible. —— IAN CHODIKOFF

I would like to dedicate my story to Svend Holsoe who introduced me to the paradox of Liberian settler architecture. Svend generously shared research and insight that shaped this story in its earliest form as "Settler Houses," in *A Land and Life Remembered: Americo-Liberian Folk Architecture* (1988), written for the Brockton Art Museum/Fuller Memorial with support from the National Endowment for the Humanities. I would also like to express my indebtedness to Max Belcher for access to his extraordinary photographs of Liberia's settler architecture. —— BERNARD L. HERMAN

I would like to thank my co-flâneur Jukka-Pekka Piimies for useful comments and observations. My thanks also go to the Eurospotters collective, who document business signs with a Euro-theme in Brussels and across the world. —— RIITTA OITTINEN

I would like to acknowledge and thank my husband Chris for all his help reading and revising this story. His insight and editing were invaluable and this story would not have been possible without him. I would like to thank Theresa Collins for lending me all the pictures, newspaper articles and books that she has collected of her home of St. Kyran's. Finally, I would like to thank all the people I have spoken to over the years who were resettled or displaced from their homes in Newfoundland and Labrador for sharing their stories with me. —— MAUREEN POWER

I would like to thank Wells Coates, for his magnificent voice, which accompanies the reader through all his writings, as well as for his persistence in the face of the many challenges and disappointments which marked his career. I'm grateful to Laura Cohn, for her book about her father, and also for her valuable feedback. This story would not have been possible without the careful work of previous historians, many of whom are mentioned in the accompanying reference, who have worked to give Wells Coates the prominent place in the history of Modern architecture, in Britain and in Canada, which he so richly deserves. —— PETER SEALY

I would like to acknowledge the unstinting support of Annmarie Adams and Patricia McKeever. They directed the research project on children's healthcare architecture, funded by the Canadian Institutes of Health Research, on which parts of this story are based. I'm grateful to everyone involved in that project, especially fellow team members Ellie Goldenberg and Coralee McLaren. Annmarie and Ellie graciously offered comments on an earlier draft. Finally, I would like to thank Lisa Freeman for putting me in touch with Uzma Shakir, and Uzma for generously sharing her stories. —— DAVID THEODORE

PUBLICATION

Editor
Giovanna Borasi

Editorial Assistance and Coordination
Anders Bell
Daria Der Kaloustian

Graphic Design
ActarBirkhäuserPro

Editing
Brendan Brogan
Nargisse Rafik

Fact-checking
Jennifer Harvey

Translation
Donald Pistolesi
Matt Sendbuehler

Proofreading
Lucinda Catchlove

Rights & Reproductions
Marc Pitre

EXHIBITION

Curator
Giovanna Borasi

Curatorial Team
Anders Bell
Lev Bratishenko
Meredith Carruthers
Peter Sealy

Design Concept
Martin Beck

Graphic Design
Alex DeArmond

Design Development
Laura Killam
Sébastien Larivière

The CCA is an international research centre and museum founded on the conviction that architecture is a public concern. Based on its extensive collection, exhibitions, programs and research opportunities the CCA is a leading voice in advancing knowledge, promoting public understanding, and widening thought and debate on the art of architecture, its history, theory, practice, and role in society today.

Board of Trustees
Phyllis Lambert, Chair
Pierre-André Themens, Vice-Chair
Raphael Bernstein
Stephen R. Bronfman
Jean-Louis Cohen
Tony Comper
Niall Hobhouse
Peter R. Johnson
Bruce Kuwabara
Sylvia Lavin
Frederick H. Lowy
Philip M. O'Brien
Charles E. Pierce, Jr.
Tro Piliguian
Pierre Pomerleau
Robert Rabinovitch
Gerald Sheff
Mirko Zardini

The exhibition catalogue is prepared in part, thanks to the financial support of Hydro-Québec. The CCA would also like to thank the Ministère de la Culture, des Communications et de la Condition féminine, the Canada Council for the Arts, and the Conseil des arts de Montréal for their continuous support.

Published by the Canadian Centre for Architecture and Actar to accompany the *Journeys: How travelling fruit, ideas and buildings rearrange our environment* exhibition, presented at the CCA from 19 October 2010 to 13 March 2011.

© 2010 Canadian Centre for Architecture
© 2010 Actar

All rights reserved under international copyright conventions.
No part of this book may be reproduced or utilized in any form or by any means, electronic or mechanical, including photocopying, recording, or any information storage and retrieval system, without permission in writing from the publisher, or in Canada, a license from the Canadian Copyright Licensing Agency. For a copyright license, visit www.accesscopyright.ca or call (800) 893-5777.

Legal depot: B-36388-2010

Printed and bound in the European Union
First edition

Printed on acid-free paper.
G-Print Matt and Offset ON premium

Typeset in Sabon, Courier
and Berthold Akzidenz Grotesk

978-0-920785-90-4
Canadian Centre for Architecture
1920 Baile street
Montréal, Québec
Canada H3H 2S6
www.cca.qc.ca

978-84-92861-54-5
Actar
Roca i Batlle 2
08023 Barcelona
Spain
www.actar.com

Distributed by
ActarBirkhäuserD
Barcelona–Basel–New York
www.actarbirkhauser-d.com

Bibliothèque et Archives nationales du Québec and Library and Archives Canada cataloguing in publication

Main entry under title :
Journeys : how travelling fruit, ideas and buildings rearrange our environment

Catalogue of an exhibition held at the Canadian Centre for Architecture, Montréal, Québec, Oct. 19, 2010 to Mar. 13, 2011.
Issued also in French under title: *Trajets*.
Co-published by Actar.
Includes bibliographical references.

ISBN 978-0-920785-90-4 (Canadian Centre for Architecture)
ISBN 978-84-92861-54-5 (Actar)

1. Architecture and society - Exhibitions. 2. Architecture - Environmental aspects - Exhibitions. 3. Emigration and immigration - Exhibitions. I. Borasi, Giovanna, 1971-   . II. Amemiya, Kozy, 1947-   . III. Beyer, Erika. IV. Canadian Centre for Architecture.

NA2543.S6J68 2010
720.1'037471428
C2010-942024-1